D1053402

LEARNING FROM LOSS

The Democrats' decision to nominate Joe Biden in 2020 was hardly a fluke but rather a strategic choice by a party that had elevated electability above all other concerns. In *Learning from Loss,* one of the nation's leading political analysts offers unique insight into the Democratic Party at a moment of uncertainty.

Between 2017 and 2020, Seth Masket spoke with Democratic Party activists and followed the behavior of party leaders and donors to learn how the party was interpreting the 2016 election and thinking about a nominee for 2020. Masket traces the persistence of party factions and shows how interpretations of 2016 shaped strategic choices for 2020.

Although diverse narratives emerged to explain defeat in 2016 – ranging from a focus on "identity politics" to concerns about Clinton as a flawed candidate – these narratives collectively cleared the path for Biden.

Seth Masket is Professor of Political Science and Director of the Center on American Politics at the University of Denver. Masket writes regularly for *Mischiefs of Faction* and *FiveThirtyEight.* His work has also appeared in *Politico,* the *New York Times,* the *Los Angeles Times,* and the *Washington Post's* Monkey Cage. He is the author of *The Inevitable Party: Why Attempts to Kill the Party System Fail and How They Weaken Democracy* (2016) and *No Middle Ground: How Informal Party Organizations Control Nominations and Polarize Legislatures* (2009).

LEARNING FROM LOSS

The Democrats, 2016–2020

Seth Masket

University of Denver

CAMBRIDGE
UNIVERSITY PRESS

University Printing House, Cambridge CB2 8BS, United Kingdom

One Liberty Plaza, 20th Floor, New York, NY 10006, USA

477 Williamstown Road, Port Melbourne, VIC 3207, Australia

314–321, 3rd Floor, Plot 3, Splendor Forum, Jasola District Centre,
New Delhi – 110025, India

79 Anson Road, #06–04/06, Singapore 079906

Cambridge University Press is part of the University of Cambridge.

It furthers the University's mission by disseminating knowledge in the pursuit of
education, learning, and research at the highest international levels of excellence.

www.cambridge.org
Information on this title: www.cambridge.org/9781108482127
DOI: 10.1017/9781108699709

© Cambridge University Press 2020

First published 2020

Printed in the United States of America by Sheridan Books, Inc.

A catalogue record for this publication is available from the British Library.

ISBN 978-1-108-48212-7 Hardback

To my parents Barbara and Sam Masket, who instilled in me a love for politics, and my brother Harris Masket, who is that kind of doctor

Contents

Figures

Tables

Acknowledgments

The book you're reading was an unusual one to write, and I really wasn't sure how or whether it was going to come together when I began. When the 2020 caucuses and primaries started, things seemed to be going in several different directions at once. Then it looked like Bernie Sanders might become the nominee. Then it looked like there was going to be a contested convention. Then suddenly the party coordinated and everything fell into place almost overnight. And then I had to retreat to my basement to avoid the COVID-19 pandemic. It is under these conditions that I finished this book.

I wish to start by thanking the dozens of political activists, campaign consultants, political journalists, and other seasoned professionals in Iowa, New Hampshire, Nevada, South Carolina, and Washington, DC, who took the time to speak with me and share the benefits of their wisdom and experience. I learned so much from these conversations, and I am grateful for them offering so many revealing, entertaining, and deeply personal stories with me. If this book project had resulted in nothing more than those conversations it still would have been worth it.

I am truly appreciative of Sara Doskow and her colleagues at Cambridge University Press for believing in the idea of this book and being willing to take a chance on it. Her encouragement and guidance have been exceedingly helpful.

Throughout the creation of this book I especially drew upon the insights, feedback, and support of Julia Azari and Hans Noel, two of the most thoughtful scholars of political parties working today. Hans has been one of my most trusted colleagues in this discipline for nearly a quarter century.

Julia helped to shape the scope of this manuscript, reliably pushes me toward better scholarship, and invariably steals my best ideas a year or two before I think of them. I know if I've written something Hans and Julia find interesting then I've done something worthwhile. So here's hoping they find this interesting.

The two of them were also part of a book conference in the winter of 2020 that was one of the most intellectually intense and gratifying days of my career. The detailed critiques I received from the two of them, along with that from Sara Chatfield, Laurel Eckhouse, Pavielle Haines, Anand Sokhey, Ismail White, Josh Wilson, and Christina Wolbrecht, changed the direction of this book and massively improved it. I hope to be as much help to these excellent scholars as they were to me that day. If you end up not liking this book, just thank your stars you didn't read the version that existed before that book conference.

I received invaluable research support from the Kluge Center at the Library of Congress during the summer of 2018. I am beholden to Ted Widmer and John Haskell for selecting me for the fellowship there. I am particularly in the debt of Jennifer Nicoll Victor for recommending me for that fellowship, for reading early concepts of this work, and offering me constructive and thoughtful guidance and encouragement.

Mohammed Alsardar was a research intern at the Kluge Center and was greatly helpful with collecting historical documents about Henry Clay and Andrew Jackson. Andi Schlut and Noelle Strom collected endorsement information from gubernatorial primaries. Colin Phipps tracked media coverage in the wake of the 2016 election and staffing patterns between 2016 and 2020. I didn't know much about text analysis and received some valuable training from Rachel Blum, Justin Gross, and Mary Kroeger. Kevin Reuning provided some useful public opinion data. I am grateful to Stephen Ansolabehere, Adam Bonica, Brandice Canes-Wrone, Hans Hassell, Nolan McCarty, Byron Shafer, Danielle Thomsen, Sarah Treul, and Hye Young You for feedback on various chapter drafts.

I wish to thank a few folks who helped open some doors for me and provide me with guidance as I learned about their states. Dave Peterson supplied me with some useful background on Iowa politics, shared a lot of valuable data, and introduced me to some impressive local beers. Peter and

Rebecca Sallee Hanson were kind enough to invite me in for dinner and talk politics. Caroline Tolbert gave me a chance to present some of this work in Iowa and attend the caucuses there. John Pérez and Elaine Kamarck shared their wisdom at a meeting of the Democratic National Committee and generally made it easier to speak with others. Dana Singiser and Scott Faber gave me insightful background material over numerous meals in Washington. Chris Galdieri taught me how to spot political celebrities in New Hampshire. My in-laws Paula and Stuart Boxer provided me with a place to stay, a hearty breakfast, and some thoughtful conversations about Granite State politics. Dave Darmofal, Tobias Heinrich, Chris Witko, and Neal Woods gave me a chance to present some of my early research in South Carolina. Jon Ralston gave me the lay of the land in Nevada. My aunt and uncle Andi and Mark Rubin offered me a bed in Las Vegas and some delicious chicken and ice cream.

A lot of the research support I received came from the Center on American Politics at the University of Denver. Yeah, I direct that center, so that helped, but I am deeply grateful to Chancellor Rebecca Chopp for helping to bring it to life, and to Lynn Schofield Clark, Jennifer Garner, Sam Kamin, Tonya Kelly, Gregg Kvistad, Corinne Lengsfeld, Lisa Martinez, Aleesha McDowell, Danny McIntosh, Susan Schulten, and Chancellor Jeremy Haefner for their ongoing support and encouragement for this program. I also want to thank my department chair Lisa Conant for her patience and support while I've worked on this project and tried, mostly unsuccessfully, to weasel out of various service commitments.

I received considerable support and encouragement, and occasional feedback, from my own family members. My wife Vivian, my kids Eli and Sadie, my parents Barbara and Sam, my brother Harris, and my sister-in-law Sirena all checked in on the project and occasionally read drafts and gave me ideas.

I had thoughtful discussions about this project with two dear friends, Laresh Jayasanker and Danielle Signoracci Solomine, and I hope this is a book they would have enjoyed reading.

Thanks to the students of my suddenly-online University of Denver Political Science Capstone class in the Spring of 2020, who were kind enough to read portions of this book and supply me with useful critiques.

Thanks as well to students in Hans Noel's Presidential Nominations Lab class at Georgetown for their comments, especially the student who demanded more Michael Bennet content.

Beyond those I've mentioned above, I am indebted to the various Klugies who listened to my stories from this project and gave me feedback on Facebook, on Twitter, at the Palmer House Hilton, and in many other venues. And although I didn't consult with him extensively on this project, I remain guided by the example of John Zaller and the respectful way he collects and treats evidence both quantitative and qualitative.

I am particularly grateful to various journalists and editors who were open to me publishing some early versions of this research and working through some ideas on their sites. Nate Silver, Sarah Frostenson, and Colleen Berry gave me a lot of extremely thoughtful and methodical edits at *FiveThirtyEight* and caught a fair number of errors of mine. Ezra Klein of *Vox* hosted the *Mischiefs of Faction*, where I worked through a number of the ideas in this book. Max Ufberg and Ben Rowen gave me free rein to pen some thoughts at *Pacific Standard* while that fine publication still lived. Terry Tang invited me to write up some of this research at the *Los Angeles Times*. Larry Ryckman and John Frank at the *Colorado Sun* provided helpful support. All these efforts helped me build up an audience and get some invaluable critiques for this project, for which I am grateful.

I engaged in detailed conversations with a lot of Democratic actors over the course of researching and writing this book. Regardless of my own personal history in politics, it was important for me to remain neutral in the presidential nomination contest throughout this process. I did not endorse or otherwise support any candidate until casting my own (private) vote in the Colorado primary. I did not donate to any campaign (with the one accidental exception of when I purchased a t-shirt for a relative and it turned out that was recorded as a contribution). On the few occasions when I attended ticketed Democratic Party functions to interview attendees, I donated equivalent amounts to the respective state Republican parties.

My interview research agenda was examined by the Office of Research and Sponsored Programs at the University of Denver and determined to not require a full IRB review. The survey experiments detailed in

Chapter 6 were reviewed and approved as project 1163550 and determined to be exempt. This was, at times, a stressful book to write on the deadline I'd created for myself, but it's also some of the most rewarding and fascinating research I've ever done. I hope I have conveyed some of this in the pages ahead. Thank you for reading it.

CHAPTER 1

When the Fools Were Right

LIGHTOLLER : "I've been at sea since I was a boy . . .. I've even been shipwrecked before. I know what the sea can do. But this is different."
GRACIE : "Because we hit an iceberg?"
LIGHTOLLER : "No, because we were so sure. Because even though it's happened, it's still unbelievable. I don't think I'll ever feel sure again, about anything."

A Night to Remember, 1958[1]

Activists are so traumatized by 2016, and they're so terrified of revisiting that night and having it all happen again.

Iowa political activist, 2019

I'm not putting another fucking dime in until someone tells me what just happened.

Democratic Party donor, December 2016[2]

This was supposed to be a book about Republicans. In the summer of 2016, I had an idea for a book chronicling how the Republican Party dealt with their embarrassing loss to Hillary Clinton. Surely they were going to have to rethink how their presidential nomination system worked, why it utterly failed in 2016, and how a patently unelectable candidate like Donald Trump somehow got the nomination and cost them an election that was obviously theirs to win. It would be a difficult period of self-

[1] ITV Archive.
[2] Tina Nguyen, 2016. "Democratic Donors Say Their Money Buys Them an Explanation." *Vanity Fair*, December 16.

1

reflection for the GOP, and it seemed like something that would be fascinating to observe in action.

Yeah, it would have been. Obviously, and much to nearly everyone's surprise, something very different happened that fall. That period of Republican self-reflection has been postponed. Instead, that mantle was passed to the Democrats, who engaged, both at an organizational and personal level, in an extensive and grueling conversation about what exactly happened in 2016 and what to do about it.

This is a book about that conversation. Everything that you've heard about the challenges and weirdness of the Democratic presidential nomination of 2020 stems, I argue, from that conversation about 2016. And the Democrats' ultimate decision to nominate former Vice President Joe Biden, and the divisiveness within the party that followed from that, similarly was a product of the party's conversations and fights about the previous election.

I want to start off by giving an example of such a conversation. Imagine a meeting of the Coca-Cola product development team in 1986. (I doubt this exact meeting happened, but let's assume something along these lines did.) The company is still reeling from the surprising and embarrassing failure of New Coke a year earlier. It had seemed like a smart idea at the time, and all their sophisticated market research had suggested it would sell well. Instead, it quickly became a laughingstock, and the company lost crucial market share to Pepsi-Cola.

Importantly for this example, the people in this meeting room can't agree why New Coke failed. Some think the flavor just wasn't that good. Others think the flavor was fine – possibly better than the earlier version of Coke – but that they had advertised the product poorly and scared off the customers they were trying to woo. Others think that soft drink consumers were far more resistant to new products and new ideas than originally thought. Still others blame things totally outside Coca-Cola's control – FDA product warnings, small independent soft drink products, etc., – for the catastrophe.

But the argument in this meeting room is vitally important, because coming up with a narrative for New Coke's failure is vital to figuring out what to do about it. If the room decides New Coke failed because it tasted bad, they may abandon it altogether and scramble to find a better flavor. If they decide it was good but marketed poorly, they might keep the product but change their advertising strategy. If the problem was independent soft drink manufacturers, maybe they try to co-opt some of them. And so forth. But if they simply can't agree on what went wrong, they might just choose what they see as the safest possible response – going back to the old formula that worked for them previously.

Without drawing out the analogy too far, this is essentially what the Democratic Party faced after the 2016 presidential election. The party, broadly defined, struggled to come up with a reason why Hillary Clinton had lost to Donald Trump. That election's outcome was stunning and disorienting for people in the party. They couldn't agree on a narrative – was the problem Hillary Clinton? Her gender? Her policy stances? Her speeches? Was it the way the party campaigned for her? The messaging her campaign used? Did it have something to do with Russian interference? Or James Comey? Or Bernie Sanders? Was the electorate more sexist or racist than Democrats had calculated after two terms of Barack Obama's presidency?

And as in the above example, the narrative is vital for telling the party what to do next. Should the party avoid nominating a woman or a person of color to avoid alienating moderate white men, or should it definitely nominate such a candidate to boost minority turnout? Should it nominate a Midwesterner? Should it move to the center or to the left? Should it strengthen or weaken its own control over the nomination process? Or was 2016 just the electoral equivalent of an act of God, meaning the party shouldn't try to change how it operates or the sort of candidate it nominates?

This is a book about election narratives, the stories we concoct about why a complex set of events came out as it did. These narratives, regardless of how accurate they are, can be very powerful in guiding the behavior of parties and political actors, especially for a party that lost. They have a substantial impact on the decisions a party and voters attached to that party make for the next nomination contest. Importantly, when a party can't agree on a narrative, that makes the job of picking the next nominee that much harder. And sometimes, as Coca-Cola did, a party might just decide to reject innovation and fall back on a formula they believe worked in the past. This, I will demonstrate, is what happened to the Democratic Party in the lead up to 2020.

Now "product innovation" means something very different for a party than it does for a soft drink manufacturer. The Democratic Party is an ideological organization, and its core ideology is inclusiveness. Like any party, it will periodically struggle with how much of its core ideology to sacrifice to the god of electability. The Democrats, struggling with determining a narrative about 2016 and facing a daily onslaught of Donald Trump's policies, norm violations, and tweets, settled on what they perceived as a safe option, determining that a moderate white man, the sort of nominee they've turned to in past competitive elections, was the best way to secure a win. This wasn't an overtly declared party position, of course, but as the evidence I'll present in this book suggests, this was the subtext of a great many conversations going on within the broader party. This conversation made the nomination of Joe Biden, or someone like him, a lot more likely than it would have been in a different political environment.

Some news coverage of the political events of late February and early March 2020 made it seem like Joe Biden's nomination was a last-minute fluke, that his flailing campaign was rescued by a lucky combination of timing and candidate withdrawals. The research I present here suggests otherwise. A substantial portion of Democratic insiders, including activists and donors and party leaders, had already decided on him as the party's standard-bearer long before anyone started voting in Iowa. They had done so in large part due to their interpretations of 2016 and their strong desire to avoid repeating that election's outcome.

For this book, I examine the Democratic Party during the process political scientists refer to, with some inconsistency, as the Invisible Primary. I define the Invisible Primary as stretching from the day after the November 2016 presidential election to just before the February 3, 2020 Iowa Caucuses. It is the period in which Democratic leaders and insiders tried to comb through the wreckage of the Clinton campaign, determine what happened, and make some decisions about how to change the party and which candidate to pick the next time around. Notably this time period ends just before voters and caucusgoers weighed in. Obviously, their input is vital to a presidential nomination, and I will discuss some of those early contests toward the end of the book. But I am mainly interested in how party leaders, insiders, and organizers made (or failed to make) decisions before they had direct guidance from voters. This is instructive about just what a modern party is capable of.

My focus on one party during one presidential cycle is important for two somewhat contradictory reasons. For one, the 2016 presidential election was an unusual one, with surprising results in both the major party nomination processes and in the general election. It was a stunning outcome that was disorienting and even traumatizing for Democratic activists and other political observers. For another, despite how unusual this example is, it is highly revealing about the behavior, capabilities, and limits of a modern American political party. If we want to understand how a party responds to a shock, absorbs information and attempts to learn from it, and both guides and is guided by perceptions of what voters will and won't accept, we could hardly find a better example.

A SHOCK TO THE SYSTEM

I want to be transparent about the environment in which these party decisions were taking place and the motivation for this book. The disorientation experienced by many within the Democratic Party in the wake of 2016 was shared by quite a few political observers and political scientists, including me.

In the summer of 2015, I was interviewed by Graeme Hamilton, a political reporter with Toronto's *National Post*, about the developing contest for the Republican presidential nomination for 2016. Canadian readers, Hamilton informed me, were hearing quite a bit about Donald Trump, and he wanted to know my assessment of Trump's chances. "Donald Trump won't be nominated," I confidently told him, "and he won't be elected president." Hamilton seemed surprised by my certitude. "You're making a very strong claim," he noted. "Do you worry about your academic reputation?" "If I'm wrong about this," I responded, "my academic reputation will be the least of our concerns."

I wish to be clear that this book is neither a partisan diatribe nor a strategic memo for one party or the other. The book is about reaction to a set of shocking events. The first of these events was, of course, the nomination of Donald Trump as the Republican candidate for president. Lacking previous political or military experience, he was obviously not the sort of candidate major parties typically nominate for the presidency. But perhaps more importantly, he won the nomination without the blessing of party leaders. He was precisely the sort of wealthy political neophyte who occasionally runs for high office and fails because the party does not trust him to follow through on issues they care about, and he won its nomination anyway. His nomination ran against most leading theories of the way party nominations work and against a good deal of my own scholarship. In general, only the fools think the candidate with nothing more than an early lead in public opinion polls will win the nomination; wise people will focus on the candidate with the bulk of party insider support. In 2016, the fools were right.

The second event was Donald Trump's election in the fall. To be sure, if the history of presidential elections tells us anything, it's that open-seat elections in middling economies are tossups. With more typical nominees, 2016's presidential race should have been a very competitive one. But Hillary Clinton was leading by substantial polling margins – sometimes in the double digits – throughout the year. It wasn't like political observers were making up some esoteric theories to predict a Clinton victory. We predicted a Clinton victory because we asked voters how they planned to vote and that was what they told us. The idea that reliably Democratic states like Wisconsin and Michigan, where polls reported healthy Clinton leads right up until election day, would somehow go Republican at the last minute seemed too bizarre to believe.

As a scholar, I needed to understand just what had happened. Were these one-off events, driven by unusual political conditions and the unique aspects of Trump's fame, wealth, and personality? Or had the political system changed? Were parties now running under new rules, and were elections far less predictable than previously thought? The Democratic Party was suddenly in the position of evaluating what had happened, as well. Were they just as vulnerable as the GOP to a famous outsider taking their nomination? Did they need to change their nomination process? What exactly did "electability" mean? And what kind of candidate were they supposed to nominate next time around to address this situation?

THE IMPORTANCE OF NARRATIVE

The way a political system generally deals with these questions is through the construction of narratives. "What unites people?" asked Tyrion Lannister in the final episode of *Game of Thrones*. "Armies? Gold? Flags? Stories. There's nothing in the world more powerful than a good story. Nothing can stop it. No enemy can defeat it." He made some bad calls that season but this was a pretty good observation. Narratives are a convenient way of breaking down a complex event like a national election into an understandable story or moral. As political scientist Marjorie Hershey notes,[3] an election is a terribly blunt tool for representation and accountability. For any given electoral race, voters usually just have two choices and don't get to say why they're voting the way they're voting. (And polling questions after the fact are filled with all sorts of biases.) A politician may just be told she received 52 percent of the vote – it's a win, but what did it mean beyond that? Did it mean the ads she ran were effective? If so, which ones? Did it mean her efforts were better than her opponent's, or that the district was already drawn to be favorable to her? Did it mean her volunteers were appropriately enthusiastic, or not enough? Was she well positioned on the issues, or should she move to the left or the right? One won't learn these things by poring over election returns.

This is where the narrative comes in. Political reporters and observers, campaign staff, pundits, scholars, and others will examine the race, look at polling and spending and turnout data, perhaps review experiments conducted during the campaign testing the effectiveness of various campaign activities, and look at many other things and render a verdict about just why the candidate lost.

Here's the uncomfortable part – a lot of what we think is important in elections turns out not to matter that much. Let's just focus on presidential elections for a moment here. Since 1988, no major party presidential nominee has received less than 45 percent of the two-party vote. That doesn't mean it can't happen – Reagan, Johnson, and Nixon won by twenty-point blowouts in the decades preceding that. But we're in a more

---

[3] Marjorie Randon Hershey, 1992. "The Constructed Explanation: Interpreting Election Results in the 1984 Presidential Race." *The Journal of Politics* 54 (4): 943–76.

stable partisan era at the national level[4] and presidents just don't win in landslides anymore. Which means that around 90 percent of the vote is already accounted for before the campaign even starts. Voters are largely going to vote for the party they are already leaning toward.

Now, that still leaves some portion of the electorate open to influence. But it turns out a great deal of their behavior can be explained by the "fundamentals" of elections. These include things like the performance of the economy, conditions of war or peace, and the length of time the incumbent's party has held control of the White House. You can come very close to predicting a November election several months earlier, long before the major portion of the campaigning takes place, just by knowing how well the economy is performing and how long the president's party has controlled the White House.

And then you have some degree of random chance. You might get bad weather in one area of the country that lowers turnout. A new voting machine might fail. A ballot might turn out to have a confusing design that advantages one candidate over another. A news story might break at the last minute that casts a candidate in a bad light. All of this is possible but still very hard to predict, and it is largely outside the campaigns' control.

So after voter partisanship, the campaign fundamentals, and random chance, just how much of the electorate is left for the campaigns to actually influence through advertisements, speeches, yard signs, and door-knocking? That's difficult to measure, and the numbers will jump around from election to election depending on the circumstances, how much people already know about the candidates, etc. But it's not a large number.

This is often where political scientists and political consultants get into fights. Political scientists often speak of the relatively small or "minimal" effects of campaigns, pointing instead to the vast influence of the fundamentals. Consultants tend to argue that the campaign strategies they honed, the advertisements they deployed, the speeches they wrote, etc., were pivotal in the election.

[4] Frances E. Lee, 2016. *Insecure Majorities: Congress and the Perpetual Campaign.* Chicago: University of Chicago Press, 2016.

And honestly, scholars and consultants aren't disagreeing about all that much. Consultants know that a good deal of the electorate is immune to their handicraft, but they must be focused on that portion of the electorate that they can influence. They just might disagree with scholars about how large that portion is.

But regardless, we're not talking about big differences. Yet there will only be one winner, no matter how close the election was, and at that point some familiar narratives will kick in. Anything the winner did will be presumed to be the correct thing to do to win an election. But the loser will be presumed to have *done something wrong*. Any decision the loser made during the campaign will be suspect. The narrative will quickly be constructed based on the idea that the loser and winner would change places if the loser had just done that one thing differently.

A familiar refrain, almost to the point of a punchline, was that Hillary Clinton "should have gone to Wisconsin." Indeed, Clinton did not make any campaign stops in Wisconsin in the fall of 2016, while Trump made five,[5] and the Badger State went for a Republican presidential candidate for the first time since 1984. So it seems on the surface that Clinton's decision to ignore the state was a costly error. But what does the evidence say? For one thing, Clinton was up by an average of five points in tracking polls in the state just prior to the election. All the publicly released polls in the final two weeks had Clinton ahead, from one to twelve points. Diverting campaign resources from states that seemed competitive right before the election to one that looked safe would have looked like a grave miscalculation at the time.

What's more, it's not remotely clear that this would have helped her. According to pre-election polls, Clinton was up by similar margins in Wisconsin, Michigan, and Pennsylvania. She devoted only minimal resources to Wisconsin, modest resources to Michigan, and massive resources, including advertisements, visits, and field organization, to Pennsylvania. She lost all three states by about a percentage point. If all

---

[5] Candace Smith and Liz Kreutz, 2016. "Hillary Clinton's and Donald Trump's Campaigns by the Numbers." ABCNews.com, November 7. https://abcnews.go.com /Politics/hillary-clinton-donald-trumps-campaigns-numbers/story?id=43356783.

that campaign effort couldn't save her in Pennsylvania, why would we think it would matter in Wisconsin? But the critique sticks nonetheless.

Narratives will also be created about the nature of the country itself. Think for a moment about the descriptions of the American electorate immediately after the 2016 election. Pundits were taken aback by the results. They described the racial resentment, outrage, and anxieties motivating the electorate. Those election results painted a picture of a divided society that was making little progress toward its goals of equality and justice; people lived in silos and did not understand one another. Rural whites felt frightened by the pace of social change, while coastal elites ignored or belittled them.

Now think about the descriptions immediately following Barack Obama's election in 2008. The *New York Times* described Obama as "sweeping away the last racial barrier in American politics." His election was "a national catharsis . . . a strikingly symbolic moment in the evolution of the nation's fraught racial history, a breakthrough that would have seemed unthinkable just two years ago."[6] A Tom Toles editorial cartoon claimed that the proposition in the Declaration of Independence that "all men are created equal" was ratified on November 4, 2008. Michael Goodson, writing in the *Indiana Post-Tribune*, reflected,

> The phrase, "never in my lifetime," overused in the past, is very appropriate in the election of Barack Obama. Certainly, there are cultural characteristics that pass from one generation to the next, and the troublesome aspect of racial prejudice is one of them. It took over 100 years to get from slavery to civil rights in the 1960s, and almost 50 years more to get to this transformational plateau of electing an African-American to our highest office.[7]

Accounts of those two elections depicted two vastly different countries. Yet those elections occurred only eight years apart. The country had changed little in the interim. Indeed, the country was more racially

---

[6] Adam Nagourney, 2008. "Obama Elected President as Racial Barriers Fall." *The New York Times*, November 4. www.nytimes.com/2008/11/05/us/politics/05elect.html.

[7] Michael Goodson, 2008. "Americans Seem to have Arrived with Obama." Indiana *Post Tribune*, November 20, p. A10.

diverse and probably more tolerant in 2016. The economy was in far better shape in 2016. The Democratic nominee won the popular vote in 2008 by around seven points; she won it in 2016 by around two points. Is it possible that we overstated the lessons of both those elections? Is it possible that America in 2008 wasn't dramatically different from the one of 2016, and that the idea that we'd overcome our prejudice and the legacy of slavery after one election was as overwrought as the idea that we were hopelessly siloed and divided after the other?

It's also worth noting here that narratives are heavily influenced by the simple fact of who won or lost the election, a simple and binary outcome that grossly ignores a great deal of subtlety, variation, and bias. Clinton and Trump could have received the exact same number of votes, but if roughly 80,000 of Trump's votes had been cast in Texas, Florida, and North Carolina instead of Wisconsin, Michigan, and Pennsylvania, pundits would have devoted their creative abilities to explaining the genius of the Clinton campaign, the GOP's irresponsibility in blowing a winnable election with a flawed candidate, the overblown hype of Russian campaign activities, the self-defeating nature of trying to run a race-baiting campaign in a nation that had elected Barack Obama twice, and so forth.

So election narratives aren't necessarily perfectly correct or apt for the elections they describe. But they're powerful. A Democrat who came away from 2016 believing that Hillary Clinton lost because she was a woman or because she spoke about redressing racial inequalities might be inclined to nominate a more moderate white male candidate in 2020. A Democrat who came away believing that she lost because she failed to stimulate African American turnout the way Obama did in 2008 and 2012 might be inclined to nominate a candidate of color for 2020. Neither one of those narratives is obviously wrong, but they lead in very different directions. The campaign to win the election is quickly replaced by a contest to define the loss, for whoever can define just *why* the election occurred a certain way has a great deal of power over what the party will do next. Control the narrative, control the future.

UNDERSTANDING NOMINATIONS

As I suggested above, the 2016 nomination contests were disorienting to party scholars. Defying expectations, the Republican Party nominated a presidential candidate who seemed neither particularly committed to – nor familiar with – many longstanding party priorities and who, at least at the time, seemed uncompetitive for the general election. Democratic Party insiders, meanwhile, converged early on a popular favorite with policy stances broadly acceptable across the party and largely cleared the field for her, only to find that insider support fueling an insurgent campaign that nearly derailed her nomination and undermined her legitimacy as the party's standard-bearer. Both parties revealed themselves to be vulnerable to outsider candidacies – Trump had little history with the Republican Party, and Bernie Sanders came surprisingly close to taking the Democratic nomination despite not even identifying as a Democrat.

One of the main questions for those who study American political parties was whether Democrats in 2020 were in the same situation as Republicans were four years earlier. Were they still capable of coordinating behind a preferred candidate and seeing that candidate to the nomination? Or were they just as vulnerable to the appeals of outsider candidates and unable to prevent their rise? The results of 2020 were surprising. Amidst a tumultuous contest with the largest candidate field ever, Democrats suddenly converged behind Joe Biden in early March of 2020. The party, it seemed, was still capable of making a decision.

But that decision didn't just suddenly happen in 2020. It was the product of conversations and debates that had been happening for three years. And those conversations and debates were rooted in interpretations of the 2016 election. The Biden decision, meanwhile, was far from unanimous. Important divisions and factions within the Democratic coalition remained throughout 2020. But explaining how the party came to its decision and sought to navigate its factional divides is the purpose of this book.

THE PLAN OF THE BOOK

The book examines different aspects of the Democratic Party – activists, members of the Democratic National Committee, donors, voters, and candidates. It approaches them in roughly chronological fashion, beginning with the journalists and longstanding activists seeking to make some sense of the 2016 election and then proceeding through the following years, culminating with the primaries and caucuses of 2020. Those looking for detailed descriptions of all the candidates and the decisions they made may be disappointed; my focus is far less on the presidential candidates than on those attempting to decide among them, using the knowledge they have gleaned from earlier contests.

I want to be as clear as possible about the terminology I'm using in this story. Chapter 2 offers some definitions that are vital to this book, getting into the concepts of electability, ideology, and identity. Perhaps most importantly, the chapter attempts to define the modern Democratic Party. Scholars sometimes disagree about what the Democratic Party is, whether it is a coalition of different identity groups or a platform for liberal ideology. Identity and ideology are two sides of the same coin; equality among different groups is the motivating ideology of the Democratic Party, and it is one that the party struggles with depending on its narrative from the last election. There is often a vocal faction within the party that believes that the way to win the next election is to ease back on the party's commitment to equality. That struggle was particularly salient and divisive during the 2020 cycle. At a time when an unusually high percentage of voters said that electability was their primary consideration (that is, they were willing to give up a lot to get Trump out of the White House), party insiders were choosing among the largest and most diverse field of presidential candidates ever, and most of the leading candidates of color were winnowed out of the race before voters even had a say. This chapter examines the Democratic Party's complex and often painful history with African American voters. And it describes just how presidential nominations usually work and the degree to which that, and our understanding of it, is changing.

Chapter 3 introduces evidence from a series of interviews and surveys I conducted among party activists between 2017 and 2020 in the early-contest states of Iowa, New Hampshire, South Carolina, and Nevada, as well as Washington, DC. These are the people who largely constitute the labor force of the party and the presidential campaigns, and their decisions can affect which direction the party goes. I look at the variety of narratives they offered for why Hillary Clinton lost in 2016. They put forward a wide range of answers – some blamed the candidate, some blamed the campaign, some focused on identity politics, some ascribed events to external factors like Russia or James Comey, some simply said there was a strange and unpredictable mood in the electorate, some blamed racism and sexism, and more. I then compare these answers with a look at media narratives in the wake of the 2016 election, by journalists and pundits seeking to explain the surprise outcome. Both among the activists and the seasoned election observers, the overall consensus about that election is a lack of an overall consensus. The election was close enough that almost any explanation *could* be right – switch a few votes here and there and you've got a different president. However, the bulk of diagnoses embraced by activists tended to suggest Joe Biden as the remedy. I look at how these activists made decisions among the candidates, or ultimately decided to sit back and wait.

Chapter 4 is a look inside the formal Democratic Party, examining what happens when narratives compete with each other as party insiders seek guidance from a recent election. It draws on some historical examples of parties trying to fix themselves, going as far back as the 1820s and efforts to resist the norm-breaking, imperious, and often racist behavior of President Andrew Jackson. It also looks at Democratic attempts to figure out why they lost in 1968 to a controversial Republican nominee and to determine what changes they needed to make to avoid such problems in future elections. (Yes, some of this may sound familiar.) But much of the chapter looks at more recent efforts by the formal Democratic Party to discern lessons from 2016 and change the party from within. As some discussions among the Democratic National Committee reveal, one of the narratives of the 2016 election concerned the divisive nomination contest between Hillary Clinton and Bernie Sanders, and many in the party were determined to avoid such skirmishes in future nomination contests at all costs. Much of the activity by the Unity Reform Commission, the Rules and Bylaws Committee, and later the Democratic National Committee as a whole, in 2017 and 2018, was focused on repairing what it saw as dangerous divisions within the party and restoring the perceived legitimacy of the party's decision-making processes. In doing so, as we will see, the party reopened some old and deep wounds along racial lines that stood to divide the party further. The consequences of following one narrative to its conclusion may have made the party more vulnerable to factional rifts.

Chapter 5 is an attempt to dig into factional divisions within the modern Democratic Party. In particular, it looks at how divisions between Clinton and Sanders supporters in the 2016 presidential nomination contest spilled over into other intraparty contests in 2017 and 2018. I focus especially on campaign donation patterns, finding that many gubernatorial primary contests in 2017 and 2018 had an "establishment" candidate and a "progressive" candidate (to use some very imprecise terms), and that those donors who backed Clinton in 2016 were very likely to back the establishment candidate in the next cycle, while Sanders supporters backed the progressive. I then look at the Democratic presidential candidates of the 2019–2020 nomination cycle to see which were aligned with which of the party's earlier factions. The evidence presented in this chapter strongly suggests that the divisions seen within the Democratic coalition in 2016 were not temporary, nor were they limited to that presidential contest. They run deep and have considerable historical roots.

Chapter 6 looks at the effects of post-election narratives on voters, showing how beliefs about the last election affect the sorts of candidates we prefer for the next one. In particular, I investigate the power of one particular narrative, the "identity politics" narrative, which argues that Hillary Clinton lost because she focused too much on the needs of women, people of color, the LGBT community, and others, without reaching out to working-class whites, who abandoned the Democrats as a result. I report the details of several survey experiments in this chapter. One of these experiments reveals that people shown this argument became less supportive of women and candidates of color as a result. Another experiment shows that African Americans and white women shown the argument shifted the kind of candidates they wanted to see win the Democratic presidential nomination; they moved their support toward more conservative white male candidates. The identity politics message actually made their preferences look more like those of white men. The evidence presented in this chapter suggests that the narrative a party chooses to accept after an election loss is highly consequential – it can greatly affect what sorts of candidates do well in the next nomination contest, and what sorts of policies he or she ends up championing.

Chapter 7 returns to the early-contest activists, examining how they ultimately lined up behind various presidential candidates. I then sum up what we have learned from the Democrats' Invisible Primary between 2016 and 2020. I examine how Democrats largely came to a decision about the type of candidate they wanted, and look at the dynamics of the race through the lens of some of the last remaining competitors: Joe Biden, Bernie Sanders, and Elizabeth Warren. I also note how the cycle is beginning anew. Should the Democrats lose in November 2020, there will be plenty of recriminations across the party toward one group or another which will likely affect the nomination process for 2024. Should they prevail, Republicans are due for a substantial reassessment of their candidate selection process.

CHAPTER 2

What We Know About Identity, Ideology, and Electability, and What We Don't

We have to realize that we're getting out of touch with normal, regular people. We're forgetting that the white middle-class is rejecting us. We're being wagged by the tail of Jesse Jackson, of feminists or gay activists. The average voter is saying, "What about me?"

Democratic political consultant, 1984[1]

"I'm a Moderate," Says Racist Democrat.

Reductress, 2019[2]

The first debate of the 2020 Democratic presidential nomination cycle occurred in June of 2019. It was spread across two nights to accommodate twenty candidates in the largest and most diverse presidential candidate field in American history. The last debate was held in March of 2020 in a CNN studio with no audience, consisting of two white men in their late 70s standing several yards apart to prevent virus transmission. Understanding how the former yielded to the latter requires getting a handle on a number of key topics. I'll review some of those topics and explain just how they're relevant to current American political parties. I describe them in the context of answering a key question: What is the Democratic Party? What are its constituent parts, and what motivates them? How do we distinguish it from the Republican Party, or even

---

[1] Quoted from Marjorie Randon Hershey, 1992. "The Constructed Explanation: Interpreting Election Results in the 1984 Presidential Race." *The Journal of Politics* 54 (4): 959.

[2] https://reductress.com/post/im-a-moderate-says-racist-democrat/.

from the Democratic Party of the past? And what role do narratives play in guiding its behavior?

The key topics I address in this chapter are as follows:

- *Ideology* – This is the concept of a unifying set of principles that guide a party.
- *Identity* – This is a rather large topic concerning the idea of how people group and identify themselves and how those identities become connected to politics.
- *Electability* – This is the idea that some candidates will have an easier time prevailing in a general election than others, and that this difference can be adequately measured during a nomination contest.
- *Post-election narrative* – This is the lesson drawn from a previous election, especially an election loss, about why the party lost and what it needs to do to win future elections.
- *Party nomination* – This is the process by which a party picks a nominee, and the extent to which that decision is driven by party leaders, activists, voters, or someone else. I'm mostly focusing on the presidential level here, but these lessons apply down the ballot.

Obviously, these concepts are all intertwined. For example, when Democrats were considering whom to nominate for president in 2020, they used polling and intuition to estimate each candidate's electability, and weighed that against the candidates' adherence to the party's ideological commitments and their perceived ability to turn those into laws. Party leaders were also trying to develop narratives about 2016 and 2018 to help them understand what sorts of candidates might prevail in 2020.

But these concepts need to be understood on their own terms, as well. I'm going to do what I can in this chapter to decompose this salad into its constituent parts before throwing them back into that nice bowl you use when company comes over.

THE DEMOCRATIC PARTY: IDEOLOGY OR GROUPS?

What exactly is the modern Democratic Party? It's the oldest party in the nation (actually one of the oldest in the world), having been a driving force in American politics for roughly two centuries. It is so intertwined with the

American political system and its history that it's difficult to define it on its own. But like any major party, it should be thought of as a *coalition*.

Coalitions, of course, can shift over time, and that certainly applies to the Democrats. Today, the dominant groups within the Democratic Party include African Americans, Latinos, environmentalists, labor unions, poorer Americans, secular Americans, and others. This coalition, of course, does not see eye to eye on all issues and candidates. One of the prime functions of a political party is to create a system for reaching collective decisions in a way that members can agree upon.

But the party, like its Republican counterpart, is not simply a collection of groups; it contains ideas for governance. And those ideas have shifted a lot over the decades and centuries. Indeed, today a reasonably informed Democrat would probably be bothered by a great deal of what her party stood for prior to 1965, and might even view the pre-1932 Democratic Party as the bad guys.

The relationship between the *groups* that comprise the Democratic coalition and the *ideology* to which they adhere is a tricky one, and political scientists disagree over this a lot. But I want to get into this a bit here, since these concepts are vital for understanding the rest of the book.

Obviously ideology is relevant to understanding the modern Democratic Party. News coverage, especially since the 2018 elections, has noted the party's leftward turn, highlighting the young progressives driving the effort and the more moderate party regulars worrying about the party's declining competitiveness. One of the party's most influential young members is US Rep. Alexandria Ocasio-Cortez of New York, who famously unseated the more moderate and experienced Joe Crowley in 2018 at a time when he was chair of both the House Democratic Caucus and the Queens County Democratic Party. Although the primary upset was an atypical outcome in 2018, it caught the attention of political observers and suggested the rise of a less compromising progressive left, perhaps even a liberal mirror of the Tea Party movement from a decade earlier.[3] And ideology seemed important in the early parts of

---

[3] Tom Davis, 2019. "Are Democrats Facing Their Own Tea Party-Style Reckoning?" *Politico*, March 18. www.politico.com/magazine/story/2019/03/18/democrats-aoc-ocasio-cortez-socialists-pelosi-congress-left-tea-party–225813.

the 2020 Democratic presidential nomination. Moderate candidates like former Rep. Joe Sestak and Montana Gov. Steve Bullock had a hard time finding support in the field, while debates ended up dominated by the center-left and progressives arguing about extending voting rights to felons, decriminalizing unlawful border crossings, and extending Medicare. It certainly seems like ideology is a good way to understand what's going on within the Democratic Party today.

Or is it? In their book *Asymmetric Politics*, Matt Grossmann and David Hopkins argue that the Democratic and Republican parties are very different organizations doing fundamentally different jobs.[4] The Republican Party, they maintain, is an ideological organization. It is marked by an "intense electoral pressure from Republican activists and primary voters to maintain doctrinal purity [that] exerts visible influence on the behavior of the party's elected officials."[5] Its candidates speak at great lengths of their commitment to conservatism as a guiding principle. (In a 2012 Republican presidential primary debate, "conservative" was the third most spoken word, after "taxes" and "economy."[6]) By contrast, the Democrats are a coalition of interest groups. Their candidates speak not of their fealty to liberalism or progressivism but rather about their commitments to the different interests – women, people of color, the LGBT community, unions, young people, environmental groups, working families, etc. – that comprise their coalition, and they are held responsible for those.

These differences in organizational goals and styles are significant and underappreciated, the authors maintain, leading to various errors on the part of political observers. If Democrats are interested in hammering out workable governing compromises between different interests, that will be seen very differently by a party that's primarily interested in advancing an ideology of low taxes and minimal government regulation. The parties are, quite simply, in different lines of work.

The evidence that the authors amass is compelling. Yet in some ways the distinctions seem overstated. Is the GOP really not a group-oriented party? Any speech by a modern Republican president or presidential

---

[4] Matt Grossmann and David A. Hopkins, 2016. *Asymmetric Politics: Ideological Republicans and Group Interest Democrats.* Oxford: Oxford University Press.

[5] Ibid., p. 4.   [6] Ibid., p. 71.

aspirant will feature numerous appeals and identity claims for people and groups within the party, from veterans to coal miners to businesspeople to gun owners. Some of those appeals are partially shrouded ("the working class" is often a shout out to downscale whites, "job creators" are referenced instead of millionaire CEOs, many appeals are for traditionally male jobs, etc.), but it's clear that the party is seeking to manage a coalition.

And Democrats are clearly running their coalition on some sort of an ideology, even if it is not as neatly packaged or branded as conservatism. As political scientist Hans Noel writes, the left ideology "would involve something like egalitarianism, but more importantly, that the government ought to intervene to help establish egalitarianism. This means intervene *on behalf of marginalized groups.* So when you talk about it, it sounds like group-benefits, because group-benefits is the ideology."[7] For an example of this, see a July 2019 interview with Democratic presidential candidate Julián Castro, in which he was asked the best ways for Democrats to push back against racist tweeting by the president. "How do you combat that effectively? Well, you do that in part by building coalitions. And that coalition is going to be built of people of different backgrounds, different skin colors, different religions from throughout the country, that actually believe that we're a nation that will be more prosperous, more successful if we appreciate our differences."[8] That's the language of groups, to be sure, but it is also making an ideological claim about rejecting hierarchy and embracing diversity.

Just as Republicans judge each other by their commitment to the principle of conservatism, Democrats judge each other by their commitment to the principle of egalitarianism. However, there is considerable disagreement on what this should mean in practice. That is, Democrats generally are committed to the idea of equality, but they disagree about how much work they, their party, and the government should apply to

---

[7] Hans Noel, 2015. "Democrats are as Ideological as Republicans. And Republicans are as Group-Centric as Democrats." *Mischiefs of Faction*, March 13. www.mischiefsoffaction.com/2015/03/democrats-are-as-ideological-as.html.

[8] Scott Detrow and Lauren Chooljian, 2019. "Julián Castro Says Trump Is 'The Biggest Identity Politician' In Recent History." National Public Radio, July 23. www.npr.org/2019/07/22/744107709/juli-n-castro-says-trump-is-the-biggest-identity-politician-in-recent-history.

effecting it. Importantly, some Democrats believe that advancing equality is costly to their party; it can hurt their chances of winning in the next election. This doesn't mean that party leaders will always abandon minority groups in the name of electability; like any ideological commitment, egalitarianism will be evaluated and fought over in the context of a nomination. Party activists may pursue a party goal even believing that they will lose some support for doing so.

IDENTITY

The concept of "identity" has rarely been more salient in an election cycle as it was in 2020. The Democratic Party, which nominated an African American presidential candidate in 2008 and 2012, and a woman presidential candidate in 2016, was considering among its most diverse candidate field ever in an effort to prevent the reelection of Donald Trump, who traded on the politics of race and gender more overtly and provocatively than any president in at least a century.

A term we hear a lot these days in political discourse is "identity politics." This is a freighted term that means a lot of different things to a lot of different people. Political scientists and pundits hear *very* different things when you use that term. But generally, we're talking about how people's identity becomes politicized and how politicians will tap into those identities for political advantage.

This is hardly unique to one political party. Indeed, a common refrain among political scientists is that *all* politics is identity politics. That is, political movements begin with a group explaining who they are, how they have been aggrieved, and what they expect the government to do about it. (The Declaration of Independence is a great example of this.) Political campaigns are often attempts by a politician to speak to and relate to people of particular identities (residents of a particular neighborhood, members of a particular racial group, veterans of a particular war, parents of children with a particular malady, etc.) and explain how he or she will improve their lot. Even ostensibly neutral government actions like fixing potholes are tied into identity: "Which potholes in front of whose houses is identity politics," explains political scientist Christina Wolbrecht.[9]

Political pundits and campaign professionals have come to use a different concept of identity politics in recent years, referring specifically to efforts by Democrats (often women or people of color) to win over voters by expressing support for marginalized groups. *Washington Post* columnist Ruth Marcus mocked Hillary Clinton's 2015 campaign announcement video for engaging in this sort of politics through its depiction of a diverse range of American supporters:

> Working mom, check. Hispanic entrepreneur, check. Retiring grandma, check. Gay couple, check. African-American family, check. Hardworking small-businessman, check. South Asian, inter-racial, lesbian, check, check, check. If your demographic was not featured, you should write the campaign and it will probably splice you in.[10]

"The preoccupation with identity has clashed with the need for civic discourse," scholar Francis Fukuyama explained on the pages of *Foreign Policy*.[11] This, he argues, prevents the nation from resolving serious issues like economic inequality.

Political scientists John Sides, Michael Tesler, and Lynn Vavreck wrote an important rejoinder to this essay, describing identity politics not as an aberration of American democracy but the key to it: "Identity politics hasn't led to the breakdown of democracy; rather, it has helped democracy thrive." Identity politics, after all, is not just practiced by marginalized groups, but also by dominant ones; white supremacy is a form of identity politics. For marginalized groups to have political power, they need to activate their political identities. And it's not like there was a golden era when public policy was divorced from race.[12]

---

[9] https://twitter.com/C_Wolbrecht/status/1153348666268299264.

[10] Ruth Marcus, 2015. "Hillary Clinton's Insultingly Vapid Video." *The Washington Post*, April 13.

[11] Francis Fukuyama, 2018. "Against Identity Politics: The New Tribalism and the Crisis of Democracy." *Foreign Policy*, September/October.

[12] John Sides, Michael Tesler, and Lynn Vavreck, 2018. "Identity Politics Can Lead to Progress." *Foreign Policy*, September/October.

A substantial number of books on race and politics in the United States have been published just since 2016, in a clear effort to explain the crucial role race played in that year's presidential election. That race was important to that election hardly seems in dispute. But why that election? How did we somehow come to the conclusion that racism cost a white woman a presidential election when the previous two presidential elections were won handily by an African American man?

While much literature has focused on the role racial identity played in the 2016 general election, I'm particularly interested in the role it plays *within* the Democratic Party as it decides between candidates. I recognize this is fraught ground and I wish to be as clear as possible in my claims: I am not claiming that the Democratic Party is rife with racism or that Democrats who prefer white presidential candidates are doing so out of racial animus. Racial identity within the party is more nuanced than that, but to ignore it would be to miss a substantial part of the story.

In her pathbreaking book *White Identity Politics*,[13] Ashley Jardina makes an important distinction between out-group prejudice – disdain by whites toward people of other racial groups – and in-group identity – whites' feeling of solidarity with other whites and their perception that their identity as white people is important. Feeling good about your race and resenting other races are related but not the same, and one does not automatically lead to the other. Notably, as Jardina points out, the concept of white identity is a relatively new one; whiteness, for most twentieth-century American whites, was largely perceived as the absence of an identity. American whites might cling to an ethnic heritage – Polish, Irish, Jewish, etc. (Indeed, stoking ethnic solidarity was once seen as a way to stir racial solidarity among whites without appearing outwardly racist.[14]) But for the most part, *other people* had race; for whites, whiteness was as invisible as water is to fish. As Robert Terry phrased it in 1981, "To be white in America is not to have to think about it."[15]

---

[13] Ashley Jardina, 2019. *White Identity Politics*. Cambridge: Cambridge University Press.

[14] Thomas J. Sugrue and John D. Skrentny, 2008. "The White Ethnic Strategy." In Bruce J. Schulman and Julian E. Zelizer, eds., *Rightward Bound: Making America Conservative in the 1970s*. Cambridge, MA: Harvard University Press, 171–92.

[15] Robert W. Terry, 1981. "The Negative Impact on White Values." In Benjamin P. Bowser, and Raymond G. Hunt, eds., *Impacts of Racism on White Americans*. Thousand Oaks, CA: SAGE, 119–51.

Recent years, however, have seen the rise of whiteness as a coherent identity. Using recent surveys, including the 2012 and 2016 American National Election Studies (ANES), Jardina examines the rise of white identity as a distinct phenomenon, driven in part by rapid demographic changes within the United States. In those surveys, whites were asked, "How important is being white to your identity?" Jardina distinguishes this identity from white *consciousness*, a more politicized version of group attachment. This can be measured with ANES questions like "How likely is it that many whites are unable to find a job because employers are hiring minorities instead?" White identity and consciousness are themselves distinct from resentment or hatred toward those of other racial groups, even if they're related. Politicians can use any of them to mobilize white voters – sometimes different subsets of them. But it's worth noting that white identity doesn't automatically lead to resentment, and may even help whites recognize their own privilege.

Sides, Tesler, and Vavreck's *Identity Crisis*[16] offers considerable evidence that issues of race and gender were crucial to the outcome of the 2016 election. White prejudice toward immigrants, Muslims, African Americans, and others was considerably more correlated with vote choice in 2016 than it was in 2012. Trump voters in 2016, in particular, were especially likely to find African Americans as undeserving, while seeing "average Americans" as deprived. The election also activated sexism among white men, with the more sexist shifting more toward the Republican candidate than they had in previous presidential elections. But again, some of this is going on within the Democratic Party, as well.

In Table 2.1 below, I examine several questions pertaining to race in the 2016 ANES, examining the results for white Republicans and white Democrats. (Here I am including self-described independents who claim they lean toward a party as being part of that party.) The first question is a more traditional racial resentment question, asking whites whether they believe the federal government treats black people better than white people. And here, we see sharp differences by party, with more

---

[16] John Sides, Michael Tesler, and Lynn Vavreck, 2018. *Identity Crisis: The 2016 Presidential Campaign and the Battle for the Meaning of America.* Princeton: Princeton University Press.

TABLE 2.1 *Percentage of whites who believe . . .*

	The federal government treats blacks better than whites	Their white identity is very/extremely important to them	It is very/extremely important that whites work together to change laws unfair to whites
Republicans	35.1%	32.5%	41.7%
Democrats	9.2%	22.9%	31.1%

Source: 2016 ANES

than a third of white Republicans but less than one in 10 white Democrats agreeing. In this case, it seems clear that there are substantial partisan differences in terms of racial resentment.

The second question, in which respondents are asked whether their white identity is important to them, is more one of in-group identity rather than out-group resentment. And while there are differences across party lines, they are not nearly so stark. About a third of white Republicans and a quarter of white Democrats felt that their white identity was very or extremely important to them. (These numbers were down a few points from those in the 2012 version of the study.) The third question, asking whether whites should work together to change laws unfair to them, is more one of racial consciousness. And again, we see substantial agreement, with more than 30 percent of white Democrats agreeing, only ten points behind the white Republican figure.

Attitudes toward gender are also of vital importance within the Democratic coalition. Hillary Clinton's strong performances in both the 2008 and 2016 presidential nomination contests and the presence of several prominent female senators in the 2020 contest, combined with a dramatic rise in the number of women interested in running for Congress, state legislature, and other offices in recent years, has forced the party to grapple with what the presence of female candidates means for voters. Quite a few studies suggest that women lack the kind of politicized group solidarity that other historically marginalized groups demonstrate in elections.[17] Yet there remain important differences in

---

[17] Kathleen Dolan, 2008. "Is There a 'Gender Affinity Effect' in American Politics? Information, Affect, and Candidate Sex in U.S. House Elections." *Political Research*

male and female voting behavior in the USA, with women voting several points more Democratic than men for several decades now. In 2016, women preferred Hillary Clinton over Donald Trump 54–41 percent, while men preferred Trump to Clinton 52–41 percent.[18] This 13-point gender gap is historically large and has been growing over time, and while it doesn't appear closely tied to the identity of the candidates, evidence suggests that gender is becoming an even more salient political identity since the 2016 election.[19]

As with African American political identity, there are several dimensions of women's political identity. These include an emotional connection to other women, a distinct conception that women have been deprived as a group, a belief that an individual woman's chances of success are related to the successes of women at large, and a collective political consciousness suggesting a need to work together for redress.[20]

To what extent are beliefs about women in conflict within the Democratic coalition? I have examined a similar set of questions as above related to discrimination against women. The first question here asks whether women complaining about discrimination ends up causing more problems most of the time or always. We might consider this a harder sexism question, as it is overt in dismissing concerns about persistent sexism. The numbers answering in the affirmative are not huge, although the percent of Republicans claiming this is double the percent of Democrats doing so, and there aren't substantial differences between men and women within the parties on this question.

Quarterly 61 (1): 79–89; Patricia Gurin. 1985. "Women's Gender Consciousness." *Public Opinion Quarterly* 49 (2): 143–63; Leonie Huddy, Francis K. Neely, and Marilyn R. Lafay, 2000. "Trends: Support for the Women's Movement." *Public Opinion Quarterly* 64 (3): 309–50; Pamela Paxton, Sheri Kunovich, and Melanie M. Hughes. 2007. "Gender in Politics." *Annual Review of Sociology* 33: 263–84.

[18] CNN 2016 Exit Polls, www.cnn.com/election/2016/results/exit-polls.

[19] Eric M. Gomez, Danielle M. Young, Alexander G. Preston, Leigh S. Wilton, Sarah E. Gaither, and Cheryl R. Kaiser, 2019. "Loss and Loyalty: Change in Political and Gender Identity Among Clinton Supporters after the 2016 U.S. Presidential Election." *Self and Identity* 18 (2):103–25.

[20] Pamela Johnston Conover, 1998. "Feminists and the Gender Gap." *The Journal of Politics* 50 (4): 985–1010; Sue Tolleson Rinehart, 2013. *Gender Consciousness and Politics*. London: Routledge.

TABLE 2.2 *Percentage who believe . . .*

	Women complaining about discrimination just cause more problems most of the time or always	Many women interpret innocent remarks or acts as being sexist	Most women fail to appreciate fully all that men do for them
Rep. men	18.2%	48.1%	29.7%
Rep. women	17.6%	45.9%	27.4%
Dem. men	9.7%	33.6%	22.0%
Dem. women	9.6%	28.2%	17.3%

Source: 2016 ANES

We see somewhat broader bipartisan agreement in the "softer" sexism questions, however. Asked whether many women interpret innocent remarks or acts as being sexist, 48 percent of Republican men, 46 percent of Republican women, agreed, as did 34 percent of Democratic men and 28 percent of Democratic women. Similarly, 30 percent of Republican men and 27 percent of Republican women, along with 22 percent of Democratic men and 17 percent of Democratic women, agreed that most women fail to appreciate fully all that men do for them. It's notable that on all these questions, whether someone is a Democrat or a Republican is a bigger driver of differences in answers than whether they are a man or a woman.

By the way, racial and gender identity don't exist separate from each other. Some scholarly research finds, that, for example, African American women's political identities are as influenced as much by their gender as by their race, but that different political circumstances can cause them to identify more strongly with other African Americans, or other women.[21] More recent work in this intersectional literature examines voting patterns in 2016, finding that white women were more supportive of the Republican ticket the more enmeshed they were within white, heterosexual, and Christian cultures.[22]

[21] Claudine Gay and Katherine Tate, 1998. "Doubly Bound: The Impact of Gender and Race on the Politics of Black Women." *Political Psychology* 19 (1): 169–84.
[22] Dara Z. Strolovitch, Janelle S. Wong, and Andrew Proctor, 2017. "A Possessive Investment in White Heteropatriarchy? The 2016 Election and the Politics of Race, Gender, and Sexuality." *Politics, Groups, and Identities* 5 (2): 353–63.

As these survey questions suggest, overtly racist or sexist sentiments are certainly present in both parties, but in fairly small numbers, especially on the Democratic side. Yet softer measures of sexism, and indicators of white identity and consciousness, exist in substantially larger numbers, even on the Democratic side. Roughly a third of Democratic men and Democratic whites appear to hold views consistent with white consciousness and soft sexism, respectively. The point here is neither to excoriate nor exonerate these views, but rather to note that if these views are so prevalent within a party, they will be relevant to the most crucial decisions that party makes – the nomination of candidates. This is especially true when the field of candidates is particularly diverse along lines of race and gender.

ELECTABILITY

Okay, I promised electability, so let's talk electability.

Party activists consider quite a few things when evaluating potential presidential candidates, but one of the main things they're trying to do is find the optimal balance between *fealty to party ideals* and *electability*. For example, few doubted whether Elizabeth Warren was sufficiently committed to advancing Democratic Party goals, but many were concerned about whether she could win; Joe Biden's supporters were confident he could defeat Donald Trump in a general election, but some were concerned about whether he was where the party was ideologically. This is just party activists trying to weigh their key goals. Fealty to party ideals is a reasonably straightforward notion, although obviously different factions within the party coalition will interpret fealty and weigh party goals differently. But electability is not as obvious as it may sound.

When I talk about electability, I'm referring to features of a candidate that make them more likely to prevail in a general election. A lot of us are quite confident that we can recognize electability when we see it. (A journalist said that Mitt Romney "oozes electability" in 2007.[23] A political scientist claimed that Michael Bloomberg "radi-

---

[23] David Yepsen, 2007. "In 2008, 'It's the Electability, Stupid.'" *Politico*, August 16.

ates electability" in 2019.[24]) But there's not always great evidence to back up people's beliefs about what makes one candidate more electable than another.

One thing that does seem to affect electability across a great deal of studies is the candidate's ideological positioning. Quite a few studies from congressional elections demonstrate that more ideologically extreme candidates[25] or those who vote more often with their party[26] tend to do worse in general elections. Voters, that is, seem to have some overall preference for moderation. Some additional research suggests that Democrats who voted against the Affordable Care Act in 2010 did somewhat better in their reelection campaigns than those who voted for it.[27] Support for Obama's signature health care proposal had the effect of making those members appear to be more liberal and more out of step with their districts. This finding holds internationally, as well, where moderation of party stances is associated with better prospects for the party in subsequent elections.[28] One of the most thorough recent studies of this phenomenon finds that extremists are roughly 20 percentage points less likely to win a general congressional election than moderates are,[29] although other studies suggest that the advantage for moderates may be waning with time.[30]

[24] Shane Croucher, 2019. "Michael Bloomberg Could 'Immediately Become a Heavyweight' in 2020 Race, Says Political Scientist: 'He Radiates Electability.'" *Newsweek*, November 8.

[25] Brandice Canes-Wrone, David W. Brady, and John F. Cogan, 1996. "Out of Step, Out of Office: Electoral Accountability And House Members' Voting." *American Political Science Review* 96 (1): 127–40.

[26] Jamie L. Carson, Gregory Koger, Matthew J. Lebo, and Everett Young, 2010. "The Electoral Costs of Party Loyalty In Congress." *American Journal of Political Science* 54 (3): 598–616.

[27] Brendan Nyhan, Eric McGhee, John Sides, Seth Masket, and Steven Greene, 2012. "One Vote Out of Step? The Effects of Salient Roll Call Votes In the 2010 Election." *American Politics Research* 40 (5): 844–79.

[28] James Adams and Zeynep Somer-Topcu, 2009. "Moderate Now, Win Votes Later: The Electoral Consequences of Parties' Policy Shifts in 25 Postwar Democracies." *The Journal of Politics* 71 (2): 678–92.

[29] Andrew B. Hall, 2015. "What Happens When Extremists Win Primaries?" *American Political Science Review* 109 (1): 18–42.

[30] Stephen Utych, 2020. "Man Bites Blue Dog: Are Moderates Really More Electable than Ideologues?" *Journal of Politics* 82 (1): 392–6.

A key question, then, is whether these findings apply at the presidential level, and there the evidence is more mixed. Nate Silver[31] compiled the evidence and found that more extreme candidates tend to do a bit worse even at the presidential level. However, this is hardly determinative. Voters in 2012, for example, seemed to consistently find Barack Obama to be more ideologically extreme than Mitt Romney, but ultimately preferred Obama in the election.[32] By some measures, 2016 voters were more likely to describe Donald Trump than Hillary Clinton as a moderate, but she won a greater share of the vote.[33]

As political scientists Cohen, McGrath, Aronow, and Zaller[34] found, it's actually very difficult to detect an effect of ideological extremism in presidential elections. In part, this is because presidential candidates have largely come from a pretty narrow range of the ideological spectrum in the postwar era. The major exceptions prior to 2016 were Barry Goldwater in 1964 and George McGovern in 1972. Both lost to more moderate incumbents by landslides, to be sure, but they also had the misfortune of trying to unseat moderate incumbents during strong economies. Their ideological extremism may have hurt them, but probably not by that much.

Why might ideological extremism matter less in presidential elections? It may simply be that there's enough information about the candidates available that voters don't need to fall back on ideology as an information shortcut. It may be that, particularly in more recent elections, voter partisanship is so strong that even a signal of extremism won't shake them. It may also be that we just haven't had a fair test of ideological extremism in recent presidential elections; the parties have usually been pretty successful in screening out the most

[31] Nate Silver, 2011. "Is Obama Toast? Handicapping the 2012 Election." *New York Times Magazine*, November 3.

[32] John Sides and Lynn Vavreck, 2014. *The Gamble: Choice and Chance in the 2012 Presidential Election.* Princeton: Princeton University Press.

[33] Pew Research Center, 2016. "Voters' Perceptions of the Candidates: Traits, Ideology and Impact on Issues," July 14. www.people-press.org/2016/07/14/voters-perceptions-of-the-candidates-traits-ideology-and-impact-on-issues/.

[34] Marty Cohen, Mary C. McGrath, Peter Aronow, and John Zaller, 2016. "Ideologically Extreme Candidates in US Presidential Elections, 1948–2012." *The Annals of the American Academy of Political and Social Science* 667 (1): 126–42.

extreme candidates, and Trump (the product of a relatively un-screened GOP nomination contest) was generally perceived as a moderate on many issues.

So let's just set ideology aside for now, confident that more moderate candidates have *some* advantage in elections that may be muted at the presidential level. What else seems to affect electability?

Most other things that party activists and political observers discuss when evaluating candidates' electability overlap considerably with the candidates' *identity*. Often, women and people of color are assumed to be more of an electoral risk than white men as nominees. To what extent is this true?

Despite beliefs, women seem to run as strongly as men in congressional elections. A study by Lefteris Anastasopoulos of thirty years of congressional elections found no evidence of a gender penalty.[35] Extensive research by Jennifer Lawless and Danny Hayes[36] concluded "not only that women win at equal rates, but also that the content of women's and men's campaigns looks the same, the volume and substance of the media coverage they receive is indistinguishable, and voters assess male and female candidates on a variety of issue competencies as equals."[37]

Now, there's an important caveat here. Women who run for office are often far more credentialed and experienced than men who run, often assuming that there's a greater penalty for inexperience for women.[38] That is, it's possible there is a more subtle bias in American elections against women, but that women candidates compensate for it by being more prepared than men are for the offices they seek. Another way to say that is that men feel qualified to run for office despite having a far thinner background than most women they'll run against.

---

[35] Lefteris Anastasopoulos, 2016. "Estimating the Gender Penalty in House of Representative Elections using a Regression Discontinuity Design." *Electoral Studies* 43: 150–7.

[36] Danny Hayes and Jennifer L. Lawless, 2016. *Women on the Run: Gender, Media, and Political Campaigns in a Polarized Era.* Cambridge: Cambridge University Press.

[37] Perry Bacon, Jr., 2018. "What We Actually Know About 'Electability.'" *FiveThirtyEight*, September 6. https://fivethirtyeight.com/features/what-we-actually-know-about-electability/.

[38] Kathryn Pearson and Eric McGhee, 2013. "What it Takes to Win: Questioning 'Gender Neutral' Outcomes in US House Elections." *Politics & Gender* 9 (4): 439–62.

Also, political professionals and pundits clearly have massively different expectations for women candidates than they do for men who run. As political scientist Kelly Dittmar's research shows, politics is generally seen as a masculine domain, and women candidates enter it at an immediate disadvantage trying to blunt concerns about their femininity and to shift the conversation to issues on which women are seen as better suited.[39] Women candidates are held responsible for the appearance and behavior of their families in ways that men aren't. Women who become angry or aggressive in public are often chastised for it, seen as unstable or irrational, while men in politics are often praised for the same behavior, seen as assertive.[40]

But again, overall, the women who do run tend to do about as well in elections as the men who do run. It's difficult to conclude that a female presidential candidate would do worse than a male one, all else being equal judging from the available evidence.

What about race? The evidence here is more mixed on this. Some studies of congressional elections find that African American candidates do somewhat worse among white voters.[41] Studies suggest that Barack Obama lost a few points nationwide due to this white aversion to African American candidates.[42] On the other hand, African American voters are more likely to turn out to vote for a Democratic African American candidate,[43] which could explain why African American turnout was at 65 percent when

[39] Kelly Dittmar, 2015. *Navigating Gendered Terrain: Stereotypes and Strategy in Political Campaigns.* Philadelphia: Temple University Press.

[40] Kelly Dittmar, 2016. "Watching Election 2016 with a Gender Lens." *PS: Political Science & Politics* 49 (4): 807–12.

[41] Neil Visalvanich, 2017. "When Does Race Matter? Exploring White Responses to Minority Congressional Candidates." *Politics, Groups, and Identities* 5 (4): 618–41.

[42] Brian F. Schaffner, 2011. "Racial Salience and the Obama Vote." *Political Psychology* 32 (6): 963–88; Seth Stephens-Davidowitz, 2014. "The Cost of Racial Animus on a Black Candidate: Evidence Using Google Search Data." *Journal of Public Economics* 118: 26–40.

[43] Lawrence D. Bobo and Franklin D. Gilliam Jr., 1990. "Race, Sociopolitical Participation, and Black Empowerment." *American Political Science Review* 84: 377–93; James M. Vanderleeuw and Baodong Liu, 2002. "Political Empowerment, Mobilization and Black Voter Roll-Off." *Urban Affairs Review* 37: 380–96; Michael C. Herron and Jasjeet S. Sekhon, 2005. "Black Candidates and Black Voters: Assessing the Impact of Candidate Race on Uncounted Vote Rates." *Journal of Politics* 67: 154–77; David Lublin and Katherine Tate, 1995. "Racial Group Competition in Urban Elections." In *Classifying by Race*, edited by Paul G. Peterson. Princeton: Princeton University Press, pp. 245–61; Katherine Tate, 1991. "Black

Obama was on the ballot and is usually closer to 60 percent.[44] So again, the lessons for nominating an African American candidate at the national level are not clear cut. Yes, it's possible such a candidate would do worse among working-class white voters living in states like Wisconsin, Michigan, and Pennsylvania, but could also boost turnout among black voters in those states, and it's not obvious whether this would be a net gain or loss for the party. (Boost African American turnout in those three states by just a few points in 2016, after all, and Hillary Clinton is the 45th president.)

And yet, as Perry Bacon, Jr. noted in a series of posts at *FiveThirtyEight* in 2018, many simply assume that women and people of color are less electable than men. "Electability," he notes, "at times ends up being used as an all-purpose cudgel against female and minority candidates." He cites numerous instances in which female and minority candidates are simply told not to run by influential Democrats because it is assumed that a white male candidate is more electable. Kira Sanbonmatsu[45] finds that party leaders are often predisposed against female candidates, assuming them to be less electable. Women are less likely to be recruited than men, even at the same level of qualification.[46] Indeed, as Kanthak and Woon argue, women may simply be more election-averse than men.[47] A recent survey of local party chairs, meanwhile, found that while they didn't hold female candidates in lower esteem, chairs of both parties were concerned that African American and Latino candidates were less electable than whites.[48]

Political Participation in the 1984 and 1988 Presidential Elections." *American Political Science Review* 85: 1159–76.

[44] Amir Shawn Fairdosi and Jon C. Rogowski, 2015. "Candidate Race, Partisanship, and Political Participation: When Do Black Candidates Increase Black Turnout?" *Political Research Quarterly* 68 (2): 337–49.

[45] Kira Sanbonmatsu, 2010. *Where Women Run: Gender and Party in the American States.* Ann Arbor: University of Michigan Press.

[46] Jennifer L. Lawless and Richard L. Fox, 2013. "Girls Just Wanna Not Run: The Gender Gap in Young Americans' Political Ambition." Report. Washington, DC: Women & Politics Institute.

[47] Kristin Kanthak and Jonathan Woon, 2015. "Women Don't Run? Election Aversion and Candidate Entry." *American Journal of Political Science* 59 (3): 595–612.

[48] David Doherty, Conor M. Dowling, and Michael G. Miller, 2019. "Do Local Party Chairs Think Women and Minority Candidates Can Win? Evidence from a Conjoint Experiment." *The Journal of Politics* 81 (4): 1282–97.

It is in this way that concerns about electability become a self-fulfilling prophecy. Women and people of color may be just as interested in holding office as whites, but they are regularly told that doing so would be a long shot and would hurt their party's chances, and so many of them (quite possibly the most qualified candidates) decline to run. Presumed to be unelectable, few are elected. And those that do run are often taken less seriously by political elites and observers, and are given less support and media attention.

At this point, I need to bring ideology back in. One of the reasons that party leaders are concerned that women and people of color will underperform as nominees is because voters tend to view them as more ideologically liberal. In a revealing Pew survey in 2007, respondents were asked to place some of the major presidential candidates on an ideological scale.[49] Hillary Clinton, running on relatively hawkish foreign policy credentials, was nonetheless placed to the left of Barack Obama. Respondents considered Southern white candidate John Edwards to be well to the right of the others despite his regular lambasting of "two Americas" and his calls to end poverty, strengthen unions, and raise the minimum wage. Arguably, the participants in this survey were responding more to the candidates' appearances (and accents) than to their stated policy positions. Among Democrats, candidates' demographic characteristics may provide a false signal about ideological commitments.

To get a sense of this, I conducted a simple analysis of Democratic members of the 115th House of Representatives (2017–2019). A 2018 survey by the Cooperative Congressional Election Study[50] asked voters in the members' districts to place their member ideologically on a scale from -5 (the most liberal position) to +5 (the most conservative position). Ongoing work at Voteview[51] uses members' roll call votes to derive an "ideal point" of their voting behavior. By comparing these two measures, we can see how close constituents are

[49] Pew Research Center, 2007. "Both Sides Reject Compromise in Iraq Funding Fight," April 26. www.people-press.org/2007/04/26/both-sides-reject-compromise-in-iraq-funding-fight/.

[50] I am grateful to Kevin Reuning at Data for Progress for providing the data.

[51] https://voteview.com.

to estimating the ideology of their members as revealed in their congressional voting.[52] The correlation between the two measures is a reasonably strong .55; voters have a pretty good idea of how liberal or conservative their members' voting behavior is.

But a more detailed look reveals some interesting differences. Constituents generally perceive both an African American and a woman member of Congress as more liberal than a white male member of Congress with the same voting record.[53] The differences are not enormous – African Americans and women are seen as about 8 and 6 percentage points more liberal, respectively, than other House members, controlling for their roll call behavior – but these results are statistically significant, and quite possibly enough for party activists to care about when considering a nominee. In other words, this evidence suggests that voters see African Americans and women as somewhat out of step with their districts just by virtue of their demographic characteristics. By extension, voters see white men as more moderate, and thus presumably more electable, for no other reason than their being white men.

This finding is consistent with studies by Brian Schaffner and Seth Stephens-Davidowitz suggesting that Barack Obama lost several percentage points of the vote in 2008 and 2012 by virtue of his race. It's also consistent with findings by Neil Visalvanich[54] and Matthew Jacobsmeier[55] that African American congressional candidates underperform because white voters see them as ideologically extreme.

---

[52] There's no need here to get into which, if either, of these measures captures the "true" ideology of the member of Congress. Voters can certainly have flawed assessments of their elected officials based on campaign material, media coverage, and so forth, and roll call votes are highly subject to agenda control, meaning we don't get to see members' voting behavior on all issues. But the mismatch between the two measures can be revealing.

[53] I ran a fixed-effects regression analysis here controlling for states, using the roll call ideal points to predict voters' perceived ideological positions of their members. I controlled for the percent of the district that is African American, as well as the percent of the vote received by Hillary Clinton in that district in 2016.

[54] Neil Visalvanich, 2017. "When Does Race Matter? Exploring White Responses to Minority Congressional Candidates." *Politics, Groups, and Identities* 5 (4): 618–41.

[55] Matthew Jacobsmeier, 2015. "From Black and White to Left and Right: Race, Perceptions of Candidates' Ideologies, and Voting Behavior in U.S. House Elections." *Political Behavior* 37: 595–621.

But in many ways, this shows how the *discussion* of electability as a desirable quality in a candidate is, in a sense, a toxic one. Introducing an election narrative about identity, even if it has no basis in fact, can force people to reassess their candidate preferences. It can cause party elites to discount the chances of women and people of color, making them more likely to recruit white male candidates. And it can prey on the lower self-assessment of prospective female candidates, in particular, making them less likely to jump into a race. (More on this in Chapter 6.)

This doesn't mean there's no value in considering electability; it would be foolish for a party to nominate someone they knew had no chance of winning an otherwise winnable race. And indeed, a discussion of electability might lead voters and party leaders to consider how nominating someone other than a white male could boost turnout among segments of the electorate who aren't always that enthusiastic. However, this discussion is fraught, particularly for a political party that has defined itself in recent decades as the one that embraces and seeks inclusion and diversity.

THE ELECTION LOSS NARRATIVE

"I couldn't get the job done," wrote Hillary Clinton in her 2017 book *What Happened*, "and I'll have to live with that for rest of my life."[56] In that book, Clinton detailed a number of different reasons why she believed Donald Trump defeated her, including voter partisanship, cultural anxieties toward immigrants, sexism within the electorate, media coverage of the e-mail investigation, and more. Political scientists Michael S. Lewis-Beck and Stephen Quinlan analyzed the various explanations in her book and found a very high proportion of them supported by public opinion evidence.[57] David Roberts wrote a related piece at *Vox* tearing through many competing election explanations and finding decent evidence supporting many of them, concluding, "The truth is that we'll never know exactly which factors made the difference, or which narrative

[56] Hillary Rodham Clinton, 2017. *What Happened.* New York: Simon and Schuster.
[57] Michael S. Lewis-Beck and Stephen Quinlan, 2019. "The Hillary Hypotheses: Testing Candidate Views of Loss." *Perspectives on Politics* 17 (3): 646–65.

is 'correct.'"[58] Regardless of these stories' accuracy, though, all were important examples of post-election narratives.

The idea of the post-election narrative is central to this book. It's based on the notion that political observers, parties, and politicians try to draw a lesson from recent elections to inform their decision-making about the next one. We hear these sorts of arguments all the time – "She should've gone to Wisconsin," "Bernie would've won," etc., were common examples emerging in November 2016. Some landslide losses have produced narratives that the party's previous nominee was too ideologically extreme, as happened after Walter Mondale's 1984 loss to Ronald Reagan. But we don't often appreciate how these narratives affect the behavior of parties and politicians as they prepare for the next election cycle.

An important feature of these narratives is that they often aren't based on very much hard data. A great deal of governing involves politicians and pundits attempting to divine the "national mood." Information for such calculations often comes from polls, constituent phone calls, town hall meetings, and election results, but may indeed be conjured out of thin air. As John Kingdon[59] noted, members of Congress often claim public support for policy stances they favor in the absence of or even in contradiction to surveys or election results. And career bureaucrats often defer to members of Congress under the assumption that "politicians have their fingers on the national pulse because it is their business and their livelihood to do so." Walter Lippmann asks if, when we vote, "Have we expressed our thoughts on the public policy of the United States? Presumably we have a number of thoughts on this and that with many buts and ifs and ors. Surely the cross on a piece of paper does not express them."[60]

One of the ways election interpretations often figure into the political system is when politicians or pundits claim a "mandate" for one party or candidate. A mandate is often said to exist when a party does decisively

---

[58] David Roberts, 2016. "Everything Mattered: Lessons from 2016's Bizarre Presidential Election." *Vox*, November 30. www.vox.com/policy-and-politics/2016/11/30/13631 532/everything-mattered-2016-presidential-election.

[59] John W. Kingdon, 2011. *Agendas, Alternatives, and Public Policies*. Second edition. Harlow: Longman, pp. 148–9.

[60] Walter Lippmann, 1925. *The Phantom Public*. New York: Harcourt, Brace, pp. 56–7.

and unexpectedly well in an election, and that victory is seen as broad support by the electorate for that party's policy agenda.[61] While the definition of a mandate isn't very precise, Stanley Kelley[62] uses surveys of voters to distinguish between the motivations of the electorates across different landslides, detecting different mandates from the lopsided elections of 1964 and 1972. Lawrence Grossback, David Peterson, and James Stimson,[63] meanwhile, examined a few pivotal elections and found that the behavior of members of Congress shifted because of them, creating the conditions for the passage of the Voting Rights Act and Ronald Reagan's first budget, among other things. While mandates are constructions of political actors and the media, they can also have important consequences for public policy. "Politicians," Grossback *et al.* write, "behave differently when they come to the belief that a recent election has signaled a voter mandate."

Modern presidents often seek to develop post-election narratives to claim mandates for their governing agenda, as political scientist Julia Azari has described, especially when the legitimacy of those president's electoral victories is called into question.[64] Think of George W. Bush claiming a mandate to reform Social Security, or Barack Obama telling Republican congressional leaders "I won," or Donald Trump showing visitors to the Oval Office a map of his Electoral College victory. Azari's work demonstrates the vital role of election interpretation to modern party politics and government behavior.

But if surprise victories provide lessons that affect behavior, then surprise losses may be even more powerful. Winning, political scientist Majorie Hershey writes, has a "fairly blunt, conservatizing effect on campaigners."[65] As long as they're winning, they're going to take the

---

[61] Patricia Heidotting Conley, 2001. *Presidential Mandates: How Elections Shape the National Agenda.* Chicago: University of Chicago Press; Charles O. Jones, 1994. *The Presidency in a Separated System.* Washington, DC: Brookings Institution Press; Robert A. Dahl. 1990. "Myth of the Presidential Mandate." *Political Science Quarterly* 105: 355–72.

[62] Stanley Kelley Jr., 1983. *Interpreting Elections.* Princeton: Princeton University Press.

[63] Lawrence J. Grossback David A.M. Peterson, and James A. Stimson, 2006. *Mandate Politics.* Cambridge: Cambridge University Press, 2006.

[64] Julia R. Azari, 2014. *Delivering the People's Message: The Changing Politics of the Presidential Mandate.* Ithaca, NY: Cornell University Press.

[65] Marjorie Randon Hershey, 1984. *Running for Office: The Political Education of Campaigners.* London: Chatham House Publishers, p. 94.

view that whatever they did prior to that win was at least partially responsible for it, and they'll continue to do it. Conversely, those who lose an
election will be very open to making changes the next time they run,
figuring that at least one of the things they did last time around was
responsible for their loss. As Richard Fenno notes,[66] even a weak win can
force an incumbent to take stock and reassess his or her public behavior.
Hershey notes that election narratives are always heavily mediated con-
structs, resulting from an interplay between candidates, party leaders,
and election observers.

For example, she notes, the 1982 congressional midterms featured
substantial gains for Democrats in the US House and several state legislatures, but no change in the US Senate. Congressional Democrats
quickly defined the election as a massive repudiation of Ronald
Reagan's economic policies. The White House called it a wash.
Conservative activists claimed that it was a sign that some Republicans
weren't governing conservatively *enough*. Ultimately, the media tended to
gravitate around the narrative offered by congressional Democrats. But,
as Hershey argues, "Whether the ... explanation was 'correct' in any
objective sense is largely beside the point. It will be remembered by
attentive candidates when they make their next race, by political activists
and other campaigners in search of models" (p. 99).

To examine this narrative construction process in action, Hershey
studied hundreds of newspaper articles written in the weeks immediately
after the 1984 presidential contest between Ronald Reagan and Walter
Mondale.[67] That election was, of course, a blowout – Reagan won by
18 percentage points and took forty-nine states. According to Hershey,
the number of explanations for the election's outcome was initially
enormous – more than eighty were offered across the various news
articles – but dropped to around ten just two months later. Initially,
interpretations based on the candidates' personalities dominated the
narratives, but they faded rapidly in significance. Among the surviving

---

[66]   Richard F. Fenno, 1991. *The Emergence of a Senate Leader: Pete Domenici and the Reagan
       Budget*. Washington, DC: CQ Press, p. xii.
[67]   Marjorie Randon Hershey, 1992. "The Constructed Explanation: Interpreting
       Election Results in the 1984 Presidential Race." *The Journal of Politics* 54 (4): 943–76.

narratives, Mondale's vowed tax increase gained in importance. Another explanation will be familiar to observers of the 2016 presidential election; Mondale and the Democrats were blamed for being too attentive to the needs of "special interests" (mainly racial minorities) and not enough to working class white voters.

Building a post-election narrative is slightly different for parties than it is for candidates. A candidate that loses might take a hint and look for a different line of work. Parties, conversely, are functionally immortal. (Okay, let's pour one out for the Federalists and Whigs.) The Democratic and Republican parties have dominated American politics since the 1850s. Even when one of those parties has been massively disgraced and repudiated, such as the Democrats after the Civil War or the Republicans following the Watergate scandal and resignation of Richard Nixon, the party is often competitive again in the space of just a few years. Thus interpreting a loss is vitally important for parties; closing shop simply isn't an option. Of course, a party rarely completely reconstructs itself. As Azari notes, parties are inherently risk-averse organizations, wary of embracing new stances or reshuffling longstanding coalitions.[68] Suffering a particularly stinging loss, a party may even be more likely to trim its sails and fall back on traditional stances and candidates.

We see evidence of this in other nations, as well. The Party Manifesto Project, providing comprehensive records of party platform stances from over fifty nations across eight decades, has been vital to tracking the processes by which parties change their positions. And indeed, evidence suggests that losses, far more than victories, cause parties to moderate their stances, at least temporarily, to become more competitive.[69]

---

[68] Julia Azari, 2019. "Are Parties Inherently Conservative?" In Jonathan Bernstein and Casey B.K. Dominguez, eds., *The Making of the Presidential Candidates 2020*. Lanham, MD: Rowman and Littlefield.

[69] Zeynep Somer-Topcu, 2009. "Timely Decisions: The Effects of Past National Elections on Party Policy Change." *The Journal of Politics* 71 (1): 238–48; Tarik Abou-Chadi and Matthias Orlowski. 2016. "Moderate as Necessary: The Role of Electoral Competitiveness and Party Size in Explaining Parties' Policy Shifts." *The Journal of Politics* 78 (3): 868–81.

I will get more into this in the next section, but this loss interpretation is a vital part of the party nomination process. Members of an out-of-power party, when picking a nominee for the next election, will consider why they lost the last one – was their candidate too ideologically extreme, too uninteresting, too inarticulate, or what? This is where Hershey's theory of election narratives becomes vitally important. Constructing the dominant vision of what happened is the way to control the party's path over the next several years. And very often, those interpretations overlap heavily with conceptions of ideology and identity.

The example of the Democrats' efforts to define their 1984 loss to Ronald Reagan is instructive. As mentioned above, one of the narratives that some influential party members pushed was that Democrats had lost because they were hopelessly in the thrall of the "special interests." As a leading Democratic consultant said shortly after the election,

> We have to realize that we're getting out of touch with normal, regular people. We're forgetting that the white middle-class is rejecting us. We're being wagged by the tail of Jesse Jackson, of feminists or gay activists. The average voter is saying, "What about me?"[70]

Note here the juxtaposition of African American leaders, feminists, and gay activists against "normal, regular people" and "the average voter." This is not just simply a recurring form of Democratic self-loathing; it has a goal. There is little reason to think that Walter Mondale lost by 18 points due to the over-solicitousness of racial groups at a time when the economy was growing by seven points. Nonetheless, if enough influential people in the party *believe* that was the cause of the loss, it may lead them to make changes in the party to disempower those interests and advance those of a more conservative set of white men.

Arguably, identity is what Democrats argue about every time they lose a presidential election. The Democrats' McGovern–Fraser reform commission (more about this in Chapter 4) focused a great deal on demographic quotas for women, racial minorities, and young people among state party delegations in the wake of the party's 1968 loss, and others in

---

[70] Quoted from Hershey 1992, p. 959.

the party in turn blamed those quotas for the party's loss in 1972.[71] At least since that time, when demographic representation was elevated to a national party-level concern among Democrats, dissenters within the party have used it as a cudgel, often blaming problems for the party on its emphasis on identity.

The internal critiques became even sharper after a series of Democratic presidential losses in the 1980s: the unusual defeat of an incumbent in 1980, Mondale's landslide rout in 1984, and a rare third consecutive presidential loss in 1988, left Democratic leaders looking for scapegoats. The fact that Rev. Jesse Jackson had been a candidate in the 1984 and 1988 contests, boosting African American turnout and raising policy expectations among black constituents, suggested to more conservative whites in the party that they were losing because of the party's focus on the interests of minorities at the expense of rural whites. Senator Daniel Moynihan argued that the party was now being seen as a vehicle primarily for minority voters.[72]

In 1985, Democratic pollster Stanley Greenberg conducted a survey for Michigan Democrats to discern the attitudes of white Democrats toward African Americans, with the goal of helping to shape party strategy regarding race. The assessment was bleak:

> Greenberg found that the white Democrats "express[ed] a profound distaste for blacks, a sentiment that pervades almost everything they think about government and politics. Blacks constitute the explanation for their vulnerability and for almost everything that has gone wrong in their lives; not being black is what constitutes being middle class; not living with blacks is what makes a neighborhood a decent place to live. ... These sentiments have important implications for Democrats, as virtually all progressive symbols and themes have been redefined in racial and pejorative terms."[73]

Paul Frymer's *Uneasy Alliances* takes a broad historical view of this dynamic. This is not simply about one election or one party, Frymer

---

[71] Byron E. Shafer, 1983. *Quiet Revolution: Struggle for the Democratic Party and the Shaping of Post-Reform Politics.* New York: Russell Sage Foundation.
[72] Paul Frymer, 2010. *Uneasy Alliances: Race and Party Competition in America.* Princeton: Princeton University Press, p. 112.
[73] Ibid., p. 112–14.

argues. Rather, African Americans have generally been "captured" in one party coalition or another since the abolition of slavery, and the party to which they pledge their loyalty often ignores many of their concerns in the name of electability. Being seen as advocating too much for African Americans, that is, is historically seen as a toxic position for a party, activating the sort of white resentment Greenberg captured in his 1985 survey.

For example, newly enfranchised blacks in the late 1800s voted consistently with the party of Lincoln, but white Republicans, concerned about resurgent Democrats during Reconstruction, looked for ways to trim the party's commitment to blacks in order to maintain support among white voters. When Democrats performed well in a number of northern state legislative contests in 1867 and then made a reasonable showing in the 1868 presidential election, Republican leaders "called for further appeasement of Southern whites and an easing of Reconstruction. Some argued that if Congress were to follow the electoral results, the issue of suffrage would be dead."[74] Frymer tracks similar interpretations of the elections of 1874 and 1880, with conservative Republican leaders consistently abandoning rights for African Americans for fear of alienating white voters. Those white Republicans, "motivated by a combination of racism and a perception that their party's attachment to black voters and interests was hurting their electoral opportunities, consistently resisted entering into coalitions with black Republicans."[75]

In a telling moment in 1876, President Ulysses Grant struggled with whether to send additional soldiers to Mississippi to protect black voters. Shortly before rendering his decision, recalls historian Vernon Wharton,

> Grant was visited by a delegation of politicians from Ohio, a pivotal state which was to have an election in October. Mississippi, these visitors declared, was already lost to the party; troops would arrive too late to save the state. Even worse, the order that sent troops to Mississippi would mean the loss of Ohio to the party. The Negroes must be sacrificed.[76]

---

[74] Ibid., p. 58.   [75] Ibid., p. 72.   [76] Quoted in ibid., p. 68.

Today, of course, African Americans are perhaps the identity group most wedded to a political party, with roughly 90 percent of African Americans regularly voting for Democratic presidential candidates. (About 80 percent of white evangelical Christians voted for Donald Trump in 2016, by comparison.) As political scientists Ismail White and Chryl Laird demonstrate, African Americans continue to vote and identify with Democrats despite roughly a third considering themselves conservative, in large part due to social pressure within the black community.[77]

In Frymer's framework, all this makes African Americans a "captured" constituency within the modern Democratic coalition. It is notable that some of African Americans' greatest political gains of the past century occurred during the Civil Rights Movement when their votes were up for grabs. Frymer also cites Bill Clinton's first two years in the White House as a productive time for the Congressional Black Caucus, as Democrats held unified control of the federal government but the CBC could make or break that control at any time. At other points, when African Americans did not have that kind of political leverage, their votes were mostly just assumed and their agenda largely ignored.

As political scientist Phil Klinkner notes,[78] we can view the post-1984 Democratic Party as working to marginalize its African American supporters in the name of greater electability. One of its moves was the creation and encouragement of Super Tuesday, a collection of primaries in mostly Southern states held relatively early in the cycle and simultaneously to enhance their influence and the attention paid to them. The tactic did not initially bear much fruit – Massachusetts Governor Michael Dukakis dominated Super Tuesday in 1988 and lost the presidential election that fall (albeit by a much smaller margin than Mondale had four years earlier, and with a Texan running mate). But the process did aid in the 1992 nomination of Arkansas Governor Bill Clinton, a candidate who ran by promising to "end welfare as we know it" and by criticizing Jesse Jackson's

[77] Ismail K. White and Chryl N. Laird, 2020. *Steadfast Democrats: How Social Forces Shape Black Political Behavior*. Princeton: Princeton University Press.

[78] Philip A. Klinkner, 1994, *The Losing Parties: Out-Party National Committees, 1956–1993*. New Haven: Yale University Press.

influence within the party.[79] We can view Clinton's nomination as the product of a multi-cycle effort to define previous elections and steer the Democratic Party away from the influence of race- and gender-oriented interest groups and more toward those of white southerners.

As we'll see in the coming chapters, the Democratic Party since 2016 has been engaged in a battle to define the narrative of Hillary Clinton's surprise loss to Donald Trump. What lesson was to be learned? To some, it was evidence that the Democrats picked the wrong candidate; surely a less scandal-plagued nominee, or a more moderate one, or a younger one, or a man, etc., would have defeated Trump. But what of the fact that Clinton beat Trump in the popular vote by roughly 3 million votes? Well, that could be evidence that Republicans made an enormous mistake in nominating Trump, and that a more conventional candidate would have won handily and governed with more of a mandate, achieving more for the party. There are plenty of interpretations available to match almost any preconceived notion.

PARTY NOMINATIONS

Okay, we've talked about electability, identity, ideology, and post-election narratives. All of this comes together here, in the decision about whom the party should nominate for the next election. Ultimately, this book is an examination of a party nomination contest, and I'm writing it at a time when our understanding of American party nominations is in a state of uncertainty. There are many definitions of political parties, but the one I'll use here is the one I've used previously: A party is a network of intense policy demanders working together to control government through their control of nominations to office.[80]

The book that has been arguably the dominant theory of nominations for more than a decade, *The Party Decides*,[81] had, to put it politely, a rather

---

[79] Gwen Ifill, 1992. "Democrats; Clinton at Jackson Meeting: Warmth, and Some Friction." *The New York Times*, June 14.

[80] Seth Masket, 2016. *The Inevitable Party: Why Attempts to Kill the Party System Fail and How They Weaken Democracy*. Oxford: Oxford University Press.

[81] Marty Cohen, David Karol, Hans Noel, and John Zaller, 2008. *The Party Decides: Presidential Nominations Before and After Reform*. Chicago: University of Chicago Press.

bad 2016 (I'll get into this in a bit), but a surprisingly good 2020. Written by political scientists Marty Cohen, David Karol, Hans Noel, and John Zaller, this book sought to explain how nominations function and why nominations didn't seem to be descending into internal factional warfare within America's major political parties. As political scientist Nelson Polsby argued a generation earlier,[82] the reforms of the post-1968 period, generally known as the McGovern–Fraser reforms, created the conditions for this internal strife. It was possible, that is, for a factional candidate, passionately loved by a minority within the party but disliked by many more, to dominate early contests like the Iowa Caucuses and the New Hampshire primary, gain media attention and money as a result, and translate that into a winning nomination bid. Arguably, this is what happened in the presidential nominations of George McGovern in 1972 and Jimmy Carter in 1976, and in Ronald Reagan's near-dethroning of Gerald Ford in 1976. Yet between 1980 and 2012, parties somehow managed to produce mainstream presidential nominees who were broadly acceptable across the parties' major factions. What allowed this to happen?

By 1980, the authors argue, party insiders across both parties had largely figured out how to control the system. Yes, primaries and caucuses were still vital to amassing delegates and the nomination, but party insiders could steer the outcomes of those contests by picking a favorite candidate early and providing that candidate with endorsements, funds, expertise, and other vital campaign assets long before anyone started voting. And indeed, the authors find that from 1980 to 2000, major party presidential nominees were invariably the candidates the bulk of party insiders had endorsed prior to the Iowa Caucuses. Two thousand and four was something of a miss for the theory in that endorsements were split among the Democratic candidates and didn't necessarily suggest a John Kerry victory. But the fact that Howard Dean had failed to do well in early contests despite his dominance of media coverage and fundraising – but a lack of support among party insiders – suggested that the party had a good deal of power in determining its nominees.

---

[82] Nelson W. Polsby, 1983. *Consequences of Party Reform.* Oxford: Oxford University Press.

Yet the book's theory showed some strain shortly after its 2008 publication. Hillary Clinton was, by most accounts, the Democratic insiders' preferred candidate for the nomination prior to the Iowa Caucuses in 2008, yet she lost the nomination. It would be a stretch to call Barack Obama an insurgent candidate in 2008 – he was recruited to run for president by the likes of Senators Harry Reid and Ted Kennedy[83] – but his nomination was an inconvenient, if hardly catastrophic, data point for *The Party Decides*, making the party system look more candidate-driven than it had looked previously. On the GOP side, the model seemed to be holding, if imperfectly. John McCain was something of an irregular choice for party insiders given his past ideological apostasies (on campaign finance reform and other issues) and his disparagement of various key groups within the Republican coalition, including the Christian right. But his moves to embrace people and positions he had previously spurned to win the nomination suggested a robust party organization that exerted control over its candidates. The 2012 race was messy, with nearly every Republican candidate holding front-runner status for a short time, and some, like Newt Gingrich, remaining potent until well into the spring primaries. But Mitt Romney, who had won the bulk of insider endorsements early in the cycle, prevailed as the nominee. The model was holding.

Then 2016 happened. To be sure, the model worked just fine on the Democratic side that year. Hillary Clinton was the runaway favorite for the nomination among party insiders, and that helped her win enough primaries and caucuses to emerge as the nominee, even if that nomination took longer to clinch than previous ones had.

But *The Party Decides* simply could not explain the Republican Party's actions in 2016. In many ways, the party that year simply didn't decide. Most party insiders who issue public endorsements on the Republican side chose not to issue any in that cycle, and others were split among various candidates (none of whom were Donald Trump). So it's fair to ask just what the authors got wrong, or failed to anticipate about the Republican Party in 2016.

---

[83] John Heilemann and Mark Halperin. 2010. *Game Change: Obama and the Clintons, McCain and Palin, and the Race of a Lifetime.* New York: Harper Collins.

In a late 2016 article, the authors offered something of a post-mortem[84], explaining where they believed their theory and empirical reality diverged. In particular, they suggested that they had built the theory over a relatively stable and congenial period in the Republican coalition's history. The rise of the Tea Party in 2009 revealed and exacerbated fissures within the party that made collective action much harder to achieve within the party, and these divisions resulted in budget shutdowns and ultimately the demise of John Boehner's House speakership.

Additionally, they note that aspects of the "invisible primary" – the long, informal stage of candidate competition and winnowing that occurs prior to any actual voting or caucusing – have become much more visible in recent years thanks to cable coverage, political blogs, and a dramatic increase in the number of primary debates. This has the effect of inviting more people into the "small world" of insiders evaluating the candidates and making the decisions, making coordination much harder. Added to this problem is the rapid increase in fundraising and early spending, creating multitudes of candidates not reliant upon mainstream party sources for support.

In separate work, Jonathan Bernstein offers some suggestions as to why the Republican nomination cycle of 2016 was so unusual.[85] For one, a number of nomination norms had recently shifted rapidly or collapsed. This included the demise of Iowa's Ames Straw Poll, an early contest in the Republican Invisible Primary that had existed since 1980 but had become seen as something of a farce with no predictive value and no relationship to convention delegates. While its abandonment was hardly a major shift in the party nominating system, Bernstein notes how the straw poll had served as an early proving ground for candidates and their ability to muster party and campaign resources, and its disappearance was one of several changing norms that undermined coherent party signals to voters, caucusgoers, and other party insiders. Bernstein also

---

[84] Marty Cohen, David Karol, Hans Noel, and John Zaller, 2016. "Party Versus Faction in the Reformed Presidential Nominating System." *PS: Political Science and Politics*, October, pp. 701–8.

[85] Jonathan Bernstein, 2019. "The Expanded Party's Influence." In Jonathan Bernstein and Casey B.K. Dominguez, eds., *The Making of the Presidential Candidates 2020.* Lanham, MD: Rowman and Littlefield.

notes how media coverage of primaries was shifting, and in particular how the GOP had developed a somewhat perverse relationship with a conservative news media that thrived on resentment and bombastic criticisms of government.

Here I'll offer my own take on where the model and reality diverged in 2016. To review, the basic principles of *The Party Decides* model are as follows:

1. Party elites have a conversation to determine their ideal presidential candidate. This "conversation" is loosely defined, but it involves activists and other longstanding party hands learning about the candidates through meetings, rallies, coffee gatherings, and other forms of research and exchanging information with each other.

2. The ideal presidential candidate is some combination of fealty to the party's agenda and electability. Party insiders want someone who will deliver on a good deal of what the party cares about but will not appear so extreme as to cost the party a victory.

3. The conversation is informed by recent elections, from which insiders "learn" where the ideal spot is. A typical pattern in the postwar US is for a party to nominate a relatively extreme candidate shortly after losing control of the presidency (e.g. Barry Goldwater in 1964, George McGovern in 1972) but nominate steadily more moderate ones with successive losses (Bill Clinton in 1992, Dwight Eisenhower in 1952).

4. Once insiders reach a decision about their ideal candidate, they coordinate their resources (endorsements, donations, and expertise) behind this candidate. This tends to give this candidate a substantial advantage in the upcoming primaries and caucuses and sends a signal to non-favored candidates to drop out of the race. This doesn't guarantee a victory for the party's preferred candidate but typically is very effective.

5. The primaries and caucuses often end up ratifying what party insiders already decided.

The Republicans' 2016 nomination contest very clearly violated several of the five steps listed above. Point 2 was importantly violated in that the party's ultimate nominee, Donald Trump, was neither particularly faithful to the party's agenda (he held views on trade and social welfare wildly outside the preferences of party insiders and had been pro-choice on abortion just a few years earlier) nor appeared to be particularly electable (he trailed Hillary Clinton in polling throughout 2016, and he seemed to be alienating pivotal segments of the population – including suburban women, Latinos, veterans, and Gold Star families – at a record pace). There was another considerable violation of point 4, in that party insiders never agreed on their preferred candidate. Dramatically fewer insiders made any endorsement at all in 2016 compared to previous cycles. Those that did tended to be split between Ted Cruz, Jeb Bush, Marco Rubio, and Chris Christie. In sharp contrast with other cycles, primary votes and caucusgoers largely made the decision on their own without clear guidance from party insiders, and the insiders largely rallied behind that decision later.

All this leads to a key question: Were Democrats in 2020 in the same position as Republicans four years earlier? We know, in hindsight, that the presidential nomination contests ended very differently (I'll get more into the Democrats of 2020 in the concluding chapter), but how did the parties differ going into each contest?

Many of the factors that were undermining Republican coordination in 2016 were also working against Democrats in 2020. For example, the modern campaign finance system makes it harder for either party to pressure candidates out of a race. Political observers often overstate the impact of the *Citizens United* (2010) Supreme Court decision, which permitted corporate and union expenditures on campaign advertisements close to an election. Parties and campaigns have actually been developing innovative campaign finance strategies for decades, usually as a way of adapting to or circumnavigating existing campaign finance laws. Nonetheless, the *Citizens United* decision helped accelerate the growth of "outside" or "dark" spending with minimal spending requirements.

In recent years, it has become possible for allies of individual candidates to set up friendly Super PACs (political action committees) that allow a small number of donors to fund those campaigns even without party insiders' backing. Journalist Mark Schmitt described Newt Gingrich and Rick Santorum as "zombie candidates" in 2012 because they were being propped up by small numbers of wealthy donors long after it had become clear that they had no chance of winning the

Republican nomination.[86] A Gingrich-aligned PAC, Winning our Future, was bankrolled almost solely by Nevada casino magnate Sheldon Adelson, who contributed over $20 million to keep Gingrich's campaign afloat into the early spring of 2012.

This has contributed to an explosion in the number of candidates running for president. The threat of being deprived of funding from mainstream party sources simply isn't as demotivating today when candidates can still find a handful of millionaires to fund their television advertisements and travel. Seventeen major Republicans competed in the early presidential debates in 2015, requiring debate hosts to come up with undercard and primetime divisions of candidates. Twenty participated in the first Democratic presidential debate of the 2020 cycle.

A large number of candidates poses a significant problem for party elites trying to pick a champion. It simply makes coordination much more difficult. To think of the 2016 Republican presidential field, for example, if someone felt the smart choice was for an experienced governor who can win moderate voters, they might have been torn between Jeb Bush, John Kasich, and Chris Christie. If they thought the party would be better off with a senator with conservative credentials who could appeal to Latinos at the helm, they might have been undecided between Ted Cruz and Marco Rubio. The usual endorsers were either split or undecided. No coherent signal was sent to primary voters. This presented a great opportunity for a wealthy candidate with strong name recognition to show well in the early primaries and caucuses.

Campaign finance had a particular wrinkle in 2020, as two multibillionaires – former New York City Mayor Michael Bloomberg and California hedge fund manager Tom Steyer – mounted serious campaigns for the Democratic presidential nomination. *Citizens United* didn't cause that, either; the US Supreme Court in *Buckley v. Valeo* (1976) made it clear that unlimited self-financing in federal elections is permissible. Wealthy individuals have certainly tried to break into presidential politics in the past, but it usually hasn't led to much success. (Steve Forbes ran for the Republican nomination in 1996 and 2000,

---

[86] Mark Schmitt, 2012. "The Rise of the Zombie Candidate." *Salon*, January 11. www.salon.com/2012/01/11/the_rise_of_the_zombie_candidate/.

winning a handful of primaries but not getting very close to the nomination either time. Ross Perot ran as an independent in 1992 and 1996, getting 19 percent of the popular vote, and no Electoral College votes, on his first try.)

These campaigns ended up not garnering that many votes (although Bloomberg managed to win the American Samoa Caucuses). But they at least potentially threatened to undermine party coordination by adding candidates to debates and contests who didn't necessarily have much popular support behind them.

Another factor mitigating against party coordination is the trend toward internal party democracy. Parties have, over time, moved from boss control to conventions to primary elections, increasing expectations that voters, rather than party leaders, are the ones who make the party's key decisions. Parties may sometimes make public participation harder or easier,[87] but they rarely turn away from public input, in part because the more open process comes to be seen as vital for the party's legitimacy. If a nomination is only considered fair when a majority of party voters have weighed in, then it's hard to go back to a system where a few hundred convention delegates make that decision on behalf of those voters – the decision is no longer seen as acceptable or legitimate.

The process described in *The Party Decides*, in which elites steer a process and often determine its outcome long before voters have any chance to weigh in, is inherently a threat to the democratic ideal many political observers apply to presidential primaries. It's one thing for primary voters to start paying attention to a presidential campaign a month or two before their state's contest and be offered a range of candidates, each trying to prove him or herself in debates, through advertising, and via retail politicking. It's quite another to see a top-down effort to winnow their choices occurring right in front of their eyes in real time. Such heavy-handed party machinations are often portrayed as illegitimate.[88]

---

[87] Caitlin Jewitt and Seth Masket, 2019. "When Parties Change Their Rules: Why State Parties Make Nomination Contests More Open or More Closed." Presented at the Northeastern Political Science Association Conference in Philadelphia, Pennsylvania, November 9.

[88] Julia Azari and Seth Masket, 2018. "'The Mandate of the People': The 2016 Sanders Campaign in Context." In John Green, Daniel J. Coffey, and David B. Cohen, eds., *The*

This, at least, was the perspective of some about the 2016 nomination contest. The Democratic Party seemed to be conducting a nomination as it had for decades, with elites converging behind a favorite and the primaries ratifying that choice, while the Republican Party simply decided not to decide and just let primary voters pick who they wanted, then rallied behind that person. But in fact, one could see the parties as being similarly hampered by increased public awareness of their efforts to cull the field of candidates and similarly sensitive to claims of illegitimacy. On the Republican side, it manifested as a reluctance to steer the contest away from an early popular favorite; on the Democratic side, it fueled a populist campaign against Hillary Clinton, both to derail her nomination and to delegitimize it after the convention.

Despite these general impediments to party coordination, there were reasons to believe that Democrats might have greater capabilities in this area and might simply be a more functional modern party than their Republican counterpart.

For one thing, Democrats may be a more functional party because they have to be. They recognize that the risks of them failing to coordinate are higher than they are for Republicans. Democrats know that the geographic arrangement of the national political institutions has a substantial partisan bias built into it. Since Democrats tend to do better in more populous states, but states, rather than people, are represented equally in the US Senate, Republicans tend to win more seats with fewer votes. Democrats won more votes in the Senate elections of 2014, 2016, and 2018 but still did not control the chamber after those elections. The majority of the Senate that approved Brett Kavanaugh for the Supreme Court represented just 44 percent of the American population.

And, of course, the Electoral College has much the same bias, giving a louder voice to smaller (and often more Republican) states. This helps explain why Republicans managed to win the White House in three of the five presidential elections between 2000 and 2016 while only winning the popular vote in one of those. Indeed, as a recent analysis suggests,

State of the Parties, 2018: The Changing Role of Contemporary American Political Parties. Lanham, MD: Rowman and Littlefield, pp. 75–83.

Republicans can reasonably expect to win the White House in more than half the elections in which they lose the popular vote.[89]

All this means that Republicans have a bigger safety margin than Democrats. They can pick a bad candidate and have a fractious party and still have a decent shot of winning. Democrats, by contrast, have to be more concerned about alienating voters. As Ezra Klein writes, "Democrats can't win running the kinds of campaigns and deploying the kinds of tactics that succeed for Republicans. They can move to the left – and they are – but they can't abandon the center or, given the geography of American politics, the center-right, and still hold power."[90]

A second reason why Democrats of 2020 wouldn't behave like Republicans of 2016 was because they had the example of Republicans of 2016 to look back upon. That is, Democrats of 2020 watched Republican leaders flail repeatedly in 2016, with Mitt Romney, Lindsey Graham, Ted Cruz, the *National Review*, and others warning about the dangers that Donald Trump posed to their party and to the country, but never successfully coordinating around an alternative candidate. All those warnings amounted to very little and enabled Trump to continue to run against a fragmented field, dispatching one competitor at a time throughout the 2016 primaries and caucuses until he had an insurmountable delegate lead. For many Democrats, this suggested that the risks of just letting the nomination contest unfold and seeing what happens were too high. In a real sense, the Democratic "establishment" of 2020 saw the failures of its Republican counterpart from four years earlier and sought to learn from its loss.

A third factor favoring Democratic coordination was something that political scientists call "negative partisanship."[91] This refers to the pattern among Americans to not necessarily like their own party any more than they used to, but to increasingly despise the other party, even to the point

[89] Michael Geruso, Dean Spears, and Ishaana Talesara, 2019. "Inversions in US Presidential Elections: 1836–2016." NBER Working Paper No. 26247.

[90] Ezra Klein, 2020. "Why Democrats Still Have to Appeal to the Center, but Republicans Don't." *The New York Times*, January 24.

[91] Alan I. Abramowitz and Steven W. Webster, 2018. "Negative Partisanship: Why Americans Dislike Parties but Behave like Rabid Partisans." *Political Psychology* 39: 119–35.

of viewing it as a threat to the nation. Forty-nine percent of Democrats, on average, approved of the job Republican President Dwight Eisenhower did in office, while the same percentage of Republicans approved of the job Democratic President John Kennedy did. The average approval rating of presidents by members of their own party hasn't changed much over the years, usually hovering in the 70s or 80s, but approval by the other party has plummeted. Twenty-three percent of Democrats approved of George W. Bush's work across his two terms. Just 14 percent of Republicans approved of Barack Obama, and just 8 percent of Democrats have approved of Donald Trump.[92]

Okay, so this negative partisanship sounds potentially problematic. How might it aid party coordination? *The Party Decides* notes an important time trend after an election loss: the out party will sometimes nominate a relatively extreme candidate their first election out of office, but, losing that, will moderate with each passing cycle to increase their chances of victory. In each cycle, party insiders are trying to balance electability and fealty to party goals, but they'll update based on what happened in the most recent election. As a party spends more time out of power, they'll become increasingly desperate for a win, to the point where they're willing to give up almost everything that their party stands for. In 1952, for example, the Republicans, after five consecutive presidential losses, were so hungry for a victory that they nominated Dwight Eisenhower without even knowing to what party he belonged, no less what his issue stances were.

This pattern – increasing moderation with time out of power – certainly makes sense, but that first term, in which the out party is willing to nominate a relative extremist (think Barry Goldwater in 1964 or George McGovern in 1972) is an interesting one. Compared to how they will later act, party insiders at this point are willing to take a chance. They don't *want* to lose the election, but they are willing to accept greater odds that that will happen for the sake of nominating someone they truly believe in.

---

[92] Amina Dunn, 2018. "Trump's Approval Ratings so far are Unusually Stable – and Deeply Partisan." Pew Research Center, August 1. www.pewresearch.org/fact-tank/2018/08/01/trumps-approval-ratings-so-far-are-unusually-stable-and-deeply-partisan/.

But think how this interacts with negative partisanship. The costs of losing a presidential election seem substantially higher than they did just a decade or two ago. Negative partisanship can make the out party after just one term act more like the desperate party that has been out of power for two or three terms or more. Notably, Republicans truly did not like Barack Obama for the most part, and in 2012, after just one term out of office, they nominated Mitt Romney, a former governor of Massachusetts who had signed health care reform into law at the state level. To be sure, Romney moved rightward to become a more conventional GOP nominee, but he was actually one of the more moderate choices party insiders considered in the 2012 cycle. The Republican Party, which had become substantially more conservative in the previous few years, was nonetheless willing to nominate a conventional Republican with a history of moderation because they thought it would give them a win. They were acting like a party that had been out of power for a lot longer than one term, in part because the ongoing presence of Obama in the White House was an affront to everything they believed in.

Now apply that to the Democrats facing Trump's reelection campaign. Trump's approval rating among Democrats was about half that of Obama's approval rating among Republicans. And needless to say, Trump's governing style was far different from Obama's. Trump's whole approach was to be relentlessly in Democrats' face whenever possible, even to the point of trolling party leaders on Twitter and mocking them with nicknames. To Democrats, Trump's governing style, his policy aims, and his frequent norm violations (and impeachable offenses) were more than just wrong – they were infuriating and exhausting. For Democrats, the costs of losing in 2020 seemed far greater than they did in previous election cycles.

We can see evidence of this with polling of Democrats during invisible primaries. A series of YouGov polls taken the year prior to recent presidential elections demonstrates shifting preferences among the Democratic electorate,[93] as can be seen in Figure 2.1. In November 2003, while

---

[93] Kathy Frankovic, 2019. "In 2020, Winning is Everything for Most Democratic Voters." *YouGov*, June 11. https://today.yougov.com/topics/politics/articles-reports/2019/0 6/11/democrats-2020-winning-poll.

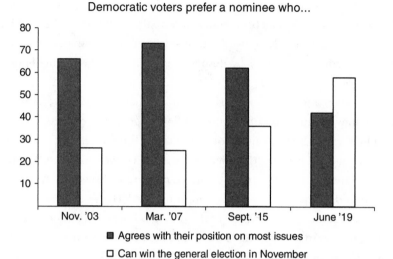

Figure 2.1 Issue preference and electability among Democrats
Source: yougov.com

Howard Dean, John Kerry, Richard Gephardt, and John Edwards were locked in a struggle for the Democratic nomination, 66 percent of Democratic voters said they preferred a nominee who agrees with their position on some issues, while just 26 percent said they preferred one who can prevail against the Republican nominee. The split was even greater in 2007, when Democratic voters preferred issue agreement over electability by a 73–25 margin. The gap had shrunk somewhat by 2015, but Democrats preferring issue similarity still outnumbered those preferring electability by 62 to 36. In June of 2019, however, the balance had shifted: 58 percent now preferred electability, while just 42 percent preferred someone who shared their beliefs. Democrats in 2019 behaved substantially differently from those in previous cycles.

A number of factors could explain the shift, especially the fact that increasing polarization means that the range of ideological opinions among one party's candidates is likely to be shrinking. So perhaps Democratic voters in 2019 were less concerned about candidates agreeing with them on issues because virtually all of them did. But a major overriding issue was simply Donald Trump. Democrats truly despised him. While Democrats were no fans of President George W. Bush, he enjoyed much higher approval ratings among Democrats than Trump did. Democratic voters were eager to see Trump's presidency limited to one term, at most. Thus it wouldn't be surprising to see many Democratic insiders after just one term of Trump acting like Republicans after five terms of Roosevelt and Truman – willing to jettison a considerable amount of their commitments for the sake of a win.

As I've suggested here, there were some important factors pushing the Democratic Party toward greater coordination than we saw among Republicans four years earlier. However, the party also faced some of the same challenges that Republicans face in the modern era. As we will see in the next chapter, one of the most important things that would affect what the party could actually do was the lesson they learned from 2016.

CHAPTER 3

Interpreting Loss

We're starting in Wisconsin because, as you remember, there wasn't a lot of campaigning in Wisconsin in 2016. With me, that changes.

Amy Klobuchar, February 10, 2019

Donald Trump got elected because, in his twisted way, he pointed out the huge troubles in our economy and our democracy. At least he didn't go around saying that America was already great, like Hillary did.

Pete Buttigieg, January 14, 2019

Why did Hillary Clinton lose? That five-word question lies at the heart of every discussion of Democratic party reform and nomination politics since late 2016. For some political observers, Clinton was a poor candidate who ran a dismal campaign. "Hillary Clinton blew the most winnable election in modern American history," concluded Damon Linker at *The Week*, "and it's her own fault."[1] How else to explain Donald Trump being within striking range of the presidency despite his range of disqualifying actions and statements? For others, though, Clinton's loss reflected long-standing biases among the electorate and the commentariat, or was the product of work of outsiders ranging from Jill Stein to James Comey to Vladimir Putin.

---

[1] Damon Linker, 2016. "Hillary Clinton Blew the Most Winnable Election in Modern American History. And It's Her Own Fault." *The Week*, December 2.

In this chapter, I examine the range of reasons given for the outcome of the 2016 election. The answers are the product of lengthy interviews I conducted with over sixty Democratic party activists in states with early presidential contests – Iowa, New Hampshire, South Carolina, and Nevada – as well as Washington, DC. I look extensively at the types of responses given and categorize them into a handful of key narratives. I also examine the narratives generated by political reporters in the months after the 2016 election.

One thing I do not do in this chapter is decide which responses are correct and which aren't. For the purposes of this book, I am less interested in the reason Hillary Clinton lost (as though that could be boiled down to a single reason) than I am in what key Democratic activists *believe* that reason is and how that reasoning informed their later decisions.

To spoil the punchline a bit, the consensus explanation of 2016 is that there was no consensus explanation of 2016. Party activists and political observers were unusually divided about just why that election came out as it did, and they *remained* divided long thereafter. The election itself was close enough, and weird enough, to provide evidence for a great range of theories. For some, it caused a rethinking of who could get elected and indeed how politics works. For others, it just reinforced their previously held beliefs. But the preponderance of narratives suggested a similar remedy: scaling back on some of the party's commitments and picking the "safe" nominee who could best guarantee a win.

WHO ARE PARTY ACTIVISTS?

I spent a few hours on the day of the Iowa Caucuses in 2020 walking around a northeast Des Moines neighborhood with Seth Silverman, an experienced canvasser in presidential campaigns. He worked through a list of houses he had on a smartphone app provided by the Elizabeth Warren campaign, knocking on the doors of registered Democrats and encouraging them to show up at their precinct caucus that night. He had a range of talking points prepared for those few instances where someone was home, willing to talk to him about their caucus choices, and still undecided between the candidates. I listened in while he spent 10 minutes talking with a middle-aged couple who were planning to caucus for

Joe Biden, but were on the fence between Bernie Sanders and Elizabeth Warren in the case that Biden's numbers came up short in the complex caucus process that night. Seth seemed to make the sale, convincing them that Warren had the right biography and policy stances to win and steer the country in their preferred direction.

A week later, I was driving around Manchester, New Hampshire, on primary day, along with Judy Reardon, an experienced campaign manager, and Kathy Sullivan, the former state party chair and current member of the Democratic National Committee. Both attorneys, they were part of the state's primary election day legal protection program, checking in on polling places around town to see if there were any disputes over ballots or other legal challenges to voting. The lawyers sitting in at the polling places briefed them on turnout and ballot issues. We also observed a campaign rally and stopped at Walgreens to buy Kit Kats.

I also spoke briefly that morning with Will Kanteres and Meryl Levin. The two have endorsed various candidates over the past several decades and volunteered their time to work on their campaigns. (Kanteres worked for Gary Hart's campaign in New Hampshire in 1984.) They are a large part of the reason Colorado Senator Michael Bennet remained in the presidential race as long as he did. Impressed with the senator's candidacy after seeing him speak, they publicly endorsed him, offered him and his family a place to stay during some campaign visits, and made introductions between the Bennets and various influential Democrats across the state.

These are the sorts of people I term *party activists*. I use this term fairly loosely. It refers to people who provide the critical labor of parties during presidential nomination cycles. They raise money, organize rallies, arrange meetings, write op/eds, and do other tasks vital to the nomination process. Importantly, most of them spend the invisible primary period learning about various presidential candidates (by attending candidate events and often speaking directly with the candidates), deciding between them, and speaking with other activists about their choices. These activists also include several state party chairs (who traditionally do not endorse candidates prior to their state contests) and some elected officials, including state legislators, members of Congress, and former governors.

Party activists often wear multiple hats. Dalton Tresvant is the Midwest area director for US Rep. Jim Clyburn's district office in Columbia, South Carolina, helping county and municipal governments secure federal funding for various projects and advocating for African American communities. But in his off hours, he's helping organize Democratic politics in Columbia, picking among candidates, speaking with other influential activists, and helping the national party direct resources around the state. Bethany Khan is a spokesperson for the Culinary Workers Union Local 226 in Las Vegas, which represents the roughly 60,000 workers in the various hotels and casinos along the Vegas Strip. The union is not an arm of the Democratic Party, and indeed will occasionally back Republicans, but it tends to lean left politically, and its endorsement is highly coveted in primaries and caucuses.[2] In addition to evaluating presidential candidates, Khan helps coordinate numerous efforts to promote turnout at presidential caucuses, running a program to arrange for workers to get time off to participate in the time-consuming events. Yvanna Cancela, a Nevada state senator and the former political director of the Culinary Union, endorsed Joe Biden early in the nomination cycle and served as a senior advisor to his Nevada campaign.

While activists like these don't technically run the Democratic Party, they are important and influential. Presidential campaigns, and even the candidates themselves, will seek them out to ask for their counsel and endorsements. The activists' expertise in the politics of their state contest and their reputations are highly prized by the campaigns. Importantly, these activists are among the most politically informed people in the country, paying close attention to news coverage, attending political events, and conferring with each other about the latest developments and the most promising candidates. Their decision-making is key to the presidential nomination process, and it was my intent to capture these decisions occurring throughout the invisible primary process. This is particularly true in the early-contest states, where activists will choose

---

[2] The union does not always endorse, and indeed chose to stay neutral in both the 2016 and 2020 Democratic presidential contests, but its voter turnout efforts during general elections are often considered crucial to Democratic victories in the state.

among a larger field of candidates and be exposed to literally years of campaigning.

I identified sixty-five such activists in the early-contest states of Iowa, New Hampshire, Nevada, South Carolina, and the District of Columbia[3] with the help of local political reporters and other political activists, and spoke with them repeatedly during a number of visits between 2017 and 2020. These included seventeen people from Iowa, fourteen from New Hampshire, eight from Nevada, eleven from South Carolina, and fifteen from the District of Columbia. Forty-two were men and twenty-three women. Fifty-six of the sixty-five were white (including all of the respondents from Iowa and New Hampshire), while the group included six African Americans, two Latinas, and an Asian American. Thirty-eight of the respondents were supporters of Hillary Clinton in the 2016 nomination cycle, while eleven were Bernie Sanders supporters in that contest, eleven were neutral, and two had campaigned for Martin O'Malley.

I do not claim that this sample of activists is representative of the larger population of party activists in each location. Notably, it was far easier to track down people who worked for or supported Hillary Clinton in 2016 than those who supported Bernie Sanders, the latter group generally having less experience within the party. Clinton activists were also more numerous than Sanders activists, even in states where Sanders culled more votes. Nonetheless, the reflections and interpretations of these activists, and the evolution of those opinions over time, are revealing about the beliefs of those most active in the party on the ground.

For interviews, I typically began by asking these people about their background in party politics. I then asked them several questions related to their interpretation of the 2016 election: (1) Why did the 2016 presidential election turn out as it did, at both the state and

---

[3] While the presidential candidates do little direct campaigning in Washington, many of the campaigns and candidates are based there, and District residents are exposed to media coverage and elite discussion about the nomination contest to a greater degree and long before most other Americans are. Moreover, a considerable number of longstanding party activists from previous successful campaigns have ended up moving to the District of Columbia and spending their professional lives there. Many are established consultants, political organizers, congressional staffers, and donors.

national level? (2) Might the general election have turned out differently had the Democrats picked a different nominee? (3) Did Bernie Sanders and his supporters do enough to help Hillary Clinton in the fall election? I found that these three questions teased out a range of interesting answers about the political environment and the role that parties, campaigns, and candidates can play in affecting election outcomes.

I additionally asked several prospective questions: (4) What does the Democratic Party need to do to become more competitive? (5) Who are you thinking about as a possible Democratic presidential nominee in 2020? These questions seemed useful for determining what respondents saw as the lessons of the 2016 election.

While I asked all the above questions, I kept the conversations loosely structured to allow the activists to feel more comfortable and forthcoming and to largely let them drive the conversation. I asked relevant followup questions and pressed them for examples when possible. With a very small number of exceptions, activists gave me permission to record their interviews, although a few requested that their names not be associated with particular comments of theirs. I have honored all the activists' requests about the use of quotes from their interviews. These conversations were mostly conducted in person, either in the activist's workplace or home, or at a coffee shop or restaurant. When in-person meetings were impossible, we spoke over the telephone.

THE EIGHT NARRATIVES

Over the course of these many conversations, the activists explained to me their understanding of why the 2016 presidential election ended as it did. I have grouped these responses into eight different categories. Let me quickly summarize those narratives before giving specific examples:

1. **Campaign activity** – Tactics deployed by the Clinton campaign were inadequate and inappropriate.
2. **Campaign message** – The messaging used by the campaign failed to resonate with the voters in the way intended.

3. **Identity politics** – The campaign reached out to women, racial minorities, and other underrepresented groups but failed to speak to working-class whites.

4. **Candidate traits** – Hillary Clinton had personality or campaigning traits that were inadequate to the task, or Donald Trump had traits that were underappreciated prior to the election.

5. **Racism/Sexism** – Voters and/or the media held to racist or sexist biases that undermined Hillary Clinton's potential vote share.

6. **Sanders/Stein** – Other candidates' activities, particularly those of Senator Bernie Sanders and Jill Stein, drew support away from Hillary Clinton.

7. **Exogenous events** – Events outside the campaign's control, particularly intervention by Russia or activities by FBI Director James Comey prior to the election, hurt Clinton's election chances.

8. **Mood of the electorate** – 2016 was somehow an unusual year, in which voters were craving atypical outcomes.

EXPLANATION 1: CAMPAIGN ACTIVITY. In one of my first interviews, I spent some time visiting with New Hampshire Democratic Party chair Ray Buckley in his office in Concord. I was a bit awestruck by his collection of campaign memorabilia collected from decades of primaries and conventions. During our conversation, Buckley summed up a frequent complaint that the Democratic presidential campaign in 2016 had a much weaker organization and less competence than other recent Democratic efforts. According to Buckley,

> I'm . . . angry about the consulting class that has an iron grip over the DNC
> in how it spends its money . . . because I believe that we didn't have to lose.
> I believe that Donald Trump is president because of the failures of the
> Democratic Party, not because of any attribute of either Hillary's or
> Donald's, and we could've fixed that.

A veteran South Carolina political strategist shared this critical assessment. The Clinton team, he told me,

> didn't have the layers of oversight that Obama had. Every time you went to
> the bathroom [during the Obama campaign], you had to check with two

people to make sure what urinal and what stall to go to. But it worked. And it was a series of checks and balances that if somebody was falling down, they would send somebody in to help them, not necessarily to replace them. [Clinton's] field effort was non-existent.

South Carolina state legislator Wendell Gilliard had a similar take, saying that the reason for the election's outcome was simply "lack of participation … lack of organizing. … The people [Clinton] used to organize her campaign, they weren't the best of the best."

These assessments didn't just come from party leadership and elected officials. Herb and Kathy Eckhouse are the owners and founders of a cured meats company just outside of Des Moines, Iowa, and are also long-term Democratic activists, having helped numerous presidential candidates and volunteered on their campaigns. Herb and I had a lengthy conversation at his office in 2017 over an enormous plate of prosciutto, speck, and nduja,[4] in which he outlined his concerns about the 2016 Democratic ground game and the doors on which he was sent to knock. "By the beginning of October," he said,

> you should not be talking to anybody who's in favor of the opposing candidate. And we were. We were bumping into Trump supporters. And that was really, that's a waste of our time, a waste of their resources. . . . I was told afterward that they [the campaign] never updated their records. So we were collecting all these forms and all of this information. They never input that data, which seems unbelievable to me.

Others had somewhat the opposite take, that the national campaign was *too* reliant on data and wasn't in touch with local organizers. In this framework, the problem wasn't poor organization or data, but a faith in that organization and data that bordered on hubris. As former South Carolina Democratic Party chair Carol Fowler explained to me over coffee, "I think [Clinton] had a lot of people on her campaign who thought they knew everything and were not listening to the people who were there on the ground. I just believe that her people thought, 'Well, we've done so many campaigns, don't tell us what to do. Don't tell us what

---

[4] I recorded this conversation and honestly it's a bit embarrassing to listen to.

to think. We know. We've got data.'" Her husband, former Democratic National Committee national chair Don Fowler, agreed that the Clinton campaign was "relying a little too much on analytics and not enough on some of the on the ground anecdotes and stories that talked about the energy level of the electorate." DC activist Chris Riddiough added,

> Hillary's campaign relied on data to tell them where to campaign and how to campaign and stuff like that, and that what they didn't do was go out to the barber shops or community centers and actually talk to people and get a sense of who was enthusiastic about Hillary, you know, who was actually going to go out and vote. And I think that is probably the important thing. I think that's probably why they lost Wisconsin.

A South Carolina political strategist also blamed campaign hubris:

> Hillary Clinton is probably the smartest person to have run for president in my lifetime. If they had moved that campaign to Chicago, where she's from, or if they had moved that campaign to Little Rock, they would've seen this coming. When you have a group of people from Washington, DC running campaigns and they don't spend any time in rural, Southern or Middle America, they're going to miss something.

Bill and Jean Shaheen have been the preeminent power couple in New Hampshire Democratic politics for decades. She's the senior US Senator and former governor, he's a prominent Dover attorney; the two host an annual major fundraising dinner for the state party. No one runs for the Democratic presidential nomination without consulting them. In a conversation, Bill Shaheen agreed with concerns about the Clinton campaign: "I just don't think [Clinton] was served well by [her] people. It's almost a natural instinct that the national headquarters wants to control everything and wants to make every decision, rather than listening to the people on the ground." Dalton Tresvant, the South Carolina activist I mentioned earlier, similarly described the campaign's approach.

> [The campaign would say,] "Okay, this is what you need to do to turn out African American voters." No. We've got a term for that. We just call them smart ass white boys. They're going to come and they're going to tell you,

'This is what you need to do to turn out black voters,' and you're like, "No, that's not."

Several Nevada activists offered an interesting angle on this explanation, noting that Democrats had an unusually good 2016 within Nevada, in part because they executed the campaign activities there that they failed to perform nationally. Not only did Clinton prevail over Trump in the Silver State, but Democrats took over Nevada's statehouse and won a competitive open US Senate race. "I think a lot of that was a product of our state party, and the organizing work that goes into a general election in Nevada, and working with all our partners – labor and progressive groups – to really run a strong field organizing effort that mobilizes our voters to get to the polls," said Stewart Boss, a Las Vegas political consultant. According to Bethany Khan, the spokesperson for the Culinary Workers union I mentioned earlier, it was a matter of proper allocation of resources: "We know that it requires deep level of investment in order to win . . . . It allowed us to do the work that needs to be done – train and develop workers to go out and talk to their co-workers and the community. . . . All of the really important things that it takes to win, we did in Nevada."

Tick Segerblom was a state senator when I spoke to him in his Las Vegas office. He has since been elected to the Clark County Commission. As he told me about Nevada election organizing, "It's a one-on-one thing. I mean, you can't try to do it by TV . . . . You have to literally grab people and make them vote. There's enough Democrats out there to do it." And all this work can sometimes only yield small dividends, a long-time Las Vegas political strategist explained to me.

> Even with all that that we had, and being in the ground for so long, the Trump campaign really didn't have much of a presence, and we still only won by two points. And so, it's just a good reminder of how hard we have to work to get our voters out to make sure they're registered. It's a lot of work.

As these activists argued, these activities were the sorts of things that Democrats did *not* do on a nationwide scale. "It was a very bittersweet election night," said state Senator Yvanna Cancela, "because in Nevada we were wildly successful; it was hard to watch what happened across the country." "I know [Clinton] should have made more trips to the Midwest," added the political strategist. State party executive director Alana Mounce contrasted the 2016 effort with her own experiences campaigning for Barack Obama's reelection in 2012: "We started doing persuasion phone calls in 2011 for Barack Obama who won here by a healthy, healthy margin in 2012, and he was incredibly popular here. I mean sometimes it's touch and go, sometimes it's tough. So then to think, fast forwarding to 2016, that there was no persuasion happening."

Several organizers in other states sounded a similar theme, lamenting the demise of the fifty-state strategy pioneered by then-DNC chair Howard Dean in 2005 and 2006. New Hampshire party chair Buckley blamed national Democrats for their party's losses over several recent cycles, saying, "When the decision was made to defund the fifty-state strategy, we began losing offices immediately. . . . I believe that if we had continued at the same level that Howard Dean was funding, over the course of the last eight years, that Hillary Clinton would be President." Buckley is proud of some recent Democratic gains in New Hampshire, and thinks that other states could learn from this example: "No other battleground state has had a record anywhere near what New Hampshire's done and it's because their grassroots have atrophied."

A South Carolina Democratic political strategist agreed in the assessment of the fifty-state strategy: "The roots of the '16 loss for us had nothing to do with the people who ran in '16. I think it was the years of neglect of the state party apparatuses across the country." A former state elected official in South Carolina agreed, "The Obama team owns a little of it because when you look at what happened after the '08 election, there was not a lot of investment in the Democratic Party from '08 'til 2016."

EXPLANATION 2: CAMPAIGN MESSAGE. The second explanation of Trump's victory is that Clinton and the Democrats simply didn't offer a compelling campaign message. This explanation is often relatively vague – it's not always clear just what the right message was or how that should have been conveyed. And this goes beyond a critique of basic campaign themes like "Stronger Together" or "I'm With Her" to include a criticism of the whole campaign approach to communications with voters. Implicit in this is an assumption that a campaign is coordinated around some sort of unifying message and that such a message allows the campaign to connect to voters and express the candidate's core set of beliefs. Indeed, one of the few things over which a campaign has direct control is its message – the themes and arguments it makes to appeal to voters. Other campaign activity, seasoned professionals will tell you, should all flow from that message. Activists focusing on this explanation generally gave credit to Donald Trump's "Make America Great Again" theme, which they saw as a simple and easily-memorized message that nonetheless connected to a great many beliefs – societal, generational, racial – implicit in the campaign.

To many activists, Clinton and the Democrats just didn't have anything along those lines. "It troubled me that we didn't have a message, and that's not just Hillary Clinton," said former Governor Jim Hodges of South Carolina. "I think from the last six or eight years there wasn't much of a message to those voters." He worried that "we fell in love with technology and fell out of love with message," arguing that the campaign innovations of the Obama years were helpful but not enough to unite a party behind a controversial nominee.

Kimberley Boggus is a longstanding community leader and environmental activist in Des Moines, in addition to being a seasoned presidential campaign staffer. The problem with the Democrats' 2016 message, she told me over coffee, was that it was little more than a criticism of Trump, offering nothing beyond that. "I don't think the Democrats' message was effective," she said. "It was not offering solutions. It was just to point out that Trump was a terribly flawed person and doesn't like X, Y, and Z. It wasn't going after his relationships with Wall Street, it wasn't going after his shady deals. It was very much, 'Let's focus on Trump' and then not saying what Hillary would do." Cancela in Nevada agreed, "Just saying, 'We're better than that guy' isn't very persuasive or inspiring." Democratic political consultant Joe Fuld added,

> I think that they did not have a clear message. It wasn't clear from the beginning. I think they did not execute their message as sort of two sides of a coin. They looked at message as one side of a coin . . . . [They said]

"Donald Trump is so bad" . . . and then they never did the other side: "This
is why we should be voting for Hillary."

According to progressive political organizer and strategist Reggie
Hubbard, who worked with the Sanders campaign in 2016, the messaging sold Clinton short, particularly among more progressive voters:

> They didn't talk about enough of what she did in civil rights. Ms. Clinton is
> the most qualified person ever to run for president. But they didn't talk
> about that. They said, "I'm with her." . . . Like, really substantial social
> programs have her influence. Even in the Senate. . . . They didn't talk
> about that. You can be establishment and talk about your track record of
> doing progressive stuff.

For some respondents, the Democratic message in 2016 was too
simplistic. Boggus expressed concern that the Clinton campaign was
afraid to engage people on multiple topics: "You can talk to me about
marriage equality and you can talk to me about jobs. You can talk to
me about how I'm going to pay back my student education loans. You
can talk to people about more than one topic, and I think that that's
what Democrats fail to do." Iowa's Eckhouse concurred, saying,

> We've got to sell our brand. We have a great brand. We have a great brand
> for fairness, equality before the law and . . . fiscal responsibility. . . . I think
> we need to have three words that describe our brand, in distinction to the
> Republican brand. And we need to have all of our candidates position
> themselves in that way and that's the only shot we've got.

For others, the Democratic message wasn't simplistic enough. Iowa's
then-state party chair Troy Price argued that a good message focuses
more on core values than policy positions, and that the Democrats'
recent approach has been to rely on a laundry list of issues to serve
as its message. "The Democratic Party has been so focused on
specific messages and specific issues. Like, we talk a lot about minimum wage, but we don't necessarily tie that to the broader vision
and broader values of our party, which is fighting for working
people. And so, I think that was where the disconnect happened."
He added:

I think it's just a message problem that we had, that we were talking about all these various messages, very specific messaging, but we were never talking about the values that the Democratic Party stood for, that Hillary stood for. It wasn't just a Hillary problem. So what always ends up happening is, when you focus so much on specific messages, and not on values, or issues and not on values, it doesn't move the needle as much and then you have no choice but to say "We're not as bad as the other people." That's ultimately what happened here.

Iowa Federation of Labor President Ken Sagar agreed, "People don't care about facts and figures. That's where the Republicans kill us. They put a bumper sticker and we say, 'Yeah? Here's a white paper.'" Cancela concurred, "It's much easier to grasp onto Trump's message than Clinton's message. And I think it's what we, as a Democratic Party, have to figure out, is how we lay out a vision for our country, not a one-off issue based on what different constituent groups may be fighting for."

Still others complained that the Democratic message was simply targeted in too many directions, or to the wrong audience. The lack of a unifying message, Hodges said, was damaging: "We tended to put together issues that were attractive to small groups of Democratic donors and Democratic supporters and believe that's enough and have not have any overarching message that sort of stitched all that together." Tammy Wawro, then the president of the Iowa State Education Association, the largest teachers' union in the state, explained to me in her office that a good message has "got to be, how do we explain to the American people what our policies are going to do to improve their lives?" Iowa political consultant Norm Sterzenbach opined, "I think Hillary Clinton didn't focus a message on Iowa. It was more of a national message."

Sagar, the labor leader, had an interesting take on campaign message, suggesting a mismatch between what some Democratic voters and what their nominee was arguing. Many union members, he said, heard more of what they cared about coming from Trump rather than Clinton:

A lot of people have said labor's message doesn't resonate. I would argue that's incorrect. Our message was we need to get rid of bad trade deals. . . . Our message was we need to rebuild our infrastructure. . . . One candidate adopted that. We said we wanted good jobs that paid decent wages. One candidate adopted that. It wasn't our candidate that adopted our issue, and he won. [It was] our messaging; we were right on the topics.

In sum, the category of campaign message is frustratingly vague and multi-dimensional. And, setting aside Clinton's loss, it is difficult to say what exactly was wrong with her campaign's "Stronger Together" theme, which had the virtues of being simple, bumper-sticker-length, and tapping into a broader campaign message of strength, inclusivity, and tolerance. Nonetheless, a great many respondents volunteered complaints about messaging and blamed it for Clinton's loss.

EXPLANATION 3: THE IDENTITY POLITICS CRITIQUE. Somewhat related to concerns about message, perhaps even a subset of it, is a worry that the party is appealing to the wrong subsets of Democratic constituencies and losing others as a result of it. Concern about "identity politics" was a potent interpretation of the 2016 election among pundits. That argument was that the Democratic Party had devoted too much attention to the concerns of African Americans, Latinos, women, the LGBT community, and other underrepresented groups and not enough to appealing to concerns of the broader group of Americans, which had the effect of alienating white Americans.[5]

My interviews suggested that this was a vibrant strain of election interpretation among Democratic activists, as well. However, the language was often somewhat more subtle than it was among conservatives and op/ed writers. Only a handful of subjects specifically chastised the party or the Clinton campaign for not appealing directly to white voters. Nonetheless, coded versions of such critiques do appear.

What's more, there's at least something of an ideological component to these criticisms. This in itself is interesting, as essentially none of my subjects explicitly volunteered ideological positioning as a cause for Democratic woes. That is, no one said the party needs to move to the

---

[5] As I note in Chapter 2, I recognize that this is a very narrow definition of the term "identity politics," which has a number of different meanings. It is a problematic definition for a number of reasons, not the least of which is that it treats identity appeals as somehow strange when they are about women or people of color but "normal politics" when they refer to white men. I am nonetheless focusing on this specific critique of the campaign offered by columnists, pundits, and some activists.

right or left to be more competitive. But a few implied as much with their discussions of identity politics.

Perhaps the most direct example of this comes from seasoned Iowa political consultant Jeff Link, who told me, "Democrats should listen to more country music, and they should stop being condescending." He expanded on this theme: "Country music is an appeal to white working-class Americans. And there are themes that run through those songs. It's like, 'Don't be condescending about where I live or how I live,' 'Don't be condescending about my way of life,' and a lot of those songs played out in the presidential election." Iowa education advocate Wawro offered a similar example, saying, "Listen to your cousin Jim that lives in rural Iowa that was a Democrat that voted for Trump. Why did he do that?"

Link further added, "I think Donald Trump made a direct appeal to white working-class voters. And I think that the Clinton campaign probably inadvertently not only made no appeal to white working-class voters, but actually ran a campaign that was offensive to white working-class voters."

Other respondents were somewhat less explicit but nonetheless sounded similar themes. Several focused on the need to reach out to downscale whites who had once been loyal Democratic voters. Nevada's Cancela asked, for example, "How do we make sure that the coal miner in West Virginia, who has voted Democratic his entire life but now voted for Trump because he's afraid of losing his job with renewable energy, how do we make sure that he remembers that the party that actually fights for him and his family is the Democratic Party?" Linda Ketner, a South Carolina activist and former House candidate, held up Rep. Joe Kennedy's response to the 2018 State of the Union Address[6] as an example of the kind of appeals Democrats should be making. "We need to talk more like Joe Kennedy did the other night about issues that are broader than the thing we got accused of – which was breaking into little groups representing ideals or ideologies – and talk about working-class people." Former local Iowa officeholder Mike Carberry said,

[6] Daniella Diaz, 2018. "Kennedy Responds to Trump: 'We all Feel the Fault Lines of a Fractured Country.'" CNN, January 31.

We need to be the Democratic Party that Franklin Delano Roosevelt could be proud of, the party of the people, by the people, for the people. For the working class, for the poor, those sorts of things that provide that rural economic development that we need in the State of Iowa. . . . That's one of the reasons we lost Pennsylvania and Michigan and the Rust Belt. Those are blue collar workers. We used to call them "Reagan Democrats" that left the party and went and voted for Ronald Reagan. Well, they left the party and went and voted for Donald Trump.

I had a lengthy conversation with Dick and Katrina Swett in their office in Concord, New Hampshire, in 2017. Dick is a former US House member, and Katrina is an historian and the president of the Lantos Foundation for Human Rights and Justice. Dick expressed concern to me that Democrats "gave the impression that the minorities and small special interest or identity groups were more important than the broader community as a whole." Katrina shared these concerns, telling me,

> We went down that path of a kind of identity politics. Really, just saying, "If we get sufficient numbers among this group, this group, this group, this group we're golden." There was always this underlying assumption that we get a certain minimum vote from that rather large identity group, white Americans. Trump again upended that because the share of white vote dropped dramatically enough across the board, including white women. Suddenly, a lot of people have said, "Yeah, I guess if you have one particular demographic group that's . . . 68–70 percent of the population, you actually still need to pay attention to their concerns."

Some activists I spoke to found this topic particularly wrenching in the Trump era. They argued that in some ways it was more important than ever to stand up for underrepresented populations, given the threats they face, while at the same time they were under the impression that doing so undermined their ability to win elections and help those populations from a position of power. "You got to call out a racist when there's a racist," said Des Moines political consultant Jake Oeth. "But every time somebody says something questionable you throw the racist flag out there and you're going to drive people away, too. Because they think you're the boy who cried wolf."

Iowa activist Brenda Kole was one of very few to specifically push back on this critique. "The United States is changing," she said,

> and we're likely not going to get the manufacturing jobs that we had before. Our Latino population is rising so fast. To me that's not identity politics; they're part of the Democratic Party. You have to put all those components together. You have to reach out to women, and Latinos, and African Americans. That's just part of who the Democratic Party is and what it looks like.

"I'm not sure that the Democratic Party talks about issues of race in a really head on way," agreed a Las Vegas political organizer. "For folks in Nevada, in a state that's incredibly diverse, with essentially a third of all the state looking like me, as a Latina, folks are just wanting more."

EXPLANATION 4: CANDIDATE TRAITS. Quite a few activists attributed the 2016 election outcome to particular qualities of the candidates themselves. "I love the lady," said South Carolina's Don Fowler of Hillary Clinton. "I really do. I'd jump off a building for her. But boy, she could have been a better candidate in 2016." New Hampshire activist Judy Reardon agreed, "I believe she would have been a very good, maybe great president. She was not a great candidate. And I think that's because. . . she doesn't need people to love her."

For others, it had less to do with Clinton's skills and more to do with Trump's atypical set of talents. New Hampshirites, in particular, noted with marvel how Trump flouted the traditional customs of that state's primary – with an emphasis on retail politics, avoiding large addresses, engaging activists one-on-one during multiple visits, spending many months in residence – and nonetheless prevailed. "Donald Trump was something so dramatically different and he didn't win the New Hampshire primary doing the things that have historically been thought to be absolutely necessary," said Katrina Swett. Clay Middleton of South Carolina expressed frustration with Trump's uniqueness.

> Look at the debates, how questions were answered or not answered by the current president. He just got away with things that others couldn't. How can you not tell the American public about your taxes and not provide

details on anything of substance? How can you say the most appalling, sexist, and racist things about women, the disabled, any minority, and get away with it? Only Donald Trump.

A number of activists offered comments along those same lines, suggesting that there were peculiarities of the candidates themselves that drove the outcome. I probed this subject further by asking respondents whether the election outcome would have been the same with a different Democratic nominee. A number felt that it would have come out similarly regardless of the nominee, but quite a few were convinced that another Democrat would have won the day.

The question of whether Bernie Sanders would have won is, of course, a vitally important one, both because it can never be satisfactorily answered and because it continues to divide Democrats. Indeed, divisions on this question are far from petty. If one believes that Sanders would have beaten Trump, then this would mean that the party, an organization whose primary purpose is to win elections, made a catastrophically bad decision. It calls into question the entire process – including a venerable infrastructure of caucuses, primaries, conventions, party rules, and so on – by which that decision was made, and indeed suggests that substantial revisions are due for those procedures. On the other hand, if a Sanders–Trump contest would have yielded roughly the same or lower vote share for Democrats, no massive rethinking of the Democratic approach is due, and perhaps some other factor was pivotal.

Those respondents who had worked for Bernie Sanders in 2015 and 2016 were generally confident that Sanders would have prevailed as the Democratic nominee. However, few expressed interest in pressing the argument. I pressed Sanders' 2016 Iowa coordinator, Evan Burger, on this question, and he explained to me, simply, "He would've won. Yeah, anyway. . . . I don't like to dwell on the past."

Some Clinton backers, meanwhile, insisted that Sanders had substantial vulnerabilities that never fully came to light in the primaries but would have proven devastating in a general election. Said Iowan Jerry Crawford, "I certainly don't think Bernie would've won. I think he would've gotten crushed. . . . He never had to answer for some of the stuff in his background. . . . he was essentially never vetted in the public discourse. He would not have stood up well to that." Several people specifically mentioned to me Kurt Eichenwald's 2016 *Newsweek* article[7] detailing various Sanders vulnerabilities. Don Fowler summed up, "Bernie Sanders wouldn't have won if he had been the nominee. Not in the least. He would've gotten his head kicked in."

Former Nevada state party chair Sam Lieberman compared Clinton unfavorably to her husband. "Sometimes she was her own worst enemy. Where Bill is very willing to not only do the substantive work but also do the hand-shaking and baby-kissing and ribbon-cutting and all of that, she's not that." Nevada's Segerblom attributed a lack of campaign skills to Clinton's own unusual path to the presidential nomination. "Most people have run for city council, dog catcher, something where you actually do the one-on-one and learn how to grovel and you come across as natural, and when you start at her level, people just see that there's nothing there." Iowa's Carberry, meanwhile, offered me a much more policy-driven reason why rural white Iowans would have turned against Democrats: the Obama administration's Waters of the United States rule.[8] Enacted in 2015, this rule created environmental protections for many waterways and wetlands, creating considerable pushback among some farmers. So perhaps groups that have typically voted Democratic were reluctant to support Hillary Clinton for purely policy-related reasons. (This was, interestingly, one of the few explanations offered that included reference to President Barack Obama.)

EXPLANATION 5: RACISM/SEXISM. Somewhat less prevalent were those who ascribed the election's outcome to the persistence of racism and/or sexism in the electorate. South Carolinian Ketner stated plainly that the reason for Trump's victory "was racism. . . . I think Make America Great Again means Make America White Again. . . . He really, in my opinion, played heavily into racializing the white working class and made them feel that he would protect them against black and brown labor, and that they could still maintain the white buddy system."

---

[7] Kurt Eichenwald, 2016. "The Myths Democrats Swallowed That Cost Them the Presidential Election." *Newsweek*, November 14.
[8] Jenny Hopkinson, 2015. "Obama's Water War." *Politico*, May 27.

A Nevada political consultant agreed, "I think sexism is one hell of a drug in our country, and that has a lot to do with [the election outcome], as well." "I give [Clinton] tremendous credit," says a long-time Democratic political strategist in South Carolina, "because there's also – and you can't deny it when you look at the numbers – some sexism that took place, too." Iowa's Wawro remarked, "I do think that rural Iowa didn't feel like it was listened to. I think there were people in rural Iowa who weren't ready for a woman president." South Carolina activist Christale Spain summarized that Clinton "was easy to dislike . . . because we live in a misogynist, racist country."

A number of activists not only blamed bigotry for Clinton's loss, but associated the bigotry with their own identity group. An African American political strategist in South Carolina blamed men of color for turning against Clinton:

> There was a drop in terms of support when looking at the Obama race between men of color. African American men came out for Obama at around 92–93 percent and dropped down to . . . I think it was about a five-point drop. Similar five-point drop in terms of Hispanics. And so the question is, why was that? I think it had to do with her gender. With all of those things playing against her, in the end it was just a little too much.

Similarly, Iowa's Brenda Kole explained to me, "Women are . . . very, very hard on each other, and women with a similar background as me (white, college educated) held [Clinton] to a standard that you would probably never hold a male candidate to. I think gender played a role in that."

As with many explanations, there is no shortage of available evidence in support of it. Although if one accepts that extant bigotry among the electorate makes it harder to elect women and people of color, it is not entirely clear what one should be doing about it. Teaching tolerance to the electorate or shaming intolerance seems like a challenging proposition at best with payoff available only in the very long term. It could mean increased voter turnout efforts to help elect women and candidates of color, or it could mean nominating more white men to get around the problem (and create others in the process). There's no one obvious direction for the party to go.

EXPLANATION 6: SANDERS AND STEIN. According to exit polls, 89 percent of self-described Democrats voted for Hillary Clinton, while 90 percent of Republicans voted for Donald Trump. These figures are roughly what one would expect in a polarized era, yet they were slightly down from 2012's numbers, reflecting the greater unpopularity of the major parties' nominees compared to those of previous years. But some activists were concerned that the less-than-perfect Democratic fealty was the result of other candidates undermining the vote. Specifically, they thought that Green Party presidential nominee Jill Stein secured many votes that would have otherwise gone for Clinton, or that Bernie Sanders and his supporters were insufficiently supportive of the Democratic ticket compared to other previous failed presidential candidates.

Iowa's Brenda Kole summed up this belief, saying, "I think that there were some supporters who supported Bernie in the caucus who didn't either vote or they voted for Jill Stein. I don't know that they necessarily voted for Trump." New Hampshire's Bill Shaheen, a Clinton supporter in 2016, told me that most Sanders supporters rallied to Clinton's side after the nomination, but a significant and potentially damaging number of them refused to: "The Bernie people and the Hillary people got together and, for the most part, we did what we needed to do. There were some renegades that voted for Jill Stein, but that is what it is." South Carolina's Middleton summed up, "I would have liked for Senator Sanders to have done more."

Christale Spain, the 2016 political outreach director for Sanders in South Carolina, drew a distinction between Sanders supporters who were loyal Democrats, and those with independent inclinations. I asked her whether Sanders supporters sufficiently helped Clinton in November 2016. "*Democrats* did," she answered. "People who supported Sanders who were Democrats, yes. And they understood the political process argument even if they didn't know the political process, they still identified as Democrats. . . . But people who . . . were not Democrats before, did not. And I feel like they really worked desperately to widen that divide."

Some Clinton supporters professed a lingering resentment over what they saw as a betrayal of the Democratic Party, either by Sanders supporters insufficiently helping Clinton or others voting for Stein. "I think there are a lot of new people that came into the party," said Wawro, "and then went out of the party. I will say it might not have been Sanders folks that didn't work hard, but I think there were Jill Stein folks that I don't appreciate, and then have come back into the party to say, 'I'm a Democrat now, and I'll run to be on the [community college board].' No, see, *we* were Democrats. We tried to get something done, and you turned your back, and we're trying to fix a big mess."

Iowan Crawford explained the situation in his state: "Iowa kind of has this one-and-a-half-hands-tied-behind-your-back political philosophy in the Democratic Party, which is that you don't attack other Democrats. So, [Clinton] was getting attacked by the Republicans, attacked by Bernie, not really allowed to fight back, and it just took an enormous toll."

In a telephone interview, South Carolina's Brady Quirk-Garvan expressed some frustrations with Sanders supporters and suggested they offered an important lesson: "I think that the '16 cycle showed, this is what happens when we as Democrats don't unify after a primary. Primaries are, to me, good and helpful. They help steer the party. They let different factions bring up different issues. They're good and healthy for any party, but at the end of the day, parties are about winning."

I asked several 2016 Sanders supporters, including Iowan Mike Carberry, about their reactions to these sorts of critiques. "I don't think those numbers [of Sanders backers who wouldn't support Clinton] were huge but I think they were blown out of proportion by the media and especially some of Hillary's backers," Carberry responded.

> And this whole story about the Bernie Bros, I think that was overblown, too. Sure there were some Bernie Bros out there but I think there's a lot of . . . I don't even know the name for them, but there was a lot of people on the other side that were just as nasty and supportive of Hillary Clinton that were just as nasty about Bernie and about Bernie supporters both in person and online.

EXPLANATION 7: EXOGENOUS EVENTS. Several activists offered the opinion that Hillary Clinton would have been elected if not for a few exogenous events outside the campaigns' control. Two specific events were offered as examples: Russian meddling and FBI Director James

Comey's late October 2016 letter regarding the Clinton e-mail investigation.

A handful of people made specific reference to Russia. Some suggested that Russian-tied advertising on social media could have exploited Democratic weaknesses and influenced the general election. "You can't win if you don't unify," said Quirk-Garvan. "I think that's much of what the Russian influence played on. I think they saw that and used that as wedge amongst Democrats to try and suppress turnout." A few simply noted Russian meddling and expressed concern about further such interference in 2018 and 2020, without affirmatively stating that Russian interference tipped the 2016 results. "Somebody, and it won't be the Republicans," said Ketner, "needs to focus on the 2018 election and Russian interference, since we know they're going to do it again."

Compared to possible Russian interference, said Iowa activist Julie Stauch, "I think the Comey memo was far more damaging." Crawford agreed, "Comey was the exclamation point. We believed, and our polling showed, that we had fought back pretty close to even in Iowa, and then the day he gave that statement, the support just cratered. Just cratered overnight. And, that was that." Don Fowler had a similar impression: "Comey's interjecting himself in that race by announcing he was reactivating the inquiry into the private server matter, I think that was the death knell." Explained Oeth, "That Comey letter was just kind of like the reminder of all the thirty or forty years that anyone in public office is going to have baggage." A few blamed journalists for focusing on these stories at the expense of ones more damaging to Trump.

EXPLANATION 8: MOOD OF THE ELECTORATE. The final category is somewhat challenging to define. Some people simply felt that 2016 was, for lack of a better term, a weird year. Think of Trump's nomination, the Cubs' World Series victory, the passing of Prince, Carrie Fisher, David Bowie, George Michael ... things were happening that year that just don't happen in a typical year. (Perhaps not as weird as 2020, but still.) Translated into politics, this means that the electorate was in an unusual mood and might vote in some unpredictable ways. This could be classified as the "fundamental conditions" of the political environment, but whereas political scientists usually define such conditions as the state of the economy or whether the nation is at war, the political activists in this case described an anti-incumbent, anti-pluralism mood that is difficult to measure. "The country was looking for change and [Clinton] could never be the change candidate," veteran DC consultant Tad Devine told me in a phone conversation.

Former Rep. Swett even drew upon John Maynard Keynes concept of "animal spirits" to describe the political atmosphere: "Trump is really not the problem. The problem is the conditions that are in the country. The loosing of the animal spirits, if you will, that allowed for a man like him to get elected." Former Gov. Hodges drew this out in a bit more detail:

> There clearly was an incredible anti-Washington, anti-establishment mood out there that no one really captured. And regardless of her many talents, the Clintons had been around a long time and not only had they accumulated some baggage, but they were symbols of the establishment. Democratic and Republican voters saw them as a symbol of people who'd been around a long time and there was this yearning for something new. I mean, we saw whiffs of it in the Democratic primary. I don't think it spoke to any deficiencies that she had as a talented, capable person. I think it just was there was this mood out there. Some of it started in '08 with the financial crisis. I think some of the seeds of it were when you looked at the Obama election in '08 that political parties had begun to hunger for somebody who was not viewed as part of the establishment. I think we over-simplify to talk about missteps in the campaign.

Iowan Nate Monson, meanwhile, said he had some inkling of this changing mood thanks to his parents, who work in a small-town tool factory:

> They were telling stories about how their co-workers were talking about the campaign. And they were just like, "Lock her up," and her e-mails and all these things. That was really resonating with these sort of working-class folks, and it was just really interesting, because no one was hearing Hillary's message at all. And it just became so focused on that anger. . . . My parents kept saying they had the baseball caps on, they had the yard signs in the yard. And I said, "If they're willing to do that, they're going to vote," and that's what happened.

Democratic Socialist organizer Christian Bowe found a similar phenomenon occurring while he was canvassing the Philadelphia suburbs prior
to the 2016 elections. These were neighborhoods consisting, as he
described it, of many working-class retirees who had belonged to the
Communications Workers of America and the International
Brotherhood of Boilermakers, and were lifelong Democrats:

> We were going to houses and people were just saying, "We're still
> undecided." So, we just kept going to these houses of undecided voters
> over, and over, and over again. Instead of pulling new D1s and D2s
> [reliable and likely Democratic votes, respectively], we keep knocking
> these potential 3s [undecided voters], that all ended up, not all of them,
> but these towns ended up being 60, 65% for Trump. . . . Then I just, it
> clicked in my head on election night when I saw some of the results come
> through. It's like, this is probably happening all across the country.

New Hampshire's Alan Reische felt there was a shift in the electorate
between 2012 and 2016, which Trump successfully tapped into, but
which blindsided Democrats. "We were driving down a road," he told
me, "looking in the rearview mirror, thinking that things were the same.
Things are not the same and they're not going to be the same."

ANALYSIS OF EXPLANATIONS

I should note that all but seven activists offered multiple explanations for
the election's outcome. A few respondents explicitly noted the interde-
pendence of these explanations. As Democratic National Committee
member James Roosevelt argued, "The Democrats lost because of the
way the Electoral College functions, and because of the Russians, and Jim
Comey. Would those things have mattered if Secretary Clinton's campaign had resonated with more people? No, probably not. Would they
have mattered if Donald Trump wasn't the consummate salesman and
showman? No, probably not. So I think it's a mix."

The typical activist offered two explanations, but some proposed as
many as six. That said, some were much more common than others.
Figure 3.1 shows the percentage of all activists who offered each explanation. More than half blamed the Clinton campaign for some sort of

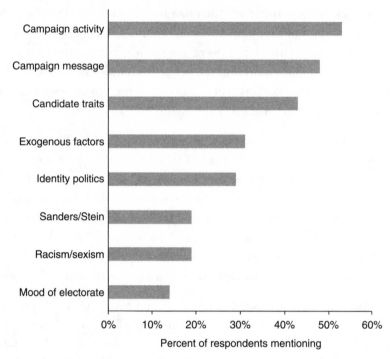

Figure 3.1 Frequency of election explanations

malpractice in its activities. Similar numbers felt that the campaign message was flawed or that the election pivoted on the candidates' traits. Indeed, all but five respondents offered at least one of these three explanations. Other explanations were less common.

In Figure 3.2, we can see how these narratives break down by various divisions among the activists. One of the sharpest divides is by sex. Men are substantially more likely to suggest that campaign messaging or candidates' traits were the problem than women were. However, women were far more likely to attribute Clinton's loss to outside events and persistent sexism and racism.

Nonwhite activists were more likely than whites to say that campaign activities and sexism/racism were to blame, although whites were considerably more likely to blame candidate traits and identity politics. Meanwhile, Clinton supporters from 2016 were more likely to blame exogenous factors,

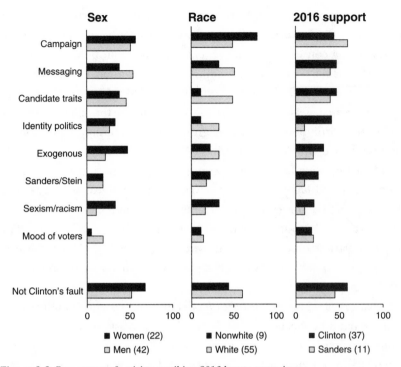

Figure 3.2 Percentage of activists ascribing 2016 loss to narratives

other candidates, and sexism/racism, while Sanders supporters from 2016 put the blame squarely on the Clinton campaign's choices.

In the bottom row of the table, I have summed the last four narratives, which blame things outside the campaign's control for the loss, into one variable called "not Clinton's fault." If an activist mentions any of those last four narratives at all, they are in the no-fault group. Women are overwhelmingly more likely than men to subscribe to such an interpretation. Whites were more likely than nonwhites to acquit the Clinton campaign, and Clinton supporters from 2016 were more likely than Sanders supporters to exonerate the campaign's role.

WHAT THEY DIDN'T SAY

This may seem like a fairly comprehensive list of explanations for the 2016 election outcome. Yet I found interesting what was left out. For one thing, the explanations offered were largely pretty separate from the ones I have been working with as a political scientist. While there certainly isn't a consensus among scholars of American politics about the causes of Hillary Clinton's defeat, a pretty common explanation (to which I largely subscribe) would go something like this:

Presidential elections are largely governed by the fundamentals of the political environment, such as the growth of the economy, conditions of war and peace, how long a party has held the White House, and so forth. Just based on such fundamental conditions, and ignoring aspects of the campaigns and candidates themselves, several political scientists published a range of forecasts in the academic journal *PS: Political Science & Politics*, as has become a quadrennial tradition in the discipline.[9] The forecasts varied somewhat, but on average they predicted Hillary Clinton receiving 50.7 percent of the two-party vote. In the end, she pulled 51.1 percent.

That's really close for a forecast model that omits so much information! But the point here is not to brag about these forecast models. Rather, the point is to note that it was already going to be a close election. In a period of good-but-not-amazing economic growth, relative peace abroad, and the incumbent party seeking a third term in office, you're going to see a competitive race. So the idea that Hillary Clinton *should* have won this election and somehow blew it isn't really supported by the available evidence. What's more, given the extent of polarization among the electorate, it's very hard to not get almost all registered members of your party voting for you if you're that party's nominee. Trump arguably did a great deal to make himself unelectable and still got elected. It's not that voters were enjoying or endorsing some of his unorthodox or offensive behavior, it's just that people will largely vote for their party, and they are capable of rationalizing or ignoring inconvenient behavior by their party's nominee.

That's not to say that these other narratives are flat-out wrong. In an election that close, it's certainly possible that James Comey's statements, or Hillary Clinton's messaging, or Jill Stein's candidacy, or something else, or some combination of them could have moved a few tens of

---

[9] James E. Campbell, 2016. "Forecasting the 2016 American National Elections." *PS: Political Science & Politics* 49 (Special Issue 4): 649–54.

thousands of votes in a few key states, and that's really all it took. But we can explain far more by just looking to the fundamentals that allowed that election to basically come down to a coin flip. The narrative that activists mentioned that comes closest to this was the "mood of the electorate" one, but for the most part, scholars and activists were speaking different languages here.

I was also surprised how little the name Barack Obama came up in conversations. Few seemed to blame him for any campaign choices he made in 2016, nor did they suggest that Clinton was the victim of an anti-Obama backlash. Bill Clinton's name didn't come up much, either, despite the role he played in his wife's nomination and campaign. No one mentioned the vice presidential candidates, either. Very few mentioned the Electoral College and the biases built into it. The activists nonetheless provided a pretty thorough list of possible explanations, each of which offer a path forward.

WHY WERE ACTIVISTS CONFUSED? A LOOK AT MEDIA COVERAGE

I want to provide some context here for the various explanations offered above. After all, post-election narratives aren't conjured out of thin air by political activists. They often emanate from journalists, pundits, and other political observers trying to attach some sort of rationale for the election results they are witnessing in real time. (And yes, cyclically, some of those observations may be influenced by the political activists who serve as sources for journalists.) I was interested in learning just what the media were saying about the 2016 election in the weeks and months that followed it.

My approach was to analyze the content of news articles about the election,[10] examining a broad range of local and national news sources.[11]

---

[10] Here I am loosely following the approach defined by Marjorie Hershey in her 1992 article "The Constructed Explanation: Interpreting Election Results in the 1984 Presidential Race." *The Journal of Politics* 54 (4): 943–76.

[11] I examined Access World News' database of 11,119 local newspapers across the United States, as well as archives for *The New York Times, The Los Angeles Times, National Review, Politico, The Washington Post, The Wall Street Journal,* and *The Hill.* Colin Phipps assisted with this research project.

I began with a search for the phrases "Clinton lost because" or "Trump won because," breaking the timeline down into the first four weeks following the 2016 election, and then examining month-by-month thereafter until November 2017. I attempted to plug each story or interpretation into one of the eight narratives I described earlier.

Figure 3.3 shows the frequencies that these narratives appeared, from election day through the end of November 2016 (left) and during the month of November 2017 (right). The percentages in each category are divided up by local and national media sources. As can be seen in the left figure, there is considerable support for all of the first four narratives – campaign activity, campaign messaging, identity politics, and candidate traits. There were some differences across local and national sources, with local sources more likely to emphasize messaging and national ones more focusing on identity politics frames, but there's broad consensus that the answer to the election lies in these four arguments.

Generally, we would expect to see the range of explanations narrow with time. However, note the range of explanations as of a year later, during November 2017, at right. Interestingly, not only has there not been concentration on a single narrative, but the range of explanations has grown. More than 40 percent of the national news sources describing

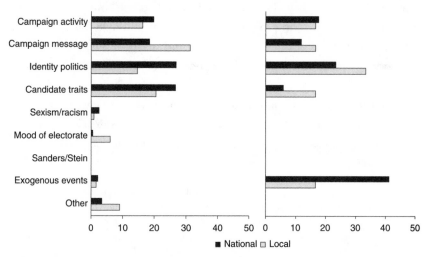

Figure 3.3 Post-election media narratives in November 2016 (left) and November 2017 (right)

the causes of the election now mention the Comey/Russia/WikiLeaks narrative. (Undoubtedly, this is due to expansions in discoveries of Russian interference into the election and the ongoing work of the Mueller investigation.) But there wasn't much decline in the other narratives, either. A year after the election, political observers were at less of an agreement on why the election came out as it did than they were in the weeks immediately following it.

To see a *decreasing* consensus on the lessons of an election is unusual. It's highly inconsistent with the work that Hershey did on the election of 1984 (see Chapter 2), when dozens of narratives about Ronald Reagan's landslide victory over Walter Mondale condensed to just a few after a few months.[12] Is it possible that as the media becomes more fragmented and American society – and particularly the Democratic coalition – becomes more diverse, that it's harder for news sources to agree on election narratives?

To examine this, I did the same post-election media narrative I described above for the elections of 2008 and 2012, dividing up the coverage into similar narratives. To measure the emergence of a single dominant narrative, I used a statistic called the Herfindahl Index. This index is often used in economic analysis to determine how much control one firm has over an industry, but it can be adapted here just as easily. Since I'm interested in knowing how much a single narrative has come to dominate public discussion about the election, I just look at the percentage that each of the eight narratives has in each month. I then sum the squares of all those percentages. The closer the sum gets to 10,000, the more one narrative has seized control of the discussion. If the media are coming to agree on a narrative, we should see this number increase over time.

Figure 3.4 presents a smoother line of the Herfindahl Index across both post-election periods for both national and local media. In both, the trend is the same – in 2008, the media agreed on a narrative (Obama's skills and personal traits) fairly quickly; in 2012, the media coverage started divided but became increasingly concentrated with time; in 2016, the media never really came to agreement on a narrative.

---

[12] Hershey, 943–76.

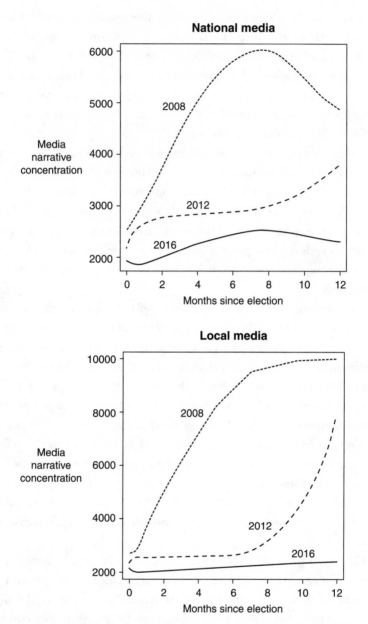

Figure 3.4 Media narrative concentration following three elections
Note: Vertical axis measures the Herfindahl Index of media narratives. Lines shown are moving averages.

The interpretation here is not that the political media have a hard time coming to an agreement over the meaning of an election; they achieved this reasonably well in 2008 and 2012. Rather, 2016 presented a difficult case for political observers of all stripes. Democrats have been confused in the wake of 2016 at least in part because the sources they rely on for understanding politics have been confused themselves.

WHAT DO YOU DO WITH A NARRATIVE?

Narratives aren't simply academic exercises. They suggest some action. I want to list a few things here that each narrative suggests as a course of action for the Democratic Party for 2020.

As the table below suggests, the first two narratives – problems with campaign activities or campaign messaging – do not necessarily call for any massive rethinking of party goals. Parties seek to refine their tactics and rhetoric all the time after losses, and can do so without dramatic changes to their coalition or core mission. Similarly, if the problem was exogenous factors (Russian interference, James Comey) or the mood of the electorate, there's no real need for the party to rethink its approach. Those are luck of the draw and not really easy to plan for. Elected

TABLE 3.1 *Narratives and the courses of action they suggest*

Narrative	Course of action
Campaign tactics	Innovations in campaign tactics, reallocation of campaign expenditures.
Campaign messaging	Innovations in campaign messaging.
Candidate traits	Nominate different type of candidate in future. Screen for problematic traits. Rethink nomination process.
Identity politics	Lessen advocacy for underrepresented groups. Nominate white man, possibly a Midwesterner.
Exogenous factors	No need to rethink.
Sanders/Stein	Seek to win over supporters for next election, or seek to defeat candidate early in nomination cycle.
Sexism/racism	Lessen advocacy for underrepresented groups. Nominate white man. Or push back.
Mood of electorate	No need to rethink.

Democrats could work to, say, battle Russian interference through their public offices, but in terms of the party and its campaign approach, that need not change.

On the other hand, if the problem is the candidate herself – if a different nominee would have won – that suggests some serious rethinking by the party. It needs to rethink just whom it nominates, figuring out exactly what candidate traits were so problematic last time and striving to avoid those in the next contest. It could also call for a reform to the party's nomination processes – changing primaries to caucuses or vice versa, de-fanging superdelegates, changing the order of state contests, and so on. If the narrative focused on other candidates, like Bernie Sanders and Jill Stein, that could call for going in several directions. Perhaps it means that the party needs to embrace those candidates' supporters and try to win them over, lessening the chances that they'll seek to hurt the nominee next time around. Conversely, it could mean trying to crush those candidacies early – going negative on Sanders as soon as he declares, for example – to limit their appeal.

Some of the most challenging narratives are those focusing on identity politics or persistent sexism and racism. One thing the party doesn't necessarily have within its power is an ability to lessen bigotry throughout society. Instead, what the party might seek to do is moderate one of its core commitments, the advancement of underrepresented groups. It could make a tactical retreat from overt support for feminism or civil rights, and it could favor the nomination of white male candidates, perhaps those from the Midwest or with strong ties to it. Conversely, one could view persistent sexism and racism as a challenge to be beaten back. Perhaps by nominating a woman and installing her in the White House, this societal challenge could be lessened.

It seems reasonable to say that we saw some version of all these approaches attempted during the leadup to the 2020 Democratic nomination contest. But it's also worth remembering that activists do not simply pick narratives at random or because of an especially effective op/ed they read. These narratives are embraced strategically. Activists may pick them precisely because they want to see the party move in a certain direction. But still, in many years, a dominant narrative emerges, and the party follows the relevant path. What happened between 2016 and 2020? Did activists settle on a narrative?

CONTINUING DISAGREEMENT

I followed up repeatedly with the activists I'd first contacted in 2017 and 2018. Between December 2018 and February 2020, I reached out to all of them every two months, asking them their thoughts on the Democratic presidential nomination. I occasionally asked related questions about the basis for their candidate choices, the lessons of 2016, and so forth. In the December 2019 survey, in particular, I asked respondents to think back to 2016 and say what the best explanation for Hillary Clinton's loss was that year.

Because I interviewed nearly all these activists in 2017 and 2018, I can compare their earlier answers to this question to the later answers. This is convenient and revealing, but I need to be up front about the limitations of this approach. I first spoke with them as part of lengthy interviews, giving them the opportunity to elaborate on the question of election loss. That's a very different experience than answering a multiple-choice question on an online survey. So we wouldn't necessarily expect their answers to these questions to match up perfectly over time.

That said, there's a reasonable amount of coherence between their answers in 2017/18 and at the end of 2019. In Figure 3.5, I show the percent of activists subscribing to each election narrative. For this figure, I only include the twenty-eight activists who provided answers in both the initial interview and the late-2019 wave of the survey. The narratives are listed in declining order of support. Again, activists can name multiple narratives, and many did; activists subscribed to an average of 2.7 narratives in 2017 and 3.0 narratives in 2019. Only two activists in each wave subscribed to just one narrative.

What the figure shows is that a few narratives had roughly the same number of adherents in 2017 as they did in 2019, but some lost favor, especially those ascribing Clinton's loss to errors of her campaign and its messaging. Meanwhile, other narratives became more popular, notably those blaming Clinton's loss on activities by Russia and James Comey, divisive efforts by Bernie Sanders and Jill Stein, and inherent sexism and

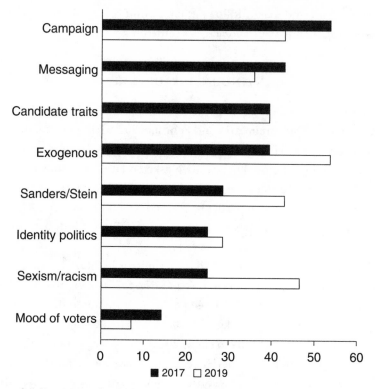

Figure 3.5 Percentage of activists supporting each narrative

racism in the electorate. In sum, these Democratic activists became less likely to blame the campaign's choices for the loss and more likely to blame things outside the control of the campaign, the candidate, and the party.

Also of note is that there doesn't appear to have been any convergence of narratives across this time span. As with the media, activists' interpretation of 2016 has become *more* dispersed with time; the mean number of narratives mentioned has increased, and there's a less sharp ranking among them.

In Figure 3.6 below, I drill down a bit into the responses given in December 2019. This is not a large sample of activists – just thirty-one of them – so the lessons we can learn by dividing them into subgroups are rather tentative. Nonetheless, I've examined adherence to the narratives based on the activists' sex, race, and experience in the party. The results are somewhat different from those reported above from the earlier surveys.

The starkest differences can be seen by sex. Most of the campaign/candidate narratives don't have meaningful differences by sex, although men are substantially more likely to mention some variant of identity politics than women are (44 to 8). But on the last four variables, which blame things outside the campaign's control for its loss, there are substantial differences by sex. Women are far more likely than men to blame Russia or Comey (77 to 33), general sexism and racism in the electorate (77 to 22), and the mood of voters (15 to zero).

We see somewhat similar divisions when we break down the results by race, with nonwhite activists considerably more likely than white activists to blame Russia or Comey, or sexism and racism, for the loss. And Clinton

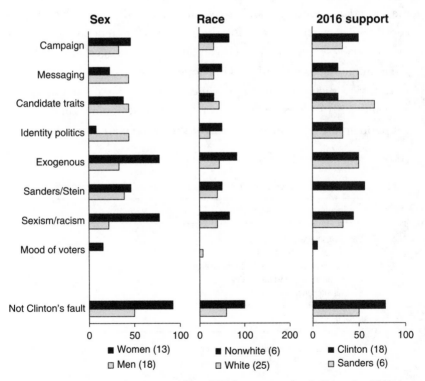

Figure 3.6 Percentage of activists ascribing 2016 loss to narratives in December 2019

supporters are far more likely to blame other candidates, and far less likely to blame choices by the Clinton campaign, than Sanders supporters are.

In the bottom row of the graph, I have again summed the last four narratives into a "not Clinton's fault" variable. Again, women are overwhelmingly more likely than men to subscribe to the interpretation that Clinton and her campaign were not at fault, and supporters of Clinton's primary bid tend to agree. In a change since the earlier interviews, more people of color than whites now agree that Clinton was not at fault.

But the most important takeaway here is continued disagreement about just why the election came out as it did. Activists offered more narratives, and those narratives were less concentrated than they were a year or two earlier. An environment in which activists are increasingly divided about why the last election came out as it did, and in which the narratives they are embracing are those that exonerate the choices that the candidate, campaign, and party made, it is difficult for the party to coordinate on a path forward. But the narratives they increasingly agreed on, especially sexism/racism and candidate traits, suggested rethinking the nomination system and possibly nominating a moderate white man.

A Civiqs survey of potential caucusgoers in Iowa, conducted in September 2019, offers some confirmation of the differences in narrative adoption across sexes. As in the activist survey, men are somewhat more

TABLE 3.2 *Iowa Democratic caucusgoer survey, September 2019*

Narrative	Men	Women
Democrats ran a bad campaign	12	9
Clinton was a flawed candidate	25	17*
Clinton focused too much on identity politics	4	1*
Clinton alienated the white working class	8	10
Russian interference	28	42*
Trump ran a more effective campaign	3	1*
Other reasons	17	10*

Notes: Online survey of 435 Democratic potential Iowa caucusgoers, conducted by Iowa State University/Civiqs between September 13 and 17, 2019. * indicates difference is statistically significant at the p ≤ .10 level. Data courtesy of David Peterson.

likely to blame Clinton and her focus on identity politics for her loss, while women are more likely to blame outside factors that do not implicate the candidate. (Russian interference was the dominant narrative overall, but hardly the consensus choice.)

HOW NARRATIVE LOSS PREDICTS CANDIDATE CHOICE

By the beginning of February 2020, just before the Iowa Caucuses, of the sixty-one activists whose candidate preferences I was able to ascertain, thirty-eight had picked a favorite candidate. Among those, the main choices were Joe Biden (backed by twelve activists), Bernie Sanders (backed by nine), and Elizabeth Warren (backed by eight).

In the chart below, I break down the percent of those candidate's supporters who ascribed Clinton's loss to each narrative in the interviews I conducted in 2017 and 2018. For example, 45 percent of Biden's supporters had said that Clinton's loss was due to campaign tactics, while 75 percent of Sanders' supporters, and 71 percent of Warren's supporters, had ascribed the loss to this narrative.

We can immediately see some important patterns. Supporters of Biden tended to favor the first four narratives, and, compared to supporters of other candidates, were particularly supportive of the idea that Clinton had lost because of candidate traits and because of the identity politics narrative. Sanders' supporters had strongly supported the idea that the campaign, its messaging, and candidate traits were to blame. They did not at all ascribe Clinton's loss to sexism or racism, and, unsurprisingly, they did not blame Sanders or other candidates for her loss. Finally, while Warren's supporters also blamed the Clinton campaign for problems, they were disproportionately likely to claim that Clinton had lost due to exogenous factors, other candidates, and persistent sexism and racism.

Here's a simpler way to look at the relationship between narratives and candidate choice. In Table 3.3, I look at all the activists who offered one of the narratives to explain the 2016 election in the early interviews, and for each group, who their top candidate was in early 2020. For example, among those who had said in 2017 and 2018 that Clinton lost due to the identity politics narrative (sixteen of the activists in total), five were endorsing Biden

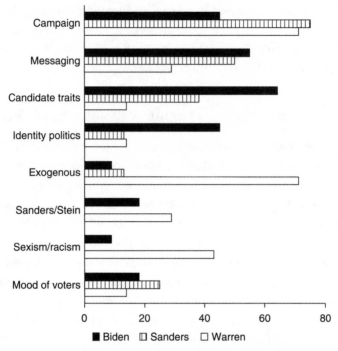

Figure 3.7 Narrative adoption in 2017–2018 and candidate support in February 2020
Notes: Bars show the percent of a candidate's supporters in early 2020 who ascribed Clinton's 2016 loss to each narrative in the 2017–2018 interviews. For example, among those who supported Joe Biden in early 2020, 45 percent had earlier said that Clinton had lost due to problems in her campaign.

by early 2020, while only one each was backing Sanders and Warren, making Biden the favorite among that narrative group.

Sanders was the favorite of those who had earlier said that campaign failures were the cause of the 2016 outcome. Among those who blamed Clinton's loss on campaign messaging, candidate traits, and identity politics, Biden was the top choice. Meanwhile, among those who said that Clinton lost because of outside factors like Russia or James Comey, or because of the mood of the voters, Warren was the top choice. The bottom two lines of the table show that among those who ascribed to any of the four narratives exonerating Clinton for her loss, Warren was the top choice, while those blaming Clinton for her loss leaned toward Biden.

TABLE 3.3 *Top 2020 candidate among adherents of 2016 narratives*

2016 Narrative	Top candidate for 2020
Campaign	Sanders
Messaging	Biden
Candidate traits	Biden
Identity politics	Biden
Exogenous	Warren
Sanders/Stein	Sanders/Biden
Sexism/racism	Warren/Biden
Mood of voters	Warren
Not Clinton's fault	Warren
Clinton's fault	Biden

The findings here do not demonstrate causality, to be sure. That is, I can't prove that some activists came to support Elizabeth Warren in 2020 *because* they had earlier believed that Russia affected the 2016 election. However, the language activists use when describing their candidate choices certainly supports this idea.

In the survey I conducted between late 2018 and early 2020, when activists told me they had decided to back a particular candidate, I invited them to explain what had led them to do so. Supporters of Joe Biden certainly sounded like those who viewed the Clinton campaign as plagued with troubles and saw electability as the main concern in choosing candidates; virtually all of them mentioned Trump in their explanations. "I think the former Vice President has what it takes to match Trump, outwork him and beat him," said one. "I believe he is the most able to beat Donald Trump," volunteered another.

Warren supporters, conversely, sounded like those who rejected the idea that Clinton lost because of who she was or how she campaigned. Rather, since they largely saw 2016 turning on events outside the candidate's control, they were supporting Warren because her policy preferences were closer to their own and they simply liked her. Said one, "I think Warren would be the best president and she closely aligns with my views." Another volunteered, "I will support any nominee. And I think Elizabeth is terrific. So why not help her now?" "The candidate's policies have been rolling out over the past few months and have been closest to my own beliefs," a third agreed.

The language used by supporters of Sanders was somewhat different. Many of his backers emerged early in the cycle, and indeed had been supporters of his in 2016 and had never really stopped backing him. They generally didn't volunteer concerns about electability, but rather spoke of a combination of policy preferences and authenticity. "Bernie is the OG when it comes to progressive policy. Why support 'Bernie Light' when you can get the real thing?" one asked. Another offered, "I am a democratic socialist and I believe Bernie Sanders is the candidate the best reflects my beliefs." Finally, said one, Sanders is "the candidate whose principled progressive policies and personal authenticity inspired a movement!"

A FIXATION ON ELECTABILITY

Party insiders spend the Invisible Primary trying to figure out the right balance between someone who can deliver what the party wants and someone who can win the general election. But what if the party can't figure out what it wants? Arguably, the confusion among Democrats I have described in this chapter paved the path for such a problem. To be sure, Democrats still believed the things they had believed for years, but they also desperately wanted Donald Trump out of office and couldn't figure out why he was there in the first place. In such a situation, possibly the easiest thing to do is to fall back on the formula believed to have worked in the past to maximize electability.

Shortly before the 2016 Iowa Caucuses, a nationwide survey asked potential Democratic voters and caucusgoers what quality was most important to them in a candidate. Forty-six percent said "a candidate who comes closest to your views on issues" while 38 percent said "the right personal style and strong leadership qualities." A mere 16 percent chose "a candidate with the best chance to defeat the Republican candidate."[13] Importantly, this was *not* the attitude among Democrats heading into 2020.

---

[13] https://online.wsj.com/public/resources/documents/NBCWSJDecember2015Poll MONDAY.pdf.

Even if activists couldn't agree on the cause of the party's last loss, they could agree on something else: electability was vitally important to them. In my June 2019 survey, I asked the activists which they considered more important in a nominee: an ability to defeat the Republican nominee, or a commitment to longstanding Democratic goals and values. Of those who responded to this question, twenty-two said defeating the Republican, while just five said a commitment to party goals. This finding is consistent with polling conducted in the lead up to 2020 showing that the focus on electability was both strong and unusual in this cycle. The 2020 contest was the first of the last four in which Democratic voters were prioritizing a candidate's electability over agreeing with them on most issues. Thanks to negative partisanship generally, and attitudes toward Donald Trump specifically, Democrats were willing to surrender quite a bit to defeat Trump.

The overall assessment among Democratic activists seemed to be that electability was the paramount issue, but it was not completely clear who the most electable candidate was early on, and this made it difficult to pick a favorite candidate. "The people who are most publicly identified with the Democratic Party, not many of them have endorsed," former DNC national chair Don Fowler explained to me. "I think those people, and I include myself in that, would rather win with Lucifer than lose to the Republicans again."

ACTIVISTS AND THEIR EMOTIONS

This combination of beliefs – a disagreement about why they had lost the last election, an overriding belief that electability was the most important feature in a candidate, but a disagreement over who the most electable candidate was – took an emotional and informational toll on party activists trying to pick a candidate for 2020. Several activists with whom I spoke described a sense of trauma when thinking back to the previous election cycle.

I want to be clear what I mean by the term "trauma." Obviously, these activists suffered no physical damage as a result of the 2016 election cycle, and whether their emotional experiences emanating from that election should be considered psychological damage is open to question. I don't mean to use the term lightly. But as many conversations suggested, that election shook them. It caused them to question their own understanding of politics, of what the American political system would and would not accept.

Some of this trauma stemmed from the surprisingly divisive and lengthy nomination contest between Sanders and Clinton in 2016. Iowa political activist Julie Stauch claimed that she and her colleagues were fearful of ripping the party apart: "One of the most negative things out of 2015 and '16 was the animosity between many Hillary supporters and many Bernie supporters. People don't want to pick too early because they don't want to get sucked into the internecine conflict."

But perhaps the more traumatizing legacy centered on Clinton's loss to Trump despite her consistent polling lead and her strong performances in the general election debates. The outcome undermined many activists' longstanding beliefs about just what sorts of candidates are electable. According to Kathy Eckhouse of Des Moines, this has had a particularly pernicious effect on women candidates. Political activists "have convinced themselves that a woman can't win," she said. "They can no longer say that an African American can't win, because that happened. But they will say, 'I just don't think a woman can win.'" According to Eckhouse and her husband Herb, some activists who otherwise would be enthusiastic supporters of Elizabeth Warren or Kamala Harris or Amy Klobuchar were hesitant to commit because they believed that voters have a bias against female candidates. (The couple themselves don't share these beliefs and claimed to have had significant disagreements with friends over this.)

"It's an emotional thing," Kathy Eckhouse continued. "[Activists] are so traumatized by 2016, and they're so terrified of revisiting that night and having it all happen again. And I think they like to think that they're just being practical and a little bit cynical and realistic." Those fears, according to Eckhouse, led some activists to support Joe Biden, not because he was their top preference, but because they thought they were playing it safe.

One additional point of anxiety activists mention is the high cost of making the wrong choice. Political consultant Jeff Link summed up, "The overriding sense I get from people is that choice matters this time more than in previous caucuses because Trump has raised the stakes." A Las Vegas political organizer agreed, "There's this [group] that's like, 'We're waiting for the field to clear out and see who's left.' . . . I've seen across the board, 'Oh, I don't want to be wrong. I endorsed Hillary, she lost.' There's still that real visceral gut reaction of not wanting to invest in a candidate who may lose."

In the October 2019 wave of the survey, I included a set of questions asking activists about their emotional state when thinking about the presidential nomination.[14] I asked them to evaluate how enthusiastic, afraid, proud, hopeful, and anxious they were on a four-point scale ranging from "not at all" to "extremely." Activists who were feeling hopeful, enthusiastic, or proud about the nomination contest were much more likely to have decided on a presidential candidate. Meanwhile, those who were feeling anxious about the contest were far less likely to have picked a candidate.

WHAT DEMOCRATS ARGUED ABOUT WHEN THEY ARGUED ABOUT THE 2020 NOMINATION

If you were to think back on some of the more memorable disagreements between Democratic presidential candidates during the Invisible Primary, you might remember some moderate candidates ganging up on Bernie Sanders and Elizabeth Warren about Medicare For All, or Pete Buttigieg coming under fire for a fundraiser in a wine cave or his days as a business consultant, or a rambling rant by Joe Biden. Judging from the evidence I've collected, though, the Democratic Party was fighting about the things it has been fighting about for decades – race, gender, and how those interact with electability. I'll break these down here to provide some examples.

RACE. In addition to being the largest presidential candidate field in the party's history, it was also the most diverse. Notably, many of the upper tier of candidates who qualified for debates throughout 2019 – including Cory Booker, Kamala Harris, and Andrew Yang – were people of color, while it was the bulk of white male candidates who ended up underperforming and withdrawing relatively early. Sometimes those

---

[14] Question text: "I'd like to ask you about the emotions you've been experiencing during this contest. Generally speaking, how do you feel when thinking about the 2020 Democratic presidential nomination contest or talking about it with others?"

candidates ended up poking fun of each other, and themselves, for their relative anonymity and, as far as reporters and many voters were concerned, interchangeability.

In May of 2019, writer Derek Davidson posted a photo of Rep. Seth Moulton on Twitter, with the text, "After a lot of soul searching I think I've found my 2020 candidate and it's Congressman Tim Ryan of Ohio (pictured), let's do this thing folks." Moulton picked up on this and responded, "No Derek, this is New York City Mayor Eric Swalwell." Tim Ryan then responded to Moulton: "Thank you for clarifying Sen. Bennet." Michael Bennet then replied to Ryan, "Thanks for all your service to the good people of South Bend. My whole family loves Chasten's Twitter feed."[15]

Race was at the core of many of the party's debates and discussions throughout the Invisible Primary. South Bend, Indiana, Mayor Pete Buttigieg, for example, was occasionally criticized by other candidates for his unconventional pedigree as a presidential candidate, representing a city of just 100,000 people. But a lot of that criticism focused on his strained relationships with African Americans in South Bend, particularly related to his 2012 firing of the city's first African American police chief, and a mid-2019 fatal shooting of a black resident by a police officer.

One of the defining features of debates throughout 2019 was frontrunner Joe Biden boasting the support of the bulk of African American primary voters,[16] and African American candidates Cory Booker and Kamala Harris trying to exploit his unpopular historical stances and awkward statements to pry some of those voters loose. Shortly before the June 2019 debate, for example, Biden gave a speech talking up his own experiences in the US Senate working with people of vastly different viewpoints. He specifically mentioned the civility he demonstrated working with the late Senators James Eastland of Mississippi and Herman Talmadge of Georgia, two ardent segregationists. "He never called me 'boy,'" Biden said of Eastland. "He always called me 'son.'"

---

[15] https://twitter.com/MichaelBennet/status/1129932450073858048.
[16] Marc Caputo, 2019. "Poll: Biden Continues to Dominate Among Black Voters." *Politico*, December 13.

At the June debate, Harris called out Biden for this comment. While conceding the importance of civility, she said, "It was hurtful to hear you talk about the reputations of two United States senators who built their reputations and career on the segregation of race in this country. And it was not only that, but you also worked with them to oppose busing." Harris then famously talked about her own experiences with busing growing up in California public schools. In the exchange that followed, Biden appeared to endorse local control of school integration.[17] Polling following this exchange saw a substantial, if ephemeral, shift, with Harris gaining several points and Biden losing some.

In the November 2019 debate, Cory Booker criticized Biden for his resistance to marijuana legalization, arguing that marijuana was "already legal for privileged people" and that "the war on drugs has been a war on black and brown people." Booker further said that black voters were angry because "we are nominating someone that . . . isn't trusted, doesn't have authentic connection." Biden defended himself by talking up his work with Barack Obama and his support within the African American community. "I come out of the black community in terms of my support. If you notice, I have more people supporting me in the black community . . . because they know me. They know who I am." He then claimed the support of "the only African American woman that had ever been elected to the United States Senate," referring to former Senator Carol Moseley Braun of Illinois, failing to mention that Kamala Harris was a US Senator and was, at that time, running against him.[18]

To many observers, it was surprising that so many African American voters were sticking with Biden. I was offered a number of explanations for this in conversations with activists and attendees at the James Clyburn Fish Fry in Columbia, South Carolina, in the summer of 2019. The Fish Fry is an annual Democratic Party event, funded largely by Rep. Clyburn and open to the public, generally running on the same night as a high-dollar state party fundraiser. The year before a presidential election, it

[17] Natalie Jennings and Eugene Scott, 2019. "The Full Kamala Harris–Joe Biden Exchange Over Race and Busing, Annotated." *The Washington Post*, June 28.
[18] Kate Sullivan, 2019. "Booker Criticizes Biden's Opposition to Legalizing Marijuana: 'I Thought You Might Have Been High.'" CNN, November 21.

becomes one of the first opportunities for people to hear from all the Democratic presidential candidates. Given that African Americans make up more than a quarter of South Carolina and a majority of the state's Democrats, and given Clyburn's prominence in the state's black political community, the Fish Fry is a highly visible event for black Democrats early in the nomination process.

Dalton Tresvant, an African American long-term staff member in Clyburn's district office, explained Biden's appeal to me. "You've got to remember that in South Carolina, black voters are more conservative in South Carolina than they are in New York. So-called progressives need to understand that." He described a conversation in a barber shop about Biden's comments on working with people like James Eastland.

> The guys at the barber shop were saying, "Yeah, he had to." He had to work with those guys because a lot of them remember Strom Thurmond. And they were saying, "Yeah, well you couldn't get anything done unless you worked with that crew." So they kind of understood. . . . Booker needs to leave that alone because it's going to backfire on him.

Don Fowler, the white former DNC chair from South Carolina, agreed with this sentiment.

> I have the highest positive regard for Joe Biden. I think he would be a good president. But he does make *faux pas* here and there. And what happened with respect to the Eastland comment, yeah, is sort of typical and I hope that he can minimize that. I think the objections that Senator Booker rose was a bunch of crap, frankly. . . . I think Senator Booker feels that he's falling behind Senator Harris and he had to do something to attract attention and so I think that's the explanation for that. But those kinds of comments are not helpful.

Biden, noted Tresvant, had deeply developed relationships with prominent African American community members that predated his time in the vice presidency. He referenced a 2007 visit by Biden to a conference of presidents of historically black colleges and universities. "I was shocked," said Tresvant. "Every one of those college presidents knew him when he went in to sit and talk to them."

Several other African American Fish Fry attendees volunteered support for Biden to me. "[Biden] seems to be better qualified than anyone else with having been Vice President. It makes him a little more qualified than anyone else" said Caroline Taylor. According to Dee Dee Washington, "President Trump has taught us, be yourself and people like you. And that's what Joe Biden does. He's himself. What you see is what you get." Asked about Biden's comments on working with segregationists in the Senate, Washington replied, "That really doesn't bother me, because once debate starts, they're going to be digging dirt on each and every one of them. So there will be comments like that about all of them, so that doesn't bother me."

As of the end of the invisible primary season, the seeds of a recurrent rift in the party had already been sown. Joe Biden had emerged as the party "regular" candidate, with the support of a broad range of insiders and, importantly, the plurality of African American voters, while Bernie Sanders was the more ideological candidate opposed to him in the early primaries and caucuses. This division, hardly uncommon in Democratic presidential primaries, is often portrayed as a regular/reform split or an insider/outsider split, but it has an important racial dimension, as well. That is, the bulk of the party's African American voters and elected officials would be more or less content with their presidential choice, while a largely white group of progressive activists would be protesting that their voice was being silenced.

Nonetheless, for many African Americans, the lessons of 2016 hung over their 2020 decisions in a particular way. The electability concern was a particularly potent one. Many African American voters would no doubt have liked to see another African American president, but many shared the concern that such a candidate would have a harder time winning than, say, a moderate white man. It's not so much that African American voters or political activists were more likely to believe in such electability concerns than whites were, just that they saw the costs of losing another presidential election as higher for them.

WOMEN AND THE NOMINATION. The final question of the December 2019 Democratic debate was asked by moderator Judy Woodruff. "In the spirit of the season," she asked, "I'd like to ask each one of you, is there someone else among these candidates that you would – you have two options, one, a candidate from whom you would ask forgiveness for something maybe that was said tonight or another time, or a candidate to whom you would like to give a gift?"[19] The responses were varied, and some more serious than others. And of course the wording of the question made no reference to gender. But the pattern that emerged was pretty clear: the five men on the stage offered gifts – a book, a private phone number, teamwork, wisdom, and so on – while the women, Senators Elizabeth Warren and Amy Klobuchar, offered apologies for their behavior.[20]

All this is to say that gender showed up in this nomination process in the ways it often does in politics, in both subtle and unsubtle ways. To be sure, the diverse candidate field included several prominent women candidates – Amy Klobuchar, Elizabeth Warren, Kamala Harris, and Kirsten Gillibrand – who dominated the debates and public discussion in 2019. This in itself was a dramatic shift from any previous presidential nomination race. But women candidates were treated differently from their male competitors, and male and female activists processed political information differently from each other.

Thirty-one activists responded to my December 2019 survey, including thirteen women and eighteen men. Among that group, six women had picked a favorite presidential candidate while seven hadn't; twelve men had picked a favorite presidential candidate while six hadn't. Throughout 2019, the men in my survey were consistently more likely to have picked a favorite candidate. There is additional evidence of this in the Civiqs Iowa poll from September 2019, in which men were approximately 7 percentage points more likely to have picked a favorite presidential candidate than women were (a statistically significant result).

Meanwhile, when I asked respondents which candidates they were *considering*, many female candidates performed well by this measure. Kamala Harris and Elizabeth Warren often led the field. Yet very few activists *committed* to supporting female candidates. These activists, that is,

---

[19] The Fix, 2019. "Transcript: The December Democratic Debate." *Washington Post*, December 19.

[20] https://twitter.com/Smilla1972/status/1207866471654789121.

were certainly open to the idea of a woman nominee, but few were willing to take the steps to make that happen.

A survey conducted by Civiqs in May and June of 2019 helps shed some light on this finding. Pollsters first asked respondents whom they would support if the primary election were held that day. Later in the poll, they asked them which candidate they would choose if they could wave a magic wand and make them president. In the first question, Joe Biden was the winner, besting all other candidates by at least ten points. In the magic wand question, Elizabeth Warren marginally beat the others. Going from a horserace to a magic wand cost Biden ten points and gave Warren five. Now, there's nothing necessarily invidious about this finding; Democratic voters were making strategic decisions about whom they liked and weighing that against who they thought could win. But then they asked respondents what they would change about their "magic wand" candidate to make them more electable. Candidate gender was by far the most mentioned factor.[21]

Figure 3.8 sheds some additional light on this question, using a similar "magic wand" survey conducted by Data for Progress and YouGov Blue in June 2019.[22] For each of the eight leading candidates, I have subtracted how the candidate did in the magic wand question from how they did in the initial trial heat question. This is essentially a measure of how much "electability" was helping the candidates – it shows how much additional support a candidate was getting because they had to win a general election against Donald Trump. I have displayed the results among different subgroups within the self-identified Democrats in the sample – white men, white women, African American men, and African American women.

As can be seen, Joe Biden was overwhelmingly the beneficiary of electability concerns. People gave him an additional seven to eight points of support, similarly across subgroups, because of concerns about the general election. The largest overall electability penalty was

---

[21] www.avalanchestrategy.com/electability.
[22] http://filesforprogress.org/datasets/pre_post_debate/FIRSTDEBATE_MEMO.pdf.

exacted from Elizabeth Warren, who lost an average of two points, with the greatest effect among white male Democratic voters. There was a similarly sized negative effect on Pete Buttigieg, concentrated mainly among white women. Interestingly, the two African American candidates, Cory Booker and Kamala Harris, suffered a modest average electability penalty that was concentrated mainly among African American men, who moved 3.5 points away from Harris and 4.4 points away from Booker out of electability concerns. That is, there were substantial numbers of African American Democratic men who would have supported Booker or Harris, but were concerned they couldn't

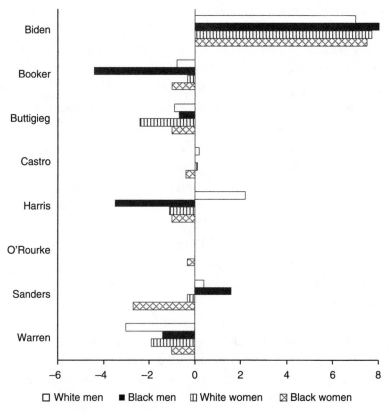

Figure 3.8 Electability effect for leading Democratic candidates, June 2019
Notes: Data from Data for Progress/YouGov Blue. Survey conducted June 24–26, 2019. Analysis limited to self-identified Democrats. Dataset includes 847 men, 1,358 women, 1,439 whites, and 433 African Americans. Data courtesy Kevin Reuning.

defeat Trump, and were backing Biden instead. Interestingly, white men thought Harris was *more* electable. Attitudes toward Bernie Sanders were mixed, with black men seeing him as more electable and black women seeing him as less so.

In Chapter 6, I will describe a survey experiment I ran showing that some political narratives had more of an effect on women than on men, causing them to change their views of what could happen in politics and who could and couldn't be elected. This was a recurring theme in my activist interviews. Many of the women I interviewed were more likely to suggest that the 2016 election caused them to update their views of politics, but that the 2018 elections did so, as well.

Conversations with two New Hampshirites suggested some important differences in beliefs about electability. Attorney Bill Shaheen, speaking in early 2019, discussed the sort of candidate he was looking for as a presidential nominee:

> I don't particularly care about a single issue. I just want to beat Trump and I want to beat him badly because we need super-majorities in both houses to fix the things he's broken. . . . I've never been that determined to say, "I want someone who thinks just like me." I don't think that candidate exists. I want a good person who's going to work hard and who's smart and who can change this country because we are really in tough shape here.

The lessons of 2016 clearly hung over Shaheen, but in a way that made him ideologically flexible. He was willing to surrender quite a few policy goals to get an overall win. Compare that with the perspective of State Representative Mary Jane Mulligan from Hanover:

> Everybody's saying, we want somebody to get rid of Trump. Well, me too, but I am not going to let Trump sell me out so that I'll vote for anything just to get him out. I won't sink that low. I will not allow him to take that control, my vote away from me. . . . I don't believe that the American people need to go that low to get him out. He's only got a base of 30 percent, and maybe they're hard core and . . . if he shoots and kills somebody, they're still willing to embrace him. But that's 30 percent, and there's 70 percent of us out there.

Some activists experienced something of a political transformation in the years since the 2016 election, and not always driven directly by that election. To provide a better sense of this, I want to highlight the example of one of my respondents, whom I will call Sandra. (Due to the personal nature of the interview, she requested to not have her actual name used.) During college, Sandra was a victim of sexual assault. She later moved to Washington, DC, and became active with an interest group with a feminist orientation. She was an early backer of Joe Biden's presidential bid, from long before he officially entered the race, due to his stances on a number of issues of personal resonance for her, and especially his advocacy for victims of sexual assault.

This began to change in late 2018 and early 2019 for Sandra. One of the catalyzing events for her was the nomination of Brett Kavanaugh to the Supreme Court. The confirmation hearings, focusing on allegations that Kavanaugh had sexually assaulted Christine Blasey Ford while in high school, ended with Republicans on the Senate Judiciary Committee angrily dismissing the charges and voting to confirm Kavanaugh. For Sandra, as with many others, the reaction was markedly personal and radicalizing:

> I've never had an abortion. And I'm primarily radicalized by things that I'm directly impacted by, as reflected by my work. But ... I was part of a group of thousands of women who immediately went and got a long-acting reversible birth control solution as soon as Kavanaugh was named to the Court. ... I started to see the personal and political coming together in a way that it hadn't for me previously.

This radicalizing process was spurred on in the late spring of 2019 by several other events. In early June, Biden reiterated his longstanding support for the Hyde Amendment, which bans federal funds for most abortions. He was promptly pilloried by Democrat leaders and other presidential candidates, as his stance, once a fairly mainstream one in Democratic circles, had become far less popular with time. Senator Warren, for one, used the moment as an opportunity to brandish her pro-choice credentials: "Women of means will still have access to abortions," she said during an MSNBC town hall. "Who won't will be poor women. It will be working women and women who can't afford to take off three days from work, and very young women. It will be women who have been raped and women who have been molested by someone in their own family."[23] After two days of such criticism, Biden reversed his position: "If I believe health care is a right, as I do," Biden said at a DNC gala, "I can no longer support an amendment that makes that right dependent on someone's ZIP code."[24]

At roughly this same time, several Republican-controlled state legislatures were forcing the abortion issue to the fore of American politics. Alabama enacted a law to fundamentally ban abortion, joining Georgia, Ohio, Mississippi, and several other states in seeking to draw a Supreme Court ruling that might overturn *Roe v. Wade*.[25]

All these events coming together over a short period of time had the effect of elevating abortion as a salient issue for Sandra. The earlier Democratic approach of welcoming a diverse range of views on the topic within the party no longer seemed adequate:

> The right are single issue voters on abortion. And the left will continue to experience this unless we all also become single issue voters on abortion. And our big tent outlook as a party is now going to directly harm women. Because we tell people that you can be neutral on abortion and still be welcomed in the Democratic Party. And that's not serving the most loyal base of the Democratic Party right now. And I think some people, including myself, are really angry about that.

Sandra ended up reevaluating her support for Biden and started looking for a woman candidate:

> I just truly don't think that these really privileged men, who have been in this work for a really long time, who in many ways are great feminists and are men that I really respect and admire. . . . I am wondering if they're the right people for this moment, because of how distinctly anti-woman this moment is.

---

[23] Ella Nilsen, 2019. "Elizabeth Warren Makes a Forceful Argument on How the Hyde Amendment Worsens Inequality." *Vox*, June 5. www.vox.com/policy-and-politics/2019/6/5/18654627/abortion-elizabeth-warren-hyde-amendment-biden-msnbc.

[24] Katie Glueck, 2019. "Joe Biden Denounces Hyde Amendment, Reversing His Position." *The New York Times*, June 6.

[25] Kayla Epstein, 2019. "This Abortion Bill is Probably Unconstitutional. A Republican Lawmaker Says That's the Point." *The Washington Post*, August 12.

Sandra, who had previously been a staunch Biden supporter in my survey, switched her affiliation to undecided in April 2019. By the October 2019 wave of my survey, she was a strong supporter of Warren.

CONSEQUENCES OF DIVISION

Perhaps the clearest conclusion of this evidence is the lack of a clear conclusion. That is, judging from conversations I had with all these activists, there was no consensus view within the Democratic Party about why they lost the presidency in 2016, and they just grew more divided about this question over time. There was no agreement that the party was too far left or too far right, that its messaging or tactics were wrong, that their candidate was flawed or that the system was stacked against her, or anything else. If, in previous years, activists might have been guided by political journalism toward developing a narrative about the election, the media provided no such help in 2016; they were just as confused and divided over its causes and meaning as other political observers.

This ongoing disagreement created an environment in which a "safe" candidate – a white, moderate man with some cross-party appeal – was increasingly seen as the smart choice. That choice would help get around some of the difficult conversations at the party's core. But as we'll see in the next chapter, those conversations would prove difficult to ignore.

CHAPTER 4

When Parties Try to Fix Themselves

We bear the burden of being a diverse party. If all we had to worry about was old white people we'd be fine. But that's not who we are.

Yvette Lewis

As abhorrent as we think Trump is . . . the truth of the matter is that the wise men and women of the Democratic Party picked a candidate who did not succeed, and the rabble rousers of the Republican Party picked the one who could.

Jeff Weaver

Mark Twain is reputed to have said that "history doesn't repeat itself but it often rhymes." Bear with me for a moment while I offer an example of a party that went through something like what Democrats went through in the wake of 2016. The example itself actually predates Twain, but its experiences bear a lot of similarities to recent political developments in the United States, and are instructive about what parties can and can't do in response to a surprise electoral loss.

If you were looking for an early-nineteenth-century version of Hillary Clinton, you could do worse than Henry Clay of Kentucky. He was a senator, a secretary of state, and a repeated unsuccessful presidential candidate, as well as one of the most prominent, intelligent, and influential leaders of his day. He was also widely accused of corruption, having bowed out of the 1824 presidential election and received a cabinet appointment from the winner, John Quincy Adams.

Clay was also the most prominent member of the National Republican Party, the precursor to the Whigs, which would dominate national politics from the 1830s until shortly before the Civil War. The National Republicans were often referred to as the Anti-Jacksonians because their primary function and orientation was opposition to Andrew Jackson, whose 1828 election and norm-breaking administration stunned political observers on a nearly daily basis.

While we're at it, if you were looking for an early-nineteenth century version of Donald Trump, you could do a lot worse than Andrew Jackson. In many ways, Jackson did the sort of things that Trump could only fantasize about, violating all manner of norms and traditions, ignoring Supreme Court decisions he found inconvenient, explicitly championing the white "common man" over the rights and even the lives of African Americans and Native Americans, and even physically beating a would-be assassin. Jackson was an extreme example of what we would call a "populist" today. It was no accident that Trump hung Jackson's portrait in the Oval Office shortly after taking office.

According to Michael Holt's detailed descriptions of this period in his *Rise and Fall of the American Whig Party*, Henry Clay and other National Republican leaders were surprised and horrified by Jackson's 1828 victory. They worried he was a potential despot who would undermine the nation's fragile institutions and democratic norms. They simultaneously dismissed his election as a fluke. "They regarded the outcome," says Holt, "as a triumph by the magnetic Jackson over the aloof and colorless [John Quincy] Adams. Hoopla, demagoguery, and Jackson's refusal to take a stand on matters of national policy, they thought, had temporarily dazzled voters, while sheer opportunism had engaged politicians with divergent policy goals in the Jackson cause."[1]

The National Republicans at first pursued a strategy of passive opposition to Jackson, confident that people would naturally turn against him once he was forced to take stances on actual policy issues. But they had misread the public and underestimated Jackson. Jackson's "vigorous advocacy of Indian removal increased his popularity in the South and the West. His demand for rotation in office among federal officeholders and his defiant contempt for . . . snobbish social pretension . . . enhanced

---

[1] Michael F. Holt, 1999. *The Rise and Fall of the American Whig Party: Jacksonian Politics and the Onset of the Civil War*, New York: Oxford University Press, p. 10.

his image as a foe of privilege and elitism" (Holt, p. 11). Jackson, that is, shored up his base through explicitly racist policies, calls for draining the swamp, and populist rhetorical appeals.

National Republicans soon recognized that the Jackson administration wouldn't implode on its own, and that defeating Jackson at the ballot box was the only way to curtail his rule. They worked under the narrative that anti-Jackson forces had lost in 1828 because they were divided, but by forging alliances with new groups, they might be able to take Jackson down in the next election. They sought an alliance with the Antimasonic Party, which were something like today's progressives, in that they were opposed to secretive elites controlling the government. The problem was that the Antimasonics weren't particularly trusting of the National Republicans, either – Clay himself was a Freemason.[2] The alliance failed. The Antimasonics nominated their own candidate, William Wirt, but even their combined vote fell well short of Andrew Jackson's, who won reelection in 1832 with 55 percent of the popular vote.

The point of this story is that what Democrats went through in the wake of 2016 is not entirely unprecedented. Other parties have found themselves losing to candidates thought unelectable, and have followed that by intense periods of analyzing past election loss and restructuring their own party, reconsidering both its purpose and functioning, trying to build alliances with those who are skeptical of the party system, and struggling with its pick for the presidency.

For some, the Democratic Party did not engage in enough of a post-mortem exercise following 2016 to determine just what went wrong. In fact, Democrats did conduct a serious self-analysis following that election. The party's formal leadership established a task force – the Unity Reform Commission – in 2016 that was tasked with addressing party practices and making recommendations for the future. The commission wrapped up its work at the end of 2017, and the Democratic National Committee spent much of 2018 debating about just what of its recommendations to implement. Throughout 2019, the party argued among itself about how to conduct candidate debates and shape the presidential field in light of what had happened in 2016. The primaries and caucuses and the

---

[2] Sean Wilentz, 2005, *Andrew Jackson*. New York: Times Books.

national convention of 2020 were heavily structured by party conversations, arguments, and decisions made in the years prior.

This chapter's main focus is attempts by people within the formal Democratic Party, especially members of the Democratic National Commission, to interpret the 2016 loss and make changes to their nomination rules in preparation for 2020. Before getting into that, I will spend a bit of time talking about an important historical parallel – the party reforms conducted between 1968 and 1972 – that gave rise to much of what we think of as the modern party nomination system. In both cases, as we'll see, race played a profound role in structuring these discussions, with representation of African Americans remaining a dominant concern and source of argument within the party for over half a century.

WHEN TO CHANGE

A great deal of attention tends to be paid to the behavior of campaigns and parties in the few months before a major election. Yet at those times, campaigns and parties are often following the tactics they've been practicing for years or even decades. The late campaign is rarely a place for innovation. Often getting less attention, however, is the period shortly after an election, when campaigns and parties seek to evaluate what just happened and to learn from past mistakes. In particular, the losing party has great incentive for reflection, and it is typically right after a major loss that we tend to see a party recalibrate its approaches or moderate its platform.[3]

In his book *The Losing Parties*,[4] political scientist Phil Klinker evaluates the major national party organizations' behavior following every presidential election loss from 1956 through 1988. As Klinkner notes, not only are the formal parties incentivized to change their ways after a loss to become more competitive, but when a party doesn't control the White House is precisely when its chair has the most freedom to make

[3] Andrea Volkens, Onawa Lacewell, Pola Lehmann, Sven Regel, Henrike Schultze, and Annika Werner, 2013. "The Manifesto Data Collection. Manifesto Project." Berlin: Wissenschaftszentrum Berlin für Sozialforschung.

[4] Philip A. Klinkner, 1994, *The Losing Parties: Out-Party National Committees, 1956–1993*, New Haven: Yale University Press.

changes to the party. He quotes former DNC chair Robert Strauss: "When the party's out of office, you're the head; when a Democrat is President, you're a goddamned clerk" (p. 3).

Klinkner goes through each post-election period methodically and finds some important differences across the major parties. Republicans tend to engage in organizational responses to loss, focusing on the "nuts and bolts" of electioneering. So, for example, in the wake of Richard Nixon's narrow loss to John Kennedy in 1960, Republican leaders noted that their party had performed worse than usual in the northern cities but better than usual in the South. They initiated a direct mail fundraising campaign to bolster party treasuries (while becoming less reliant on funders in northeastern cities) and reallocated more campaign resources to southern white communities in an effort to, in Barry Goldwater's words, "go hunting where the ducks are." This shift of focus to the South would have important consequences down the road, but it didn't involve a significant rethinking of how the party was run or whom it nominated.

If Republicans tinker with their approach but are overall pretty confident in who they are and what they stand for, Democrats are pretty much the opposite; it doesn't take much to convince them that they're doing everything wrong. Democrats, says Klinkner, "have a culture that focuses on procedure, making it a much more 'democratic' party. They are continually concerned about voice and representation within the party and they tend to see the party as both the arena and arbiter for such questions after their losses" (p. 201). As Grossmann and Hopkins explain, Democrats have been "convinced that they could succeed electorally by better balancing their constituencies."[5] These debates, over how representative and democratic the Democratic Party should be, have defined the party at least since 1968, and arguably throughout its existence.[6]

---

[5] Matt Grossmann and David A. Hopkins, 2016. *Asymmetric Politics: Ideological Republicans and Group Interest Democrats.* Oxford: Oxford University Press, p. 104.

[6] Julia Azari and Seth Masket. "'The Mandate of the People': The 2016 Sanders Campaign in Context." *The State of the Parties, 2018: The Changing Role of Contemporary American Political Parties* (2018): 75–83.

Parties will sometimes undergo massive internal reforms, substantially changing the way they nominate candidates, select convention delegates, fund campaigns, and even stand on issues. But this is no guarantee. Some years, they will essentially continue with business as usual, making few if any changes to the way they conduct business. What determines the extent to which a party reforms itself?

Political scientist Jillian Evans set out to answer this question in her dissertation research, which focused on changes in the ways state parties changed their nomination processes.[7] Evans' research found surprisingly little consistency in the reasons state parties change their rules. Sometimes change is imposed upon them by courts or voter initiatives. Sometimes the state parties make changes to improve their own electability or to enhance the ideological consistency of their slate of nominees. In some research I've done with Caitlin Jewitt, we've found that state party nomination rules changes are quite frequent. After any given presidential election, typically between five and ten state parties either switch from a primary to a caucus or vice versa, or make participation in those contests more or less restrictive. But it's not always obvious why they do this.[8]

Separate work I've done[9] has found that the Democratic Party tends to change its delegate selection rules more following (a) a general election loss, and (b) an especially contentious nomination contest. In particular, when the nomination contest creates something of a legitimacy crisis for the nominee, the party may be more willing to make significant substantive change in its rules.

For example, the most substantive changes to these rules were made shortly following the 1968 election (more on that below). That was a year with a particularly contentious Democratic presidential

---

[7] Jillian Evans, 2019. "A Primer on Primaries: Exploring the Variation in U.S. Primary Election Laws." Doctoral Dissertation, University of Illinois at Urbana-Champaign.

[8] Caitlin Jewitt and Seth Masket, 2019. "When Parties Change Their Rules: Why State Parties Make Nomination Contests More Open or More Closed." Presented at the annual conference of the Northeastern Political Science Association in Philadelphia, Pennsylvania, November 9.

[9] Seth Masket, 2018. "How Much will Democrats Tinker with their Rules this Year?" *Mischiefs of Faction/Vox.com*, August 7. www.vox.com/mischiefs-of-faction/2018/8/7/17653746/democrats-tinker-rules.

nomination contest; the nominee, Hubert Humphrey, essentially ignored the primaries (which were largely beauty contests and not determinative of delegates) while anti-war candidates like Robert Kennedy and Eugene McCarthy won the support of voters and young activists, and only got the nomination through the intervention of party insiders in the catastrophic convention held in Chicago that summer. Party members had reason to doubt whether Humphrey was truly representative of the broader Democratic Party, and they were eager to re-write rules to prevent all that from recurring. On the other hand, there was almost no change in the rules following the 2000 and 2004 elections, which saw comparatively tidy and non-controversial nominations that wrapped up relatively quickly. This doesn't mean everyone in the party agreed with the nomination of Al Gore and John Kerry, respectively, but few had reason to believe that their nominations had been arrived at unfairly or that they weren't representative of the party.

How does 2016 fit into this pattern? The nomination contest was a close and contentious one, and the party's nominee, Hillary Clinton, received 55.2 percent of the overall vote across those primaries and caucuses. (By comparison, Gore received 75 percent of the vote in 2000, and Kerry got 61 percent in 2004.) Despite her overwhelming advantages in contests and delegates won, supporters of her rival Bernie Sanders continued to call the legitimacy of her nomination into question throughout the summer of 2016, accusing the DNC of improperly involving itself in the contest to advantage her. All this controversy would lead us to expect a relatively consequential series of post-election reforms. The actual reforms to delegate selection rules that the party would approve after 2016 were not numerous, but they were substantive and controversial. However, in terms of party reform efforts, there's really no way to understand 2016–2020 without understanding 1968–1972.

RETHINKING NOMINATIONS AFTER 1968

Possibly the most substantive restructuring of a modern party charter was the Democratic Party's efforts in the wake of Hubert Humphrey's 1968 loss to Richard Nixon. Indeed, this episode makes for an exceptionally close analogy for what Democrats experienced after 2016.

As in 2016, the 1968 Democratic Party faced internal divisions over its choice of presidential nominee. Humphrey was widely regarded as the "establishment" candidate and didn't even participate in a primary election that year. At the time, one didn't need to enter a primary to secure a majority of convention delegates. However, several other candidates, notably Robert Kennedy (until his assassination in early June) and Eugene McCarthy, had been competing in primaries and rallying an anti-war constituency. The convention's ultimate choice of the pro-war Humphrey as the nominee struck many younger activists within the party as a corrupt maneuver, leaving the party divided going into November.

I don't want to overstate the parallels to 2016 here. Yes, there are *some* parallels between Humphrey and Hillary Clinton. Both were former senators strongly tied to the outgoing Democratic presidential administration. Both were strongly preferred by the Democratic establishment and won the nomination with their help. Also, like Humphrey's, Clinton's nomination was controversial, left the party divided, and was followed by a narrow general election loss to a Republican most Democrats outright despised. However, unlike Humphrey, Clinton participated in all the primaries and caucuses and won most of them; it's hard to make the case she wasn't representative of the Democratic coalition as it existed in 2016.

Added to this was the drama of the Democratic National Convention in Chicago during the summer of 1968. The spectacle of Chicago police attacking anti-war protesters became a source of contention within the convention halls. From the podium, Senator Abe Ribicoff of Connecticut accused the host city of employing "Gestapo tactics" to suppress dissent. The event laid bare a tension between working-class whites, exemplified by convention host Mayor Richard J. Daley, and college-educated liberals agitating for greater influence over the party's choices. It reinforced tensions between women, racial minorities, young Democrats, and other demographic subgroups and the older white men who had been running the party at nearly all levels for decades. The convention left party leaders looking corrupt and exclusionary, tarnishing Humphrey's nomination and leaving the party bitterly divided going into the fall.

After Humphrey's narrow loss that November, the DNC convened a task force to assess the state of the Democratic Party. The task force's quick assessment was blunt, arguing that "events in 1968 have called into question the integrity of the convention system for nominating presidential candidates." But more:

> The crisis of the Democratic Party is a genuine crisis for democracy in America and especially for the two-party system. Racial minorities, the poor, the young, members of the upper-middle class, and much of the lower-middle and working classes as well – all are seriously considering transferring their allegiance away from either of the two major parties. . . . We recommend the following principal proposals to the Convention and its principal Committees, some to validate the procedures of the 1968 Convention itself, others to be implemented prospectively, to purify – and hopefully to preserve – the power exercised by future Democratic National Conventions.[10]

The following year the party convened the committee that would come to be known the McGovern–Fraser Commission. One of the chief historic legacies of this commission's work was the explosion in the number of presidential primaries and the tying of those primaries to the selection of convention delegates. But for those within the party organization in the early 1970s, the most notable immediate effect was the dramatic change in whom convention delegates were and the demotion of longstanding voices within the party.

Over the next few years, members of this commission would conduct meetings all across the country and hear from a wide range of voices about just what ailed the party and whose voices needed to be heard. As political scientist Byron Shafer notes, many different factions within the party had importantly divergent viewpoints on what the party needed to do. From his reporting, there were three major factions within the party with different agendas: organized labor leaders, African Americans and other racial minority groups, and educated white liberal reformers.

---

[10] Quoted in Byron E. Shafer, 1983, *Quiet Revolution: The Struggle for the Democratic Party and the Shaping of Post-Reform Politics*, New York: Russell Sage Foundation, p. 25.

Organized labor, for their part, took a dim view of the whole reform enterprise. In the view of the AFL–CIO and other prominent labor organizations, they had contributed massive resources to rescue the Democratic ticket in 1968 and nearly succeeded, even while other reformers were seeking to undermine their work. Many labor officials, while eager to make the party more competitive, rejected the arguments pressed by reformers and saw little need to change the way the party had been nominating candidates for years – a process in which labor had been an influential player. "The party that had produced Roosevelt, Truman, Kennedy, Johnson, and Humphrey didn't need reform," said commissioner Bob Nelson.

Other divisions within the party reared their heads. A schism between racial minority groups and white reformers showed up repeatedly. We might call this a *representation-versus-reform* divide. For some party members, representation of the party's diverse array of interest groups was vital to its identity and needed to be encouraged. For others, representation was a side concern, and perhaps a detriment to the party's efforts to reform itself, free itself from corrupt bossism, and make itself more competitive for future elections.

This period of party reform in the early 1970s was taking place at an important moment in America's racial realignment; African Americans were voting in greater numbers thanks to the civil rights reforms of a few years earlier and were leaning steadily more Democratic. For some in the party, this was undoubtedly a point of pride, a reward for the party's efforts to isolate its segregationist wing and embrace the Civil Rights Movement. For others, the logic Paul Frymer[11] described immediately kicked in; any effort to champion the needs of African Americans would be seen as a vulnerability in the next general election, and the party had to minimize the visibility and demands of its newly captured constituency to remain competitive.

McGovern–Fraser Commissioner Sam Beer seemed surprised that minority groups weren't particularly engaged in the reform movement. "I went to Massachusetts, Philadelphia, Chicago, St. Louis, and Atlanta,"

---

[11] Paul Frymer, 1999. *Uneasy Alliances: Race and Party Competition in America.* Princeton: Princeton University Press.

Beer remarked. "I was impressed, at these meetings, by the fact that Negroes and the people in the cities were not the slightest bit interested in this whole thing. This was really a suburban, white, middle-class movement." Commissioner Jim Lindheim expressed concern about this, saying that the typical attendee at meetings was

> a white lawyer of liberal leanings who has been connected with the Kennedy-McCarthy-McGovern wing of the party. We have no definite means of getting around this problem, beyond trying to recruit people of different backgrounds, which is proving very difficult. Hence, there is a real danger that the report will simply be active liberal Democrats talking to active liberal Democrats, while a real understanding of grass-roots participation will be lost.[12]

While there was broad agreement within the commission that representation for racial minorities, women, and young people should be improved, there was little consensus on just how seriously that should be addressed and how to address it. Commission members proposed guidelines for state delegations to take "affirmative steps" to become more representative of the racial, gender, and age distributions of the states they represented. While some members didn't take these guidelines too seriously, others ultimately interpreted them as requiring strict demographic quotas. These new guidelines were adopted by the commission as strongly proscriptive.

The reforms adopted prior to the 1972 presidential nomination cycle were surprisingly disruptive of the party structure and caught longstanding party insiders off guard. Senator George McGovern struck a populist tone at a committee hearing, saying, "Really the only purpose of party reform is to provide a vehicle through which ... policies can be determined by the people rather than by the bosses."[13] In Shafer's words, "The result of all these reforms was the diminution, the constriction, at times the elimination, of the regular party in the politics of presidential selection."[14]

[12] Shafer, pp. 129–30.
[13] Sam Rosenfeld, 2018. *The Polarizers: Postwar Architects of our Partisan Era.* Chicago: University of Chicago Press.
[14] Shafer, p. 525.

Columnists Evans and Novak described reformers' attitudes toward party regulars more bluntly: "They urinated right in the face of all those people."[15] Few party regulars grasped the importance of these changes at the time.[16] Yet by the summer of 1972, many of them found themselves without credentials to their own national convention, instead having to watch from the sidelines.

The shift in party nominating procedures induced dramatic changes in the party's national convention delegation. Between 1968 and 1972, the percent of Democratic delegates that was female jumped from 13 to 40 percent, the percent that was African American went from 5 to 15 percent, and the percent under age thirty went from 3 to 22 percent.[17] At this point, the older, white, male party regulars took notice and began to complain. A delegate to the 1972 convention protested, "There is too much hair and not enough cigars at this convention." Labor leader George Meany was more specific: "What kind of delegation is this? They've got six open fags and only three AFL–CIO people on that delegation!" Another opined, "We don't want a party that consists of Bella Abzug on one hand and Jesse Jackson on the other."[18]

But the reforms the Democrats adopted prior to the 1972 cycle changed not just who got to be a convention delegate, but who got to be a presidential nominee. McGovern (one of the reforms' architects, naturally) was one of the first candidates to understand just how significantly the system had changed, and he set out to win primaries and caucuses and pledged delegates across the nation while others were relying upon their ties to a party establishment that had largely been overthrown. The campaign team McGovern put together was clever and innovative. According to political scientist Bruce Miroff, they "went about the work quietly so as not to disturb the torpor of established party elites. In these sparsely attended arenas for selecting delegates,

15 Rowland Evans and Robert Novak, 1972. "The Dethroning of Daley." *The Washington Post,* July 12.
16 David Plotke, 1996. "Party Reform as Failed Democratic Renewal in the United States, 1968–1972." *Studies in American Political Development* 10 (2): 223–88.
17 Adam Hilton, 2019. "The Path to Polarization: McGovern–Fraser, Counter-Reformers, and the Rise of the Advocacy Party." *Studies in American Political Development* 33 (1): 87–109.
18 Klinkner, pp. 106–8.

McGovernites were generally more numerous and prepared than any rivals."[19] But besides being crafty, they were legitimately hopeful, seeing themselves as transforming American government in a way that empowered average people and ended cynicism and corruption. It would not be a mistake to view this as one of the most optimistic and sincere presidential campaigns in American history, the apotheosis of many of the political movements of the late 1960s.

Bernie Sanders is probably a better parallel for George McGovern than Hillary Clinton was for Hubert Humphrey. As McGovern did prior to 1972, Sanders pressed for a number of changes to the way Democrats nominate presidential candidates, and those rule changes largely worked to his benefit when he next ran for president. Both used populist appeals to champion a young and left-leaning segment of the Democratic coalition that felt alienated or excluded by the establishment and sought significant changes to break into the power structure. And both managed to catch the rest of the party divided and flat-footed, unprepared to deal with their enthusiastic constituencies.

McGovern's campaign, while capturing the Democratic nomination and the imaginations of millions, got annihilated in the fall. Richard Nixon won 60.7 percent of the popular vote and all the Electoral College votes except those from Massachusetts and the District of Columbia. McGovern won just 37.5 percent of the popular vote, the lowest vote share for a major party presidential nominee since Alf Landon's loss to Franklin Roosevelt in 1936. The loss was a brutal one for the Democrats, who quickly developed a new narrative about 1972: they lost because they'd put the activists in charge and left the regulars out in the cold.

As political scientist Adam Hilton notes, the Democrats' loss sparked a counter-movement within the party to repeal some of its earlier reforms. Much of this movement united as the Coalition for a Democratic Majority (CDM), which consisted of a range of moderate-to-conservative white intellectuals and labor leaders seeking to pull the party back from the left. It included the likes of teacher union leader Al Shanker, political scientists Austin Ranney and Nelson Polsby, Senator

[19] Bruce Miroff, 2009. *The Liberals' Moment: The McGovern Insurgency and the Identity Crisis of the Democratic Party*. Lawrence: University Press of Kansas, p. 62.

Henry Jackson and Rep. Tom Foley, and even people who would later identify as neo-conservative thought leaders, including Jeanne Kirkpatrick, Norman Podhoretz, and Ben Wattenberg.[20]

In an early newsletter, CDM described what it saw as the main schism within the Democratic Party:

> We now face a need to draw some distinctions between the two major strands of what used to be called liberalism. One strand, with which CDM is aligned, holds that the Democratic Party must rebuild a broad coalition to win back the blue-collar, Southern moderate, Catholic, and "middle-American" voters who deserted the Democratic ticket in 1972. . . . The second strand seeks to strengthen the forces which came to dominate the party between 1968 and 1972 – an alliance of women, blacks, and youth, led by dissident elements of the affluent, educated middle class.[21]

Through a series of further reforms spurred by older party regulars and the CDM, more conservative voices found their footing in the party again, and the percentages of women, African Americans, and young delegates dropped modestly for the 1976 convention. But this divide would continue to define internal Democratic Party communications and arguments in the decades to come. In particular, the CDM and its ideological descendants would use each national loss by the party as an opportunity to blame the party's alliances with identity-oriented interest groups.

When President Carter lost to Ronald Reagan in 1980, more conservative Democratic leaders claimed that the party had become too liberal and failed to attend to the needs of the white working class. "The middle-class," said Texas Rep. Charlie Stenholm, "the small businessman and the working man – traditionally has been the heart and soul of the Democratic Party. That's where the votes are. But we lost their support." DNC chair John White agreed, "The political needs of our traditional supporters – white ethnics, urban dwellers, labor, blue-collar workers, small businessmen – have changed but we haven't changed with them. . . . For us to write off that segment of society would be a mistake. We have to capture the center."[22]

---

[20] Hilton, 2019.   [21] Quoted from ibid., 2019.   [22] Klinkner, p. 156.

Following the party's rout in 1984, Democratic leaders were quick to pin the blame on what pundits would later call identity politics: "The perception is that we are the party that can't say no, that caters to special interests and that does not have the interests of the middle class at heart," said Tennessee's Democratic chair. According to another party leader, "We ought to be just as concerned with the farmer on the tractor as that guy with an earring in his left ear." A former aide to Lyndon Johnson complained, "Blacks own the Democratic Party. . . . White Protestant male Democrats are an endangered species." Many Democratic insiders expressed concern over the influence of these new interest groups within the party. One of the internal party fights in 1984 was over the choice of a new chair, and, as reporter Dan Balz noted, many in the party sought someone who could signal an end to the tyranny of "special interests":

> The long resume reads something like this: former elected official from outside Washington with good ties with the various power blocs of the party but who can speak to new voters in the growth areas of the country, and – by the way – someone who looks and sounds great on television. The short form is more crudely put: white, southern male.[23]

More conservative voices within the party ultimately got a presidential candidate along these lines in Bill Clinton in 1992. Clinton's economic message was similar to that of previous Democratic nominees, but he importantly made a number of symbolic gestures toward racial conservatism, criticizing Jesse Jackson and Sister Soulja and calling for welfare reform and cutbacks on "excessive" unemployment benefits for undeserving recipients.[24]

THE POST-2016 DNC

The reform-versus-representation divide so visible within the Democratic Party after 1968 could also be seen in the wake of 2016. Indeed, in many

---

[23] Dan Balz, 1984. "Group Ends DNC Chairman Search." *The Washington Post,* December 17, A7. Cited from Klinkner.

[24] Frymer, pp. 4–5.

ways, the 2016 convention and its aftermath were a retread of the events of a half century earlier – less violent, to be sure, but no less divisive.

National party conventions of the modern era tend to be something along the lines of four-day love fests or branding exercises. While party primaries and caucuses can be internally divisive, typically party voters have settled on a nominee months before the convention is called to order. Rather than settle disputes or litigate grievances, modern presidential nominating conventions generally serve to ratify decisions already made and to provide several days of camera-ready speeches and advertisements for a national audience.

The 2016 Democratic National Convention was no love fest, despite Clinton having clinched the nomination months earlier. Numerous supporters of Bernie Sanders, both inside and outside the convention halls, registered their dissatisfaction with Hillary Clinton's nomination loudly and repeatedly throughout the event. Delegates and protesters booed pro-Clinton convention speeches. Some of Sanders' supporters orchestrated anti-Clinton protests at the convention – even after his endorsement of her – with marchers chanting "Hell, no, DNC, we won't vote for Hillary." One protester said he'd "rather watch the DNC burn" than see Clinton nominated.[25] Particular fire was directed at outgoing DNC chair Debbie Wasserman Schultz, who had been blamed for the DNC's perceived anti-Sanders bias as revealed in various internal DNC e-mails hacked by WikiLeaks and publicized shortly before the convention.[26]

(I should note here that "DNC" is a common target of populist anger among the American left, but it's used fairly vaguely. Sometimes it specifically (and accurately) refers to the Democratic National Committee, the formal organization of the national party. At other times it is just a label for anyone smacking of establishment, or, more specifically, anything preventing Bernie Sanders from being nominated.)

But the divisions in the party had begun well before that convention. Sanders had done surprisingly well in the early contests in 2016, roughly

---

[25] Trip Gabriel, 2016. "Bernie Sanders Backers March against Hillary Clinton in Philadelphia." *The New York Times,* July 24.

[26] Mark Z. Barabak and Michael A. Memoli, 2016. "Convention Opens to Boos, but Democrats Salvage the Night with Praise of Clinton from Sanders and Warren." *Los Angeles Times,* July 25.

tying Clinton in the Iowa Caucuses and besting her substantially in the New Hampshire primary, despite her early advantages in party endorsements and funding. Clinton nonetheless amassed a considerable array of victories, and by the end of the state contests had secured enough delegates to clinch the nomination. While they weren't decisive in the contest, Clinton was aided by support from the party's "superdelegates" – DNC members and Democratic officeholders who automatically become unpledged convention delegates (more on them below). Their overwhelming lean toward her candidacy led Sanders and his supporters to claim that the process was "rigged" against him and that party insiders were tipping the scales to make his nomination an impossibility.

According to Sanders and his supporters, it wasn't just the superdelegates who were conspiring against him. The party's scheduled primary debates were also suspect. Sanders complained that the six primary debates were too few to give him a fair airing,[27] and that they were scheduled on weekends or shortly before holidays to minimize their visibility. "In Iowa, you know when the debate was held? It was the night of the big football game in Iowa. You think that's a coincidence? ... I think there is a desire on the part of the leadership of the DNC to protect Secretary Clinton," Sanders said in December 2015. "I guess Christmas Eve was booked," remarked one of his staffers.[28]

These various events conspired to make the 2016 Democratic convention arguably the most internally conflicted one since 1968. Although it concluded with strong speeches by First Lady Michelle Obama, Presidents Bill Clinton and Barack Obama, and the presidential nominee herself, the party emerged somewhat divided. A spring 2016 poll suggested roughly a quarter of Sanders' supporters wouldn't vote for Clinton in the fall.[29] While studies suggest defections weren't that high by November,[30] supporters of the losing

[27] Bernie Sanders, 2016. *Our Revolution: A Future to Believe In.* Basingstoke: Macmillan.

[28] Jesse Byrnes, 2015. "Sanders: Timing of Debates Structured to Help Clinton." *The Hill,* December 21.

[29] Nick Gass, 2016. "Poll: 1 in 4 Sanders Supporters Won't Vote for Clinton." *Politico,* April 6.

[30] Danielle Kurtzleben, 2017. "Here's How Many Bernie Sanders Supporters Ultimately Voted for Trump." *National Public Radio,* August 24.

candidate for the Democratic nomination were considerably less enthusiastic about their party's ticket than those of previous failed candidacies.

THE UNITY REFORM COMMISSION. Sanders' supporters had sought to remake the party's nomination system during a meeting of the Rules and Bylaws Committee at the beginning of the DNC convention in July 2016. While they failed on that front, they managed to secure the creation of a Unity Reform Commission as a compromise measure. The commission would include nine members appointed by Clinton and seven by Sanders, with three more members appointed by the DNC chair. The commission was tasked with meeting promptly after the fall election, examining the various ways the party conducts its business, and producing recommendations for reform by the end of 2017. The commission's mandate included an examination of party nomination processes, delegate selection procedures, the status and existence of superdelegates, outreach to unaffiliated voters, and access to party primaries and caucuses.

The commission met at four different venues in different parts of the country throughout 2017 – in May in Washington, June in San Antonio, August in Chicago, and October in Las Vegas. Meetings were open to the public and later posted on YouTube. Each meeting invited party leaders from different parts of the country to give presentations on various aspects of party functions, which were typically met with a variety of questions. Conversations were typically civil and informed, but occasionally during periods of questioning and debate, familiar splits within the party emerged.

Earlier, I mentioned that the McGovern–Fraser Commission meetings between 1968 and 1972 saw a recurring representation-versus-reform split between a largely white group of reformers pushing for the party's nominating systems to be more internally democratic and a more non-white membership that sought greater representation of different demographic groups within the party. In many ways, the arguments among the Unity Reform Commission in 2017 broke down along similar lines. Some white commissioners, in many cases those selected by the Sanders campaign, tended to argue that the party lost in 2016 because it lost the support of white working-class voters, and that the path to future victories lay in winning those voters back. In the May meeting,[31] Jim Zogby described the panoply of white ethnic voters who have tended to identify as Democrats but who have sometimes looked elsewhere for support:

> There are Polish American groups. There are Greek American groups. There are Italian American groups. There are people who identify with ethnicity and still live in those neighborhoods and have historically been Democrats and whose values remain Democrat. We've called them everything from Reagan Democrats to swing voters. In their hearts their tradition is still Democratic. We didn't lose them so much as we stopped talking to them. They didn't walk away from us. We simply stopped focusing on them.

Zogby went on to express concern about an overt focus on ethnic and racial differences at the expense of a unifying message. As he said, "It reminded me of the person who asked, 'What does it mean to be a Democrat?' and he pointed to the forty buttons he had on at the rally, assuming there's somehow a way to connect those dots and you can just intuit what that means." Commissioner Jeff Weaver claimed that divisions were overstated: "When you talk to voters about what they want in their family, it's amazingly consistent across racial lines." A return to a specifically economic message could help bring the party future victories, he argued.

These claims met with strong responses by several African American women who had been appointed by the Clinton campaign. They argued that the future lay in reaching out not to the working-class whites who had voted for the other party, but to the racial minority groups who had declined to vote in 2016. Rep. Marcia Fudge of Ohio took particular exception to previous references to white ethnic groups:

> There are two words I've not heard since we've been here, and that is "African Americans," who are the only real true loyal base of this party. We fought to get in, too . . . We never left, even when they stopped speaking to us. . . . What we have done, especially over the last two elections, is spend all

---

[31] https://youtu.be/zu7FuyOqA2w.

of our resources trying to get back people we are never going to get back, instead of talking to people who should be our base.

Commissioner Yvette Lewis of Maryland echoed these sentiments, "The African American community is loyal. We don't leave. We do the work other folks don't want to do. We show up faithfully. This is who you run to when you need to be *saved*. This is where you go when you need to be saved. We've got to turn out the African American base to save us." Fudge took additional exception to the oft-repeated term "working class": "When we say things like 'working class,' most of the time that doesn't include immigrants or black people. But we work too. We have to be real careful about the terminology."

The discussion of race reappeared during a segment of the June meeting[32] focusing on whether the party should be more encouraging of open primaries (in which non-party registrants are permitted to vote). Supporters of Bernie Sanders, who tended to do well in open primaries in 2016, sought to make more state contests open to independent voters. Several, like Ohio State Senator Nina Turner, framed open primaries in terms of voter enfranchisement. "We can't be the party," she said, "that says that we believe in voter enfranchisement but then in the primaries we want to disenfranchise unaffiliated voters, and that's what our party is doing." Nebraska's Jane Kleeb added, "The fastest growing party ID is nonpartisan. And I don't think it's because independents don't want to be part of a party. They do. But they feel like the Democratic Party has not shown them the welcome mat. . . . One way that we will signal that, in very clear terms, is to have open primaries."

Yvette Lewis, however, among other Clinton appointees, suggested that the move to open up primaries had the effect of undermining representation of people of color:

> While I'm all for growth and expanding our party and expanding our ideas
> and expanding our reach, I am not for diluting the voting power of the
> most reliable voting bloc in the Democratic Party. . . . We bear the burden
> of being a diverse party. If all we had to worry about was old white people
> we'd be fine. But that's not who we are.

[32] https://youtu.be/KBSFZHtha4c.

Louisiana's David Huyhn, another Clinton appointee, agreed, "We should all be wary of the unintended consequences of opening up a primary system that would dilute communities of color and their voice in the Democratic nomination process."

There is a logic to these claims. African Americans tend to be strong Democratic Party adherents (roughly 90 percent of African American voters went with the Democrats in 2016), and in some southern states make up roughly half of registered Democrats. Closed Democratic primaries thus tend to have a relatively large voice from African American members. If access to the Democratic primary ballot is extended to independent voters, that would tend to make for a somewhat whiter primary electorate. A PPIC survey of California voters, for example, found that African Americans comprised around 10 percent of Democratic adherents in that state, while whites comprised around 50 percent. However, African Americans comprised only 8 percent of Democrats plus Independents, while whites comprised 52 percent.[33] There's little reason to believe these numbers would remain static should a state shift from closed to open primaries – people would likely shift their party identifications somewhat – nor do we have much evidence that such a shift would meaningfully change who gets nominated. Nonetheless, an expanded primary electorate would likely be a somewhat whiter one.

2018 REFORMS AND THE SANDERS AGENDA. In November of 2017, following the year of Unity Reform Commission meetings, Bernie Sanders wrote an article for *Politico* outlining the three main areas for nomination reform he and his supporters were seeking: making primaries more open to independent voters, expanding access to party caucuses, and abolishing superdelegates.[34] These were, of course, inspired by the Sanders team's own interpretation of why they had lost the nomination in 2016. Sanders had performed well among

---

[33] Public Policy Institute of California, 2017. "Race and Voting in California." In *Secondary Race and Voting in California.* San Francisco, California. https://www.ppic.org/publication/race-and-voting-in-california/

[34] Bernie Sanders, 2017. "How to Fix the Democratic Party." *Politico*, November 10.

independent voters in primaries that year, had bested Clinton in twelve of the seventeen state and territorial caucuses, and was overwhelmingly opposed by superdelegates. In theory, reforms that would encourage more open primaries, make it easier for people to participate in caucuses, and reduce the role of superdelegates would help Sanders, or someone like him, prevail in the 2020 nominating contest. Over the course of 2018, the Democratic National Committee would wrestle with several of these reform proposals and enact some version of them, with some of their consequences only becoming apparent much later.

If you're reading this book, chances are you noticed that the Iowa Caucuses of February 2020 were something of a hot mess. This was a consequence, in part, of rule changes adopted by the DNC in 2018. That is, one of the changes adopted was a recommendation that caucuses record and report vote counts, in addition to the state delegate equivalents that they'd typically reported previously. This was seen as an earnest reform to promote transparency in the often-confusing caucus process, demystifying it and encouraging participation. And it responded to concerns by Sanders supporters that he may have won the "popular vote" in the 2016 Iowa Caucuses even while Clinton narrowly won in state delegate equivalents. Iowa Democrats adopted this change, committing themselves to reporting the first and second vote counts in the caucuses as well as the state delegate equivalents. But it turned out there were tons of inconsistencies across these levels. The Iowa Democratic Party decided to delay the release while they sorted through the problems, likely dampening the race's influence in the nomination contest and causing a backlash against caucuses within the party.[35]

But changes to primaries and caucuses didn't attract very much attention or controversy when they were discussed in 2018 and 2019. The reforms that did draw heat were those revolving around superdelegates and primary debates. Those controversies revealed some deep fissures within the party that were hardly resolved by the time the first voters and caucusgoers weighed in in 2020.

---

[35] Andrew Prokup, 2020. "How the Iowa Caucus Rule Changes Complicated this Year's Count." *Vox*, February 4. www.vox.com/2020/2/4/21122483/iowa-caucus-results-count-rules-change-app.

THE SUPERDELEGATE FIGHT. The term "superdelegate" gets thrown around a lot in modern political discussions, and not always very accurately, so allow me to offer a concrete definition here. Formally known as "unpledged party leaders and elected officials" (or "unpledged PLEOs"), superdelegates consist of elected Democratic members of Congress and governors, distinguished party leaders (such as former presidents), and national party committee members. Superdelegates automatically attend national conventions as delegates without being required to pledge their support to a presidential candidate. That is, regardless of how primary voters or caucus attendees in their states leaned, superdelegates can simply vote their preference. Superdelegates consisted of about 15 percent of the 4,767 delegates who participated in the 2016 national convention.

Superdelegates are themselves the product of an election loss narrative. After Jimmy Carter's loss in 1980, the DNC's Hunt Commission was established to address concerns that the party had become the creature of its most passionate activists. The Hunt Commission recommended superdelegates to give party elites automatic access to the convention (so that they wouldn't have to compete with their own constituents to become delegates) and also more influence in the presidential nomination process. They were proposed as a check on caucusgoers and primary voters should they side with a candidate perceived to be either unelectable or insufficiently committed to party goals. They were seen as a solution to the excesses of intraparty democracy following Carter's presidency, during which a candidate with virtually no ties to the congressional party had come into power, governed poorly, and failed to secure reelection. "We've reformed ourselves right out of business," lamented Wisconsin Democratic leader Suellen Albrecht at the time,[36] urging that party insiders seize back some control over the nominating system.

In fact, it is difficult to identify presidential nomination contests in which superdelegates have proven pivotal. They provided some assistance to Walter Mondale in his 1984 contest with Gary Hart – the Minnesotan was the frontrunner and the winner of most of the party's

---

[36] Klinkner, p. 158.

primary votes, but he was a bit short of a majority of convention delegates until the superdelegates helped him clinch the nomination. In most cases, superdelegate preferences have been largely in line with the party's rank and file, and when conflicts have arisen, it is the superdelegates who have generally sublimated their preferences to the voters'. Several super-delegates originally pledged to Hillary Clinton prior to the 2008 contest switched over to Barack Obama's side after he won their state's nomination contest.[37] Even if party rules grant superdelegates autonomy, they are above all politicians, and are not eager to anger party activists in their states and districts.

Where superdelegates *could* become influential is in a contested convention with several candidates close to a majority of delegates; super-delegates could tip the balance. However, the last time the Democrats had a contested convention was in 1952 – three decades before the invention of superdelegates – making the bitterness of this fight in 2017–2019 all the more remarkable.

Yet despite this relative weakness of superdelegates, Sanders and his supporters in 2016 directed much ire their way, depicting superdelegates as an anti-democratic relic interfering with the proper decision-making of the Democratic Party. Indeed, this proved to be the dominant issue in the Unity Reform Commission's deliberations and a major rallying point among the Sanders-appointed members.

During the Unity Commission's deliberations on the subject,[38] a common theme by Sanders-appointed delegates was that party insiders had no greater moral authority or decision-making ability than rank-and-file primary voters and caucusgoers. Sanders delegate Nomiki Konst argued, "Elected officials are human. And I don't think anyone in here would say that all elected officials are a moral authority." Sanders delegate Jeff Weaver said, "As abhorrent as we think Trump is ... the truth of the matter is that the wise men and women of the Democratic Party picked a candidate who did not succeed, and the rabble rousers of the Republican Party picked the one who could." Sanders delegates

---

[37] Katharine Q. Seeyle, 2008, "For Clinton, a Key Group Didn't Hold," *New York Times*, June 5.

[38] https://youtu.be/KBSFZHtha4c.

pushed a number of suggested reforms, from requiring that elected superdelegates be pledged to the vote outcome of their home state to having superdelegates vote after the first ballot at the convention to banning superdelegates altogether.

Others on the commission, mostly Clinton appointees, defended the role of superdelegates, if not the entirety of their actions. Jim Roosevelt claimed that, in his role co-chairing the party's Rules and Bylaws Committee, he occasionally met with his counterparts in the RNC, and he said that the Republicans he spoke to envied superdelegates in 2016. Such elite influence theoretically could have provided some party resistance to Trump at a key stage of the Republican nomination process. Roosevelt added that he felt it was problematic to bind a superdelegate's vote to their state's voters' preferences: "People should not be required to violate their conscience." Committee member Elaine Kamarck gave one of the more persuasive arguments in favor of superdelegates by discussing the value of their "peer review":

> The elected officials are co-partners with the president of the United States in making the grassroots vision reality. It doesn't happen only with the president. They're there not because they're some exalted species. They're there because they have a constitutional authority to either help or hinder the President of the United States. That's what the idea is in including them in the decision-making process. . . . Their judgment about the people running for president is something voters might want to know.

Throughout this year of deliberation, a few consistent patterns could be detected, and broken down largely along lines of candidate support. The Sanders appointees consistently argued for a more open and more "democratic" Democratic Party. Much like the reform wing of the McGovern–Fraser Commission, they sought to involve more rank-and-file voters in the party's nomination processes and to include independent voters wherever possible. They proposed steering the party's decision-making powers away from party insiders like superdelegates and generally demystifying the party for political novices. "The best-kept secret in American politics is American politics," said Zogby. "It's easy to get engaged, but from the sixty-page thing you get from the state

party, and the no help you get to how to get engaged, it becomes something that actually ends up discouraging people from participating."

Many of those making such arguments also argued that the path to
making the party more competitive involved reaching out to the working-
class white voters who'd abandoned the party in the 2016 election for
Trump. Conversely, those arguing in the other direction – preserving
some power for superdelegates, limiting participation in primaries to
registered partisans, and so on – tended to be walking in the path of
the racial minority groups that advanced the quota systems during the
McGovern–Fraser process. They were seeking to preserve the numerical
influence of people of color within the party, and they tended to advocate
for reaching out less to voters who turned to Trump in 2016 than to those
who declined to vote in 2016.

But the participants were doing more than walking in the footsteps of
their McGovern–Fraser forebears; they were litigating narratives from
2016. The Sanders allies largely argued that Democrats lost because
whites had abandoned their ticket, while Clinton allies largely argued
that Democrats lost because people of color had been ignored. The
Sanders allies believed the party could be saved by more democratic
reforms that would bring people into the party; Clinton's adherents
believed the party could be saved by preserving the influence of African
American voters and leaders.

The commission published its report in early December of 2017. It was
very clearly a compromise document but nonetheless committed to moving
the party in the reform direction. It embraced a number of recommendations pushed by the Sanders appointees to the Commission, including easier
access to caucuses and an encouragement of open primaries.[39]

Importantly, the report also called for a reduction in the power of
superdelegates. And here again, race is relevant, even if not always
spoken of openly. Sanders' supporters, both on the commission and
among the party's primary electorate, were largely (though hardly

---

[39] The commission's report, and the preceding discussions, notably did not address all
of reformers' pressing concerns. In an interview, Sanders appointee Jim Zogby
expressed frustration that transparent party governance and financing, which were
his main motivations in accepting appointment to the commission, went largely
unaddressed.

exclusively) white, while the bulk of the party's African American voters were supportive of Clinton, and many of her most outspoken appointees on the commission were African American, as well. What's more, the entire Congressional Black Caucus (CBC), consisting of a quarter of the Democratic Caucus in the US House of Representatives, are considered superdelegates. To Sanders supporters, disempowering the superdelegates was a blow against party corruption and a step toward open and fair nomination contests. To the CBC, it meant young white progressives were trying to silence them and limit their power.

I wish to be clear here that I am describing tendencies rather than iron-clad laws. Not all Sanders supporters were white, nor were all members of the CBC opposed to superdelegate reform. ("As a member of Congress, I don't need more power than anybody else," said Rep. Keith Ellison of Minnesota in support of the reform.[40]) But this was a major cleavage within the formal party.

The commission thus treaded lightly with its recommendation on the disposition of superdelegates. Rather than reducing the number of super-delegates or eliminating them completely, it proposed binding superdelegates to the votes of their respective states' primaries and caucuses; they would no longer be unpledged on the first convention ballot.

Over the course of 2018, the Democratic National Committee considered these recommendations and sought to make changes in the party's nomination rules. The disposition of superdelegates again proved controversial at several meetings of the party's Rules and Bylaws Committee. The bulk of the committee converged on a compromise plan to have superdelegates retain their status but to lose their first floor vote at the convention. Only if no candidate had a majority of pledged delegates at the time of the first ballot would the superdelegates have a true voice in the nomination process.

A number of DNC members resisted this compromise, however, and race was again at the heart of the matter. Bob Mullholland, a DNC member from California, wrote an open e-mail to DNC chair Tom Perez and Rep. Ellison claiming,

[40] David Weigel, 2017, "Democrats Take First Step Toward Curtailing Superdelegates." *The Washington Post*, March 10.

The two of you are conspiring with Bernie Sanders to block Congress members John Lewis, Maxine Waters, Barbara Lee and the rest of the congressional delegation, Governors, State Party Chairs and the rest of us DNC Members from entering our Convention floor in 2020 as voters. I don't know if you will have paid thugs at the doorways to beat up Congressman Lewis and the rest of us or not.[41]

DNC member William Owen of Tennessee objected, "If we don't have a vote, then what good are we?" He promised that "this will not be rubber stamped" at the DNC's full meeting in Chicago in August of 2018. Mulholland warned that the meeting would reveal a party torn apart by the issue. "While the Republicans are winning elections and taking over the Supreme Court, we'll be in Chicago looking like 1968." Senior DNC member Don Fowler, the former DNC chair, warned that the proposal contained the seeds of even worse party splits than encountered in 2016. If a plurality, but not a majority, of delegates preferred a candidate, and the superdelegates weighed in on the second ballot to give a different candidate the nomination, that could create a massive legitimacy crisis that "this party would have a very difficult time surviving," said Fowler.[42]

I attended the Democrats' convention in Chicago in August of 2018, at which these reform proposals were debated and voted upon. Delegate reform was hardly the only issue being discussed – members voted to encourage state parties to adopt primaries, to make the remaining caucuses more accessible, and to make party governance more transparent. But it was delegate reform that generated the most controversy.

Divisions broke down largely as they had at earlier meetings, and can be roughly categorized as follows:

1. Supporters of Bernie Sanders from 2016, who were eager to disempower superdelegates, whom they saw as a sign of improper insider influence in nominations.

---

[41] David Weigel, 2018. "DNC Considers Blocking Superdelegates from Voting on First Presidential Ballot." *The Washington Post,* June 8.

[42] David Siders, 2018. "Sanders-backed DNC Plan Sparks Superdelegate Revolt." *Politico,* July 11.

2. African Americans, who did not want to give up their voting powers as superdelegates to assuage the concerns of mostly white progressives with little history in the party.
3. White supporters of Hillary Clinton from 2016, who didn't want to abolish superdelegates, but were eager to demonstrate party unity and not have future nominees' legitimacy questioned.

Throughout the convention, members of the Congressional Black Caucus expressed strong concerns that they were being, in their words, "disenfranchised." They raised concerns about the declining importance of African American voters in general and those African American party members in the room specifically.

At the meeting of the Black Caucus during this convention, Randy Kelly, the caucus' Vice Chair, argued that an African American voting for the measure was like a runaway slave voting for the Fugitive Slave Act. Caucus chair Virgie Rollins told me in an interview that it took a long time for African Americans to rise to their numbers and importance in the party. She said that it's an open party, and people are welcome to join in and work on some campaigns and work their way up, but the reform supporters were effectively skipping their place in line.

When the full committee finally met to consider the reforms, the chair and the reforms' supporters simply had the numbers to prevail. When it became clear in the general session that they could not stop the effort, reform opponents withdrew their opposition and offered to vote for all the changes by acclamation. The session ended on a note of unity, although not, as the chair noted, unanimity.

The Sanders supporters and other critics of superdelegates won a non-trivial symbolic victory, and Chair Perez got the demonstration of unity he wanted. But it came at a cost. A lot of prominent African Americans in the party clearly felt sidelined and insulted. Indeed, in November of 2018, the Congressional Black Caucus passed a vote of no confidence in Chair Perez' leadership.[43]

---

[43] Nolan D. McCaskill and Josh Bresnahan, 2018. "CBC votes no confidence in Democratic Chair Perez." *Politico*, November 14. www.politico.com/story/2018/11/14/congressional-black-caucus-tom-perez–991270.

This reform measure starkly showed the racial and factional divisions within the Democratic coalition, but also demonstrated the ways that the party struggled to address the perceived lessons of 2016. For those who believed that the party's problem was a lack of unity, lack of outreach to working-class whites, and ongoing concerns about Hillary Clinton's legitimacy as the nominee, then superdelegate reform should have been a help. For those who believed the problem was insufficient enthusiasm from the party's African American voters and activists, this reform package only made the situation worse. And again, while contested conventions are exceedingly rare in the modern era, this superdelegate reform made them both more likely and potentially messier. Furthermore, while hardly ensuring the nomination of Bernie Sanders or someone else like him, the reform did reduce the power of established party elites, making such a nomination marginally more likely.

PRIMARY DEBATES. As I noted above, Sanders and his allies portrayed the broader rules of the Democratic Party of 2016 as hostile to them, interpreting the nomination contest of that year as utilizing rules and debates in ways that gave advantages to Hillary Clinton. And many within the broader party leadership clung to the narrative that the Democrats had lost in 2016 in part because the party was divided and considered the nomination processes biased and illegitimate. One way to create a more legitimate nomination system, they reasoned, was to have a more transparent and unbiased system of primary debates. But the party leadership had another reason to control the primary debates, as well – to help cull a very large field of presidential candidates, and do so in a way that appeared fair. This would prove no small feat.

It is not generally appreciated what a radical move it was for the DNC to step in to control the primary debates for 2019 and 2020. The idea of party rules for primary debates has a surprisingly brief history; the party's guidance for primary debates is largely a twenty-first-century phenomenon.[44] Debates prior to the McGovern–Fraser reforms of the early 1970s were very rare, consisting largely of a single debate between

---

[44] Julia Azari and Seth Masket, 2018. "Intraparty Democracy and the 2016 Election." In Jennifer Lucas, Christopher Galdieri, and Tauna Starbuck Cisco, eds., *Conventional*

Republicans Thomas Dewey and Howard Stassen in 1948 and a cross-partisan debate over the Vietnam War between potential presidential candidates Ronald Reagan and Robert Kennedy in 1967.

The debates that cropped up from the early 1970s onward were generally ad hoc events, either assembled by specific campaigns or by news organizations. By the 1990s, news organizations were making more of a practice of inviting all the "major" presidential candidates, although they had broad discretion in determining just who made the cut. After all, there are typically hundreds of presidential candidates in a given election cycle, with news organizations only seriously considering a handful of them.

Yet excluded candidates have sometimes challenged the media's decisions. In a 1992 New York City debate between presidential candidates Bill Clinton and Jerry Brown, for example, Irvine, California, Mayor Larry Agran, who had filed to run for the presidency, rose from the audience and demanded to be allowed on the debate stage; police dragged him out of the debate hall and arrested him for trespassing, disorderly conduct, and resisting arrest.[45] In less dramatic fashion, Fox News excluded two candidates – businessman John Cox and US Representative Ron Paul – from debates early in the 2008 presidential cycle, despite those candidates seeming to meet the network's viability thresholds.[46] In the few court cases that exist on the topic, primary elections are generally seen as public institutions, but parties themselves, along with news organizations, are accorded deference as private associations that can decide whom to include or exclude from events.[47]

One important turning point in the development of party primary debate practices came from the Republican Party's post-mortem of the 2012 presidential election.[48] That document is a preeminent case of

---

Wisdom, Parties, and Broken Barriers in the 2016 Election, London: Lexington Books, pp. 137–62.

[45] NYT Staff, 1997. "Former Candidate Loses Lawsuit Over '92 Arrest." *New York Times*, July 10, B4.

[46] Jennifer Harper, 2008. "Fox News Challenged over Paul Debate Snub." *Washington Times*, January 4, A13.

[47] Azari and Masket, 2018.

[48] Barbour, Henry, Sally Bradshaw, Ari Fleischer, Zori Fonalledas, and Glenn McCall, 2012. *Growth and Opportunity Project*. Report for the Republican National Committee. www.gop.com/growth-and-opportunity-project/.

a party attempting to learn from loss, prescribing a series of consequential reforms that would theoretically have affected the results of the most recent election. In this case, the problems that GOP leaders identified with the 2012 debates were fourfold: There were too many of them (twenty in that cycle); they were haphazardly scheduled (two were even on the same weekend); they were dominated by media moderators who were largely hostile to the party's goals; and they largely served to tear down the party's frontrunner (Mitt Romney) and to elevate the profiles of divisive and potentially disastrous challengers like Newt Gingrich.

Following the recommendations of that report, the RNC issued specific guidelines for the 2016 primary cycle, saying they would only sanction twelve primary debates, and that those had to include conservative voices like Hugh Hewitt on the panels of moderators. It would be difficult to say that the reforms produced the party's desired nominee in 2016, but the party's assertion of authority notably changed the development of primary debates.

Following its presidential loss in 2016, the Democratic Party set about making changes to the primary debate rules, as well, in the hopes of learning from the problems of 2016. Unlike the superdelegate process and other reforms, there was no public process for arguing about or developing a primary debate policy. I spent a good deal of 2018 following the party's meetings and deliberations, and was frequently told that decisions over debates would be addressed later, but I could never find anyone within the party organization who would explain to me just how those guidelines were being developed and implemented or what they would look like. Then, on February 14, 2019, DNC chair Tom Perez's office simply announced the rules via a press release.[49] "We had no vote on that. That was all Perez," Kathy Sullivan, a DNC member from New Hampshire, explained to me in early 2020.

The lack of a public process limits my ability to understand the precise motivations for the debate rules as they were introduced. However, judging from numerous conversations with journalists and influential party members, the debate rules that emerged seemed to be motivated by three main narratives about the 2016 election:

---

[49] https://democrats.org/news/dnc-announces-details-for-the-first-two-presidential-primary-debates/.

1. **Anyone is electable**: Donald Trump's victory in the 2016 general election, despite his association with many damning scandals and his repeated efforts to alienate huge segments of the electorate, suggested to candidates and donors that pretty much anyone with a major party's label next to his or her name can win. This was a huge motivator for Democratic candidates, encouraging quite a few to run who might have otherwise sat the race out or focused on more winnable races like Senate seats. This is likely a major contributor to the fact that roughly two dozen people declared for president in 2018 and 2019, and at least a dozen more explored candidacies.

2. **Large fields of candidates are unpredictable and dangerous**: Donald Trump received the 2016 Republican nomination even while many Republican leaders were clearly uncomfortable with or even hostile to him. He did so in part because the field of candidates was so large; this made it harder for party elites to coordinate their support on an alternative to Trump. While Democrats didn't precisely face a Trump-like candidate for their presidential nomination in the 2020 cycle, they did want to retain some control over the process.

3. **Party preference for some candidates over others is perceived as illegitimate**: The DNC was widely derided for appearing to be biased in favor of Hillary Clinton in 2016, and suspicion of insiders influencing the party demobilized supporters of Bernie Sanders in the general election. While the DNC actually did little of any real substance to enable Clinton's nomination, this was a persistent sore spot for the party, as the discussion of the superdelegate debate earlier suggests. The DNC thus made every effort to appear neutral in the 2020 nomination contest.

The debate rules specified a series of thresholds for candidates to participate in DNC-sanctioned debates. As in previous cycles, there was a polling threshold – candidates had to demonstrate at least 1 percent support in three polls from a DNC-approved list of polling houses to qualify for the first debate in June 2019. But there was also, for the first time, a fundraising threshold; even if candidates couldn't pass the polling test, they could qualify for the summer debates by receiving donations from at least 65,000 unique donors, including at least 200 donors from each of twenty different states.[50] What's more, these thresholds increased for subsequent debates; in order to qualify for the third debate in September 2019, candidates had to have at least 2 percent support in the polls *and* demonstrate donations from at least 130,000 unique donors, including at least 400 from each of twenty different states. By December's debate, the polling threshold was 4 percent, and participants had to show donations from at least 200,000 donors.

While both parties have utilized polling thresholds in the past, there were some new aspects to the 2020 Democratic guidelines. For one, polling thresholds have generally been used previously so that both the party and media organizations could clearly define who was invited and who was not, providing something of an objective basis for exclusion. For the 2020 cycle, the party was quite clearly trying to cull the number of candidates and hasten the winnowing process. Second, the inclusion of fundraising goals was a novel one. At least for the first few debates, it didn't really eliminate many candidates, but rather gave them a target to strive for. Billionaire candidate Tom Steyer noted that he would be disqualified from the debates if he were just financing his own campaign, so he used some of his funds to specifically target small donors, essentially "buying donations" to qualify him for debates.[51]

To no small extent, the party's goals here – eliminating a large number of candidates while not appearing to be biased against any of them – were contradictory. This is especially true given that candidates do not all compete for visibility and donations equally. Senators and governors have greater visibility and access to donors than House members and mayors typically do. Joe Biden, a two-term vice president and multi-decade Senate veteran, surely had an easier time reaching these thresholds than others. And some research suggests that women and people of color often have a more difficult time fundraising than white male candidates.[52]

[50] Dan Merica, 2019. "DNC Doubles Threshold for Third, Fourth Democratic Debates." CNN, May 29. www.cnn.com/2019/05/29/politics/dnc-threshold-democratic-debates/index.html.

[51] Eric Levitz, 2019. "Tom Steyer Bought Himself a 'Grassroots Campaign' for $10 Million." *New York Magazine*, August 19.

[52] Eugene Scott, 2019. "The Problem with Comparing Kamala Harris's Fundraising to that of her Opponents." *The Washington Post*, April 2.

These concerns were echoed by former New Hampshire state party chair Kathy Sullivan as she and I did a pre-primary drive around Manchester:

> The DNC's pretty diverse in terms of its staffing and its leadership, but no one ever thought about the unintended consequences of debate qualifiers that required a lot of money. Because to get the 200,000 supporters and do all that work costs money. And there is inherent structural racism when it comes to raising money, because who has the money in this country is white people . . . and white people give to white people.

At least initially, it appeared that the party was prioritizing winnowing over the appearance of neutrality or concerns about representation.

But the party's debate rules also mitigated against winnowing somewhat through determinations of who would appear in which debates. Rather than create a main debate with the more popular candidates and an "undercard" debate of the less popular ones, as Republicans did in 2015–2016, the Democrats determined that whenever more than ten candidates qualified for a given debate, they would divide the debate into two nights, with candidates randomly sorted across nights. (They violated this modestly in the October 2019 debate when twelve candidates graced the stage on one night.) Indeed, they made sure to match less popular candidates against frontrunners, increasing the chance that a long-shot candidacy might catch fire.[53]

Unsurprisingly, candidates negatively affected by these rules quickly began to contest their legitimacy. In August 2019, Tulsi Gabbard had reached the 130,000 donor qualification for the September debate, but fell two DNC-approved polls short of the 2 percent polling threshold. She issued a press release in late August calling for the DNC to change its list of certified polling houses, noting that she had at least 2 percent support in many other polls. As her campaign's press release stated, "The Gabbard campaign is calling on the DNC to hold true to their promise and make adjustments to the process now to ensure transparency and fairness. Crucial decisions on debate qualifications that impact the right of the American people to have the opportunity to

---

[53] Katie Galioto, 2019. "Miami Will Host First Democratic Debates." *Politico*, March 28. www.politico.com/story/2019/03/28/miami-2020-primary-debates-1242116.

participate fully in the Democratic process should not be made in secret by party bosses."[54]

Similarly, Tom Steyer's campaign complained about the DNC's exclusion of several polls favorable to him. Michael Bennet and Steve Bullock complained, as well, and lobbied the DNC to change its rules. "If we wanted to be the party that excluded people," said Bennet, "we'd be Republicans."[55] Marianne Williamson took to Twitter to more explicitly accuse the DNC of malfeasance: "Our establishment politics is run by elites within elites. DNC poll requirements are a perfect example, a situation with no transparency but with power to block candidates not anointed by a gatekeeper class. In America there should be no gatekeepers; only the people should decide." She further objected to the DNC adding "rules" to who could be president when the nation's Founders had already made those clear in the Constitution.[56]

Bullock withdrew from the race in early December 2019, saying "it has become clear that in this moment, I won't be able to break through to the top tier of this still-crowded field of candidates." *Politico*'s Bill Scher maintained that Bullock "was undercut by the DNC's awful debate rules."[57] Cory Booker, after failing to qualify for the final debate of 2019, circulated a petition calling for the DNC to change its qualification rules for the early 2020 debates. "Candidates who have proven both their viability and their commitment to the Democratic Party are being prematurely cut out of the nominating contest before many voters have even tuned in – much less made their decision about whom to support," said the petition, which most of the leading candidates signed.[58] Booker would not appear in another debate, and he ended his candidacy in mid-January 2020.

Tom Perez and the DNC's leadership remained steadfast in their debate decisions throughout the barrage of criticisms in late 2019,

---

[54] Rebecca Klar, 2019. "Gabbard Hits DNC over Poll Criteria for Debates." *The Hill*, August 23.

[55] https://twitter.com/MichaelBennet/status/1164977491901059072.

[56] https://twitter.com/marwilliamson/status/1168001717331537921.

[57] https://twitter.com/billscher/status/1201483033175457792?s=20.

[58] Tal Axelrod, 2019. "Booker Leads Other 2020 Dems in Petition Urging DNC to Change Debate Qualifications." *The Hill*, December 14.

continuing to ramp up the polling and fundraising thresholds. Yet this decision was notably keeping another candidate off the debate stage. Former New York City Mayor Michael Bloomberg decided to enter the crowded presidential field in late November 2019, vowing an unusual campaign approach: he would functionally ignore the contests in Iowa, New Hampshire, Nevada, and South Carolina, seeking ballot access in the later state contests, and would do no fundraising, bankrolling his own campaign. He immediately began a nationwide advertising blitz costing hundreds of millions of dollars, and thanks to this, some favorable news coverage, and his own history in politics as both a candidate and a generous financer of other campaigns, his support grew – from roughly 5 percent to roughly 15 percent in national polls just between mid-January and mid-February. Yet because he wasn't raising money, he did not qualify for debates.

In a rather stunning about-face, the DNC announced in late January 2020 that it was eliminating the fundraising threshold requirements for its February debates. It set a polling threshold that Bloomberg easily met, although candidates could also qualify by winning at least one delegate in a February contest. The DNC argued that, now that candidates could qualify by winning delegates, they no longer needed other indicators of grassroots support, like donations. The other candidates were sharply critical of the decision. "Changing the rules now to accommodate Mike Bloomberg and not changing them in the past to ensure a more diverse debate stage is just plain wrong," said Steyer. Warren echoed a similar theme: "The DNC didn't change the rules to ensure good, diverse candidates could remain on the debate stage. They shouldn't change the rules to let a billionaire on." Sanders spokesperson Jeff Weaver described it as "the definition of a rigged system."[59]

In our conversation, DNC member Kathy Sullivan was particularly incensed about the party's refusal to change debate qualifications when they were destroying the campaigns of candidates of color but its willingness to amend them to accommodate Bloomberg. She thought it was

---

[59] Reid J. Epstein and Matt Stevens, 2020. "D.N.C. Rules Change for Nevada Debate Could Open Door for Bloomberg." *The New York Times*, January 31.

not only wrong, but likely to increase factional dissent and undermine party legitimacy. "When Kamala Harris went out," she told me,

> at that point, you would have thought Perez would have said, "Okay, we need some flexibility here." Instead it was, "You know, these are the rules." Well you know, if the rules suck you change the rules! ... And then, to change it so Bloomberg will probably qualify ... now that sucks .... And especially knowing how the Sanders people are paranoid about every friggin' thing you do, and now they're like, "They're doing it because they don't like Bernie,' and I'm like, 'Oh my God, here we go again."

The DNC ignored the criticism, and the Democratic debates in the second half of February 2020 included Bloomberg. This turned out to be a mixed blessing for the former mayor. In the February 19 debate in Las Vegas, Warren repeatedly attacked Bloomberg for sexist and derogatory comments he'd made to female employees and his history of demanding nondisclosure agreements. Sanders and other candidates piled on. Bloomberg's quick polling rise came to an end after that debate. Bloomberg fell well short of expectations in his first actual contests on Super Tuesday, and he withdrew the next day.

THE 2017–2018 REFORMS IN HINDSIGHT

The reforms that Democrats embraced in the wake of 2016 were neither as transformative nor as revolutionary as the ones it embraced in the wake of 1968, nor as self-defeating as the ones the National Republicans attempted after 1828. But they were nonetheless profound and, importantly, controversial. They were also very clearly driven by election narratives stemming from 2016. Many in the Sanders camp saw superdelegates as a barrier to the 2016 nomination; many in the Clinton camp saw intra-party divisiveness as the reason Clinton had lost in the general election. People in the party's leadership saw tightly managed debates as a way to avoid some of the factionalism that had injured the Republican Party in 2016. At every stage, these reform efforts were perceived as harming representation for people of color, both as DNC members and as candidates, but the party was willing to risk that perception in the service of potential victory in 2020.

It is also noticeable that the party seemed to be moving in two directions at once, both toward greater and lesser control over nominations. The superdelegate decision was a move in the latter direction. In a series of public discussions, private decisions, and internal votes, the Democratic National Committee substantially changed its orientation toward party nominations. Unlike the DNC members of the McGovern–Fraser era, who didn't seem particularly cognizant of the extent of the reforms they were passing, DNC members in 2018 consciously voted to reduce their own power in selecting nominees. They did so in response to concerns by a vocal minority faction within the party that the DNC had become a powerful and corrupt agent in party nominations.

The amusing note here, of course, is that the DNC was never nearly as powerful (nor corrupt) as its critics contended. It is inherently a weak organization, often underfunded, heavily dependent on state parties and presidential campaigns, and limited by longstanding concerns that any decision it makes seen as helping a candidate will be perceived as unjust and illegitimate. If it has had a bias in the past, it has generally been to try to appear as open and impartial as possible,[60] even to the point of allowing *twenty* presidential candidates to participate in debates, because to appear otherwise is to look corrupt.

Yet even while the party was stepping back from nominations control in one way, it was asserting greater control in another, by aggressively setting and adjusting the rules for primary debates and using those debates to shape the candidate field, even while there were candidates running. Of course the party was the target of some accusations of bias, particularly from candidates who failed to qualify for increasingly stringent debate thresholds. But there was clearly a logic to these rules and a considerably different set of outcomes if the party had declined such a role.

It's hard to know how the presidential candidate field would have shaped itself had the debates been organized like they were in the late twentieth century, with news organizations taking the lead role in inviting

---

[60] Julia Azari, 2019. "Of Course the DNC Didn't Want to Have a Climate Change Debate." *Mischiefs of Faction*, August 29. www.mischiefsoffaction.com/post/of-course-the-dnc-didn-t-want-to-have-a-climate-change-debate.

candidates and the party largely operating on the sidelines. Perhaps news organizations might simply have invited whom they saw as the mostly competitive candidates – possibly creating a much smaller group of candidates than we saw on the debate stages in mid-2019. On the other hand, perhaps twenty or more candidates would have competed in prime time and undercard debates as the Republican candidates did in 2015. Perhaps Bloomberg would have been included in earlier debates, further boosting his visibility and chances in the early-contest states (or being knocked out by Warren and other candidates earlier). Perhaps news organizations would have been more cautious about excluding prominent candidates of color like Cory Booker, Kamala Harris, or Julián Castro. The party might end up with the same nominee regardless of the approach, but the process itself would have looked very different if not for the DNC's strong hand here. A different system might well have left more candidates and their supporters feeling marginalized, increasing concerns about the contest being "rigged."

As the Democratic Party prepared for the first primaries and caucuses of February 2020, it was facing a peculiar set of circumstances. The DNC, the source of much derision from four years earlier, had stepped back from power in some ways but asserted itself in others, making itself a target for voter outrage should there be substantial dissatisfaction in the ultimate choice of nominee. These party decisions were rife with racial tensions, with many African American party members and presidential candidates complaining that they'd been sidelined by the party's leadership. And the party had taken these steps in response to concerns about 2016 – that the DNC had overstepped in the nomination contest and that both parties' debates from that year were problematic. The building blocks for significant discord within the party in 2020 were all present.

CHAPTER 5

The Persistence of Faction

There are comments that we all make like, "Oh, they're a Bernie Bro." I still hear that. I find myself doing that, too. I know that's not right to do and that's not a good policy thing to do or to build the party, but I know that happens all the time, still.

Former Martin O'Malley Iowa staffer, 2017

As the evidence in the past few chapters suggests, divisiveness within the Democratic Party was a source of substantial concern among party leaders and activists following the 2016 election, and many of the party's decisions in the wake of that loss were motivated by a desire to mitigate such factionalism in the future. These concerns were bolstered by media coverage following the election that suggested that internal divisions would likely plague the party for many years to come. "It's clear that the party is divided, split on issues including free trade, health care, foreign affairs and Wall Street. They even disagree over the political wisdom of doing deals with Trump," wrote Philip Elliott.[1] Supporters of 2016 Democratic presidential nominee Hillary Clinton and those of her primary rival Bernie Sanders continued to mistrust each other and blame each other for the party's presidential loss.

Yet both major parties have experienced factionalism and bitter intra-party nomination contests in the past, but have gone onto periods of significant unity in governance and successful election cycles shortly thereafter. Indeed, despite some hard-fought nomination battles in 2018, Democrats enjoyed a great range of successes in that fall's general elections at the national, state, and local level.

---

[1] Julia Elliott, 2017. "A Divided Democratic Party Debates Its Future." *Time*, September 21.

In this chapter, I seek to determine just how split the Democratic Party is. Were the internal party fights in 2016 just a feature of disagreements between Hillary Clinton and Bernie Sanders, limited to that particular contest? Or are they a deeper and persistent schism within the party, spilling over into other years and contests? If it's the latter, that presents a serious barrier for any sort of collective action by the party, whether that involves making policy, running elections, or picking a presidential nominee.

I examine this question in a particular way – by studying campaign finance patterns in the 2017 and 2018 Democratic gubernatorial primaries across the country. This is by no means the only way to study factionalism, nor does it necessarily tell us about every important aspect of the Democratic Party. But how partisans allocate money tells us a great deal about their priorities, and if party donors are deeply divided across factional lines, that's instructive about how the modern Democratic Party thinks of itself and behaves.

DO FACTIONS PERSIST?

Factionalism is hardly new to the major political parties in the United States. The modern parties are actually enjoying a period of relative internal harmony when compared with earlier eras. Southern Democratic delegates walked out of the party's 1948 national convention rather than approve a civil rights plank, for example, and placed an alternative segregationist ticket atop the party's ballot in their states. Influential Republican Party elites called for the defeat of their own party's presidential ticket in 1964, and some Democratic elites did the same in 1972. As recently as 2008, a faction of Hillary Clinton supporters called PUMA (People United Means Action, or Party Unity My Ass) threatened to vote Republican in the general election after their preferred candidate was deprived of the Democratic nomination, and by some estimates, roughly a quarter of Clinton's supporters that year ended up voting for John McCain in the fall.[2] Today's factionalism has not quite attained such levels.

---

[2] Jeff Stein, 2017. "The Bernie Voters Who Defected to Trump, Explained by a Political Scientist." *Vox.com*, August 24. www.vox.com/policy-and-politics/2017/8/24/161940 86/bernie-trump-voters-study

What exactly are factions? They're more than just supporters of two different candidates vying for the nomination. Political scientist Nelson Polsby defined them pretty succinctly as a group operating within a political party in pursuit of a common interest.[3] Political scientist Daniel DiSalvo added a bit more detail, saying a faction has (1) ideologically consistency, (2) organizational capacity, and (3) durability over time, and uses those to (4) move the party in one direction or another.[4] These factions seek to shape what a party stands for, generating new ideas and shaping what a party does when it finds itself in the position of governing. Recent divisions within the Democratic Party certainly meet these definitions.

A Brookings research project[5] examined Democratic party factions peculiar to 2018. The researchers reviewed the websites of Democratic US House campaigns, dividing them up between those that referred to their candidate as "progressive" and those that did not (presumed to be "establishment" candidates). The study found that establishment candidates were more likely to prevail in the primary election (35 percent received the nomination, as opposed to 27 percent of progressives who did so), while progressives were somewhat more likely to win the nomination in more conservative districts (presumably because fewer establishment candidates contested those).

It's not always clear just where the factional lines are drawn within the broader party coalition, or what they mean. Sometimes, it appears that "progressives" and "establishment" party leaders seem to roughly agree on policy – expanded health care access, a commitment to racial and gender equality, protections for abortion rights, regulations on gun ownership, and so on – but just disagree on the means to get there.[6] At other times, though, there appear to be significant policy disagreements. Note

---

[3] Nelson W. Polsby, 1983. *Consequences of Party Reform.* Oxford: Oxford University Press, p. 65.

[4] Daniel DiSalvo, 2012. *Engines of Change: Party Factions in American Politics, 1868–2010.* Oxford; Oxford University Press.

[5] Elaine Kamarck and Alexander Podkul, 2018. *The Primaries Project at Brookings.* Washington, DC: The Brookings Institute. www.brookings.edu/series/the-primaries-project-midterms–2018/.

[6] Hans Noel, 2016. "Ideological Factions in the Republican and Democratic Parties." *The Annals of the American Academy of Political and Social Science* 667(1): 166–88.

the divide among the 2020 presidential candidates over whether to expand health care access with a "public option" (a government-backed health insurance option) or via Medicare For All, essentially a government takeover of the health insurance industry.

Political scientists Hans Noel and Rachel Blum[7] have attempted to use social network analysis across multiple presidential election cycles to tease out the different persistent factions within the Democratic Party. They identify an establishment core (who generally get their preferred candidate although failed to do so in 2008), congressional leaders, New Yorkers, white Southern moderates, labor unions, and so forth. Each of these factions is loyal to the party and stays intensely involved with its presidential nomination process, but in some cycles one may be more or less powerful relative to other factions, while in other cycles the factions may appear relatively unanimous in their support of a candidate. A snapshot of donor address sales in the 2004 presidential cycle showed similar factional splits within the Democratic Party,[8] with large factions of environmental groups, media organizations, and general interest liberal advocacy organizations competing in nominations but generally cooperating on core party missions. Meanwhile, a group of political scientists attempted to discern the differences between "liberals" and "progressives." They found that the differences were far more social than policy-based; progressives were more likely than liberals to hold sexist attitudes.[9]

But if you want to get a sense of typical factional patterns within the Democratic Party, just look at the last half century or so of presidential nomination contests. There are often between five and ten viable candidates (more so in recent years), whose ranks are thinned out quickly after the Iowa Caucuses and New Hampshire primary. Within a few weeks, we typically see two main candidates vying for the nomination. The first is

[7] Rachel Blum and Hans Noel, 2016. "Presidential Nominations and Coalition Politics: Detecting Party Factions in Network Data." Paper presented at the annual conference of the Southern Political Science Association, San Juan, Puerto Rico.

[8] Gregory Koger, Seth Masket, and Hans Noel, 2010. "Cooperative Party Factions in American Politics." *American Politics Research* 38: 33–53.

[9] Kevin K. Banda, John Cluverius, Lilliana Mason, and Hans Noel, 2019. "A Distinction with a Difference? Investigating the Difference Between Liberals and Progressives." Presented at the annual conference of the Southern Political Science Association in Austin, Texas, January 17–19.

what we might call a party regular. This is typically a center-left pragmatist, usually with a range of allies within the party leadership – prominent members of Congress, governors, union leaders, and others. They typically have many years of experience within the party, have served at a high level of state or national office, and have been vetted through numerous election cycles. The second candidate is what we might call an ideologue or a progressive. This tends to be someone who prioritizes ideological purity over compromise and is often popular among more liberal activists, college students, and others. Such regular/ideologue rivalries as those between Walter Mondale and Gary Hart (1984), Bill Clinton and Jerry Brown (1992), Al Gore and Bill Bradley (2000), and John Kerry and Howard Dean (2004) stand as exemplars of this divide.

This doesn't mean there are only two factions within the broader party, of course. Organized labor has long been a powerful constituency within the party (although has perhaps waned somewhat in recent years), and presidential candidates rarely win the nomination without substantial support from that community. The African American community tends to be prominent, as well, and it's rare for anyone to win the nomination without the bulk of black leadership in their corner. The so-called "wine track" liberals often have considerable resources to expend in nomination races. It's rare for a nominee to have all the factions on their side during the nomination race, but usually the bulk of them.

Indeed, such divisions go back at least as far as the 1960s, when the New Deal coalition was beginning to fray along lines of race, age, class, and attitudes toward war. When the Democratic Party was debating massive reforms in its nomination system in 1970 in the wake of its humiliating 1968 loss, DNC chairman Larry O'Brien remarked, "We had lost in 1952 and 1956 and remained reasonably united. But in 1970 the bitter divisions of 1968 still existed – hawk versus dove, liberal versus conservative, reformer versus regular – and no reconciliation in sight."[10] Other observers of what would become known as the McGovern–Fraser Commission noted the persistence and the rigidity of the factionalism: "The split of the executive committee appeared to be developing along

---

[10] Byron E. Shafer, 1983. *Quiet Revolution: The Struggle for the Democratic Party and the Shaping of Post-Reform Politics.* New York: Russell Sage Foundation, p. 249.

roughly the same lines as the 1968 division between the supporters of [Vice President Hubert] Humphrey and those of Senator Robert F. Kennedy of New York. One source characterized the fight as 'an argument between young and old, establishment and innovators, stand-fast and antiwar' elements" (p. 246).

The 2016 contest between Hillary Clinton and Bernie Sanders fit well within this historical pattern. As with other modern Democratic presidential nominations, a "regular" or "establishment" candidate backed by much of the party's leadership and officeholders, but sometimes criticized for her pragmatic deal-making, squared off against an "ideologue," widely praised for his ideological consistency but with support largely limited to white progressives and college students. Yet in some ways, this division seemed sharper and more durable than previous ones. Importantly, Sanders performed far better in primary and caucus contests than most earlier ideologue challengers, essentially tying Clinton in Iowa and substantially besting her in New Hampshire.

Additionally, Sanders wasn't just running as an ideologue, but also as a populist. This taps into a somewhat older division within the Democratic ranks.[11] The Populist Party of the 1890s was largely subsumed into the Democratic coalition, along with its many moralistic appeals about the virtue of rank-and-file party members and the corruption of wealthy insiders and elites.[12] William Gibbs McAdoo exploited these populist sentiments in his presidential nomination campaign against Al Smith in 1924. While he failed to secure the presidential nomination, McAdoo's claim that he had the "mandate of the people" helped split his party internally and arguably contributed to his party's loss in the fall.[13]

[11] Julia R. Azari and Seth Masket, 2018. "'The Mandate of the People': The 2016 Sanders Campaign in Context." In John C. Green, Daniel J. Coffey, and David B. Cohen eds., *The State of the Parties, 2018: The Changing Role of Contemporary American Political Parties,* London: Rowman & Littlefield, pp. 75–83.

[12] John Gerring, 2001. *Party Ideologies in America, 1828–1996.* Cambridge: Cambridge University Press; John Donald Hicks. 1931. *The Populist Revolt: A History of the Farmers' Alliance and the People's Party.* Minneapolis: University of Minnesota Press; Charles Postel. 2007. *The Populist Vision.* Oxford: Oxford University Press.

[13] Robert K. Murray, 1976. *The 103rd Ballot: Democrats and the Disaster in Madison Square Garden.* New York: Harper & Row.

A main question for this chapter is whether the factional split in one contest maps onto another one. For example, just as the 2016 presidential election was coming to an end, the 2017 Virginia gubernatorial election was beginning to heat up. That contest saw a fiercely competitive Democratic primary between Rep. Tom Perriello and Lieutenant Governor Ralph Northam. Bernie Sanders, and the Our Revolution organization closely tied to him, endorsed Perriello, while many party establishment figures backed Northam, who prevailed in the June primary election. But to what extent did Democratic activists follow their patterns from 2016? Did the Sanders/Clinton divide hold for another nomination for another office?

ACTIVIST VIEWS OF FACTIONALISM

In my visits with the Democratic activists in early-contest states, I asked about their perceptions of factionalism within the Democratic Party. In particular, I asked about the degree to which party splits from 2016 mapped on to midterm contests in 2018, especially gubernatorial primaries. Importantly, many rejected the idea, suggesting that the contests and candidates were sufficiently different from year to year that factional splits didn't really survive from one contest to the next. However, some felt that the ongoing factionalism was important. This came up quite a bit in discussions about the 2018 Nevada Democratic gubernatorial primary between two Clark County Commissioners, Chris Giunchigliani (generally referred to as Chris G.) and Steve Sisolak, who prevailed. Nevada state Senator Yvanna Cancela, for example, argued, "I think what we're seeing play out is a fight for where the Democratic party in Nevada wants to go. Are we a more moderate party? Are we a more liberal, progressive party? And I think the gubernatorial primary is the manifestation of that." In my conversation with former Nevada Democratic Party chair Sam Lieberman, he described the candidates explicitly in terms of their factional alliances from 2016: "Chris G. has all the Clinton people and all, Chris G. is the one that can build bridges between Clinton and Bernie. In other words, no Bernie person would ever vote for Steve Sisolak, and a lot of Hillary people would vote for Chris G."

Kimberley Boggus, a longstanding Democratic campaign worker in Des Moines, similarly sized up the 2018 Iowa gubernatorial candidates in terms of their presidential loyalties:

> So Kathy Glasson is the Bernie person. Nate Boulton is the Obama, and Andy McGuire is the Hillary. And then it's John Norris, who had a role in the Obama administration, from a rural part of Iowa. He's like the rational kind of Democrats ... he's like that person where the sane Democrats go.

Nate Monson, a Martin O'Malley campaign staffer in Iowa in 2016, conceded an anti-Sanders bias among many party regulars, as evidenced by comments on the state party's Facebook page:

> There are comments that we all make like, "Oh, they're a Bernie Bro." I still hear that ... I find myself doing that, too, sometimes and I dismiss people who are in that position that I classify as kind of a Bernie Bro .... I know that's not right to do and that's not a good policy thing to do or to build their party, but I know that happens all the time, still. They're a Bernie person, so that means just dismiss them, they're crazy, instead of working together on a common issue. But yeah, that's something I've noticed a lot, is where we're still so divided.

CAMPAIGN FINANCE DIVISIONS. Judging from the conversations I had across these states, some were convinced that the factional divides of 2016 were affecting the divisions within gubernatorial primaries in 2017 and 2018, or indeed might just be the same divisions. To examine this more systematically, I looked at campaign donation patterns across the two election cycles. I focused my analysis on the thirty-three states that had Democratic gubernatorial primary elections in 2017 and 2018. I have excluded California from this analysis due to the unusual nature of its top-two election system, which is functionally different from a party primary election. For each of the states, I gathered complete records of donations to Democrat presidential candidates prior to the state's presidential primary or caucus in 2016. I then gathered complete records of donations to Democratic gubernatorial candidates prior to the primaries in 2017 (New Jersey and Virginia) and 2018 (thirty-one other states).[14]

It's one thing to show that there's a divide. But I was particularly interested in knowing, for each gubernatorial primary, who was the "party's choice." Now, I want to be clear what I mean by that. Obviously, whoever wins the primary is the party's choice, both politically and legally, but I was interested in knowing who the bulk of party insiders were backing *before* the primary. I recognize that these concepts aren't perfectly precise, but there are definite differences in who funds "establishment" candidates and who funds the "ideologues."

To examine this, I drew on an approach from Hans Hassell,[15] who studies people who donate both to a candidate and to a party committee (the DNC, the DCCC, the Colorado Democratic Party, etc.). I gathered complete records of donations to state formal party committees in 2016 and 2018 in the thirty-three races under study. I then matched all the donors who had contributed both to a party committee and to a gubernatorial primary candidate in 2017–2018. This turns out to be a fairly high threshold for donors. There were some 354,646 donations recorded to Democratic gubernatorial candidates in the primaries under study, but only 25,602 donations to party committees in those states. Of these, just 7,362 donors contributed to both a party committee and a Democratic gubernatorial candidate. As Hassell notes, those who donate to both a party committee and a candidate (I'll call them "party-aligned donors") are a good indicator of the overall party's leanings.

Table 5.1 displays the overall number of party-aligned donors who contributed to each gubernatorial candidate in the primary. This turns out to be a pretty strong predictor of a candidate's successes in the nomination contest. Of the thirty-three nomination contest winners, twenty-seven had received the plurality of party-aligned donations. Among the six cases where the party donors' choice did not receive the nomination, two were cases in which the plurality recipient did not reach a majority, and which might be

---

[14] Campaign finance data were made available by the National Institute on Money in Politics (followthemoney.org).
[15] Hans J.G. Hassell, 2018. *The Party's Primary: Control of Congressional Nominations.* Cambridge: Cambridge University Press.

TABLE 5.1 *Gubernatorial candidates and party donations*

State	Candidate	Number of candidate-and-committee donors			State	Candidate	Number of candidate-and-committee donors		
AL	Cobb	4	(	20.0)	IL	Biss	74	(	67.3)
	Countryman	1	(	5.0)		Daiber	5	(	4.5)
	Fields	0	(	0.0)		Hardiman	0	(	0.0)
	Maddox	15	(	75.0)		Kennedy	25	(	22.7)
	White	0	(	0.0)		Marshall	0	(	0.0)
AR	Henderson	3	(	75.0)		Pritzker	6	(	5.5)
	Sanders	1	(	25.0)	KS	Anderson	0	(	0)
AZ	Farley	64	(	29.8)		Bergeson	0	(	0.0)
	Fryer	3	(	1.4)		Brewer	0	(	0.0)
	Garcia	148	(	68.8)		Kelly	0	(	0.0)
CO	Johnston	99	(	16.6)		Svaty	0	(	0.0)
	Kennedy	279	(	46.8)	MA	Gonzalez	111	(	91.0)
	Lynne	60	(	10.1)		Massie	11	(	9.0)
	Polis	158	(	26.5)	MD	Baker	39	(	12.8)
CT	Ganim	4	(	20.0)		Ervin	1	(	0.3)
	Lamont	16	(	80.0)		Jealous	200	(	65.6)
FL	Gillum	230	(	48.1)		Madaleno	26	(	8.5)
	Graham	203	(	42.5)		Ross	24	(	7.9)
	Greene	0	(	0.0)		Shea	14	(	4.6)
	King	15	(	3.1)		Vignarajah	1	(	0.3)
	Levine	30	(	6.3)	ME	Cote	65	(	21.4)
	Lundmark	0	(	0.0)		Dion, D	0	(	0.0)
	Wetherbee	0	(	0.0)		Dion, M	7	(	2.3)
GA	Abrams	142	(	80.7)		Eves	73	(	24.0)
	Evans	34	(	19.3)		Mills	97	(	31.9)
HI	Caravalho	0	(	0.0)		Russell	14	(	4.6)
	Hanabusa	16	(	44.4)		Sweet	48	(	15.8)
	Ige	20	(	55.6)		El-Sayed	177	(	38.1)
IA	Boulton	188	(	31.8)	MI	Thanedar	1	(	0.2)
	Glasson	115	(	19.4)		Whitmer	286	(	61.6)
	Hubbell	162	(	27.4)		Murphy	5	(	23.8)
	McGuire	40	(	6.8)	MN	Savior	0	(	0.0)
	Norris	86	(	14.5)		Swanson	1	(	4.8)
	Wilburn	1	(	0.2)		Walz	15	(	71.4)
ID	Balukoff	0	(	0.0)	NE	Davis	0	(	0.0)
	Dill	0	(	0.0)		Krist	5	(	100)
	Jordan	11	(	100.0)	NH	Marchand	70	(	100)
NJ	Brennan	0	(	0.0)	VT	Ehlers	2	(	18.2)
	Johnson	7	(	9.6)		Hallquist	6	(	54.5)
	Lesniak	2	(	2.7)		Siegel	2	(	18.2)
	McGreevey	1	(	1.4)		Sonneborn	1	(	9.1)
	Murphy	60	(	82.2)	WI	Evers	444	(	41.3)
	Wisniewski	3	(	4.1)		Flynn	47	(	4.4)
NM	Apodaca	24	(	4.0)		Gronik	60	(	5.6)
	Cervantes	16	(	2.7)		McCabe	82	(	7.6)

TABLE 5.1 *(continued)*

State	Candidate	Number of candidate-and-committee donors		State	Candidate	Number of candidate-and-committee donors	
	Grisham	557	(93.3)		Mitchell	72	(6.7)
NV	Giunchigliani	37	(56.9)		Pade	1	(0.1)
	Sisolak	28	(43.1)		Roys	122	(11.3)
	Thorns	0	(0.0)		Soglin	4	(0.4)
NY	Cuomo	284	(26.2)		Vinehout	110	(10.2)
	Nixon	801	(73.8)		Wachs	134	(12.5)
	Cordray	212	(70.0)	WY	*Throne*	5	(100)
OH	Kucinich	43	(14.2)		Wilde	0	(0.0)
	O'Neill	0	(0.0)				
	Schiavoni	48	(15.8)				
OK	*Edmonson*	11	(84.6)				
	Johnson	2	(15.4)				
	Brown	189	(100)				
OR	Jones	0	(0.0)				
	Neville	0	(0.0)				
	Brown	3	(1.8)				
RI	Dickinson	0	(0.0)				
	Raimondo	160	(98.2)				
	Noble	6	(20.0)				
SC	*Smith*	23	(76.7)				
	Willis	1	(3.3)				
TN	*Dean*	36	(62.1)				
	Fitzhugh	22	(37.9)				
	Davis	0	(0.0)				
	Mumbach	0	(0.0)				
	Ocegueda	0	(0.0)				
TX	Payne	0	(0.0)				
	Valdez	5	(100)				
	Wakely	0	(0.0)				
	White	0	(0.0)				
VA	*Northam*	100	(75.2)				
	Perriello	33	(24.8)				

Note: Percentages of party-aligned donors appear in parentheses. Nomination winners appear in italics.

considered unusual cases for other reasons. In Colorado, for example, Cary Kennedy received 44 percent of these donations, but lost the nomination to Jared Polis, a multi-millionaire member of Congress who largely self-financed during the contest, and party support was split as a result.[16] Iowa, meanwhile, saw a large field of primary candidates and no clear

[16] John Frank and Natalie Weber, 2018. "Jared Polis Wins Democratic Primary for Colorado Governor." *The Denver Post,* June 26.

party consensus, and the plurality donor choice, Nate Boulton, ended up withdrawing from the race shortly before the primary election when allegations of sexual misconduct surfaced.[17] The total *number* of party-aligned donors is a somewhat better predictor of nomination success than the total *amount* contributed by these donors, which only predicts the nominee in twenty-five of the thirty-three cases. For the purposes of this analysis, I treat the recipient of the plurality of party-aligned donations as the party's choice in the nomination contest.

Persistence Across 2016 and 2018

I next investigate whether donor patterns in 2016 predict similar patterns in 2018. Across the thirty-three states under study, 330,897 people donated to the Democratic presidential candidates of 2016 prior to their state's primary or caucus. Only 24,792 people contributed to both a 2016 presidential nomination candidate and a 2017–2018 gubernatorial nomination candidate. I am just examining this subset of presidential-and-gubernatorial donors here, excluding donations made by the presidential candidates themselves.

If Clinton supporters and Sanders supporters were backing different sorts of candidates in the 2017–2018 gubernatorial primaries, it's presumably because they were responding to different signals about whether those gubernatorial candidates were "establishment" or "progressive." I look at different political environments where the signal was more or less prominent to see how donor behavior varied. For example, if a clear majority, rather than a plurality, of party-aligned donors backed a candidate, that presumably sent a louder signal to donors about that candidate belonging to the establishment. Or if allies of Bernie Sanders backed someone who was not the party choice, that also would send a loud signal about whom to support.

Figure 5.1 offers some insight here, showing the percentages of people who donated to the various 2016 Democratic presidential candidates and how they donated in the 2017–2018 gubernatorial primaries. (This only includes those who donated to either Clinton or Sanders in 2016 and to a Democratic gubernatorial candidate in 2017–2018 – obviously

---

[17] Daniel Strauss, 2018. "Iowa Democrat Boulton Suspends Campaign Following Sexual Misconduct Report." *Politico*, May 24.

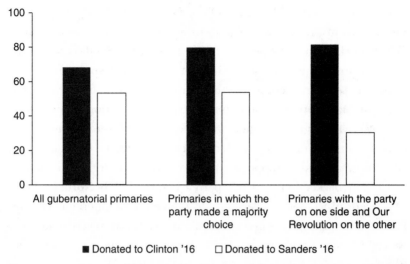

Figure 5.1 Percentage donating to party choice in 2017–2018, by candidate support in 2016

there were many donors only active in one of those cycles.) As the figure shows, supporters of Hillary Clinton were somewhat more likely to support the party's choice in a gubernatorial primary than supporters of Bernie Sanders were, 68.5 percent to 53.3 percent.

Differences in these levels of support grow substantially when we just limit the analysis to cases in which a majority of party-aligned donors picked a favorite. (This omits Colorado, Florida, Iowa, Kansas, Maine, and Wisconsin.) In these states (depicted in the middle group of columns), there is now roughly a 26-point gap between supporters of Clinton and Sanders, with the former supporting the party's gubernatorial choice 80 percent of the time and the latter doing so only 54 percent of the time.

The differences become far starker when we limit the analysis those cases where there were conflicting factional signals. In the third group, I have just examined those cases in which Our Revolution, the Sanders-affiliated advocacy group, endorsed a different gubernatorial candidate than the party donors' choice.[18] There were seven of these contests –

[18] https://ourrevolution.com/results/.

Iowa, Massachusetts, Michigan, Ohio, Oklahoma, Rhode Island, and Virginia. In just these states, Clinton supporters donated to the party's gubernatorial choice 82 percent of the time, while Sanders supporters did so around 31 percent of the time – a more than 50-point gap.

We can see a few examples of these divisive gubernatorial primaries in 2018. In Massachusetts, for example, party-aligned donors picked Jay Gonzales, while Our Revolution endorsed Robert Massie. Eighty-two percent of Clinton supporters ended up contributing to Gonzales, while 68 percent of Sanders supporters gave to Massie. In Virginia, 62 percent of Clinton backers gave to the party's choice, Ralph Northam, while 61 percent of Sanders backers gave to the Our Revolution choice, Tom Perriello. In Michigan, 79 percent of Clinton backers donated to the party-backed Gretchen Whitmer, while 77 percent of Sanders supporters contributed to the Our Revolution-backed Abdul El-Sayed.

All this raises the question of the importance of the Our Revolution endorsement. Does that signal of difference from the mainstream Democratic Party cause donors to shift their alliances in Our Revolution's direction? Or is Our Revolution simply choosing to back those candidates who already seem to have a substantial base of support distinct from the party's choice?

I investigate this in Figure 5.2 by breaking down the donation records so that we can examine divisiveness both before and after the Our Revolution endorsement. As the figure suggests, there are already pretty substantial divisions before Our Revolution gives any public statement, with Clinton supporters donating to the party's choice in the gubernatorial primary 83 percent of the time but Sanders supporters doing so only 42 percent of the time. But that difference becomes far greater after the endorsement, with a difference of 77 to 19 percent – a nearly 60-point gap. The evidence here suggests that Our Revolution tended to insert itself in a race only when there was already substantial support for someone other than the party's favorite, but that their activity tended to boost support for such a candidate.

Primary Donor Behavior in General Elections

Another aspect of donor behavior that can provide insight into party factionalism is the donors' activities in the general election cycle. How involved are primary donors in the general election cycle, and how much

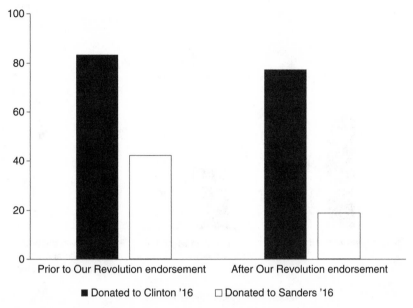

Figure 5.2 Percentage donating to party choice in 2017–2018, by presidential support in 2016 before and after Our Revolution endorsement

does it matter if their candidate won the primary? In a more factional system, that is, donors whose candidate was denied the nomination might be less likely to help out that party's nominee in the fall election.

To examine this question, I looked at the behavior of donors to primary campaigns and examined how, or whether, they contributed in the general election. Figure 5.3 displays some of the results of this inquiry. The first set of columns shows the percentage of contributors across all the examined states who also donated to a candidate in the general election, broken down by whether the candidate the donor initially supported won or lost the party's nomination. As this shows, there are notable differences in general election involvement based on the identity of the nominee – 48 percent of those whose candidate won the nomination went on to donate in the fall, while only 32 percent of those whose candidate lost the nomination did the same.

In the middle of the graph, we see just those states in which party-aligned donors had a majority preference for one primary candidate.

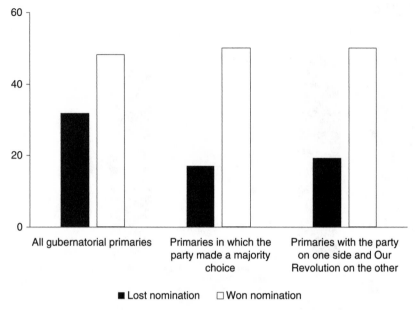

Figure 5.3 Percentage of primary donors contributing to general election campaign in 2017–2018, by success of primary candidate

Those contests appeared to be more divisive, with half of the nominee's supporters going on to donate in the general election but only 17 percent of other candidates' backers doing the same. It was a similar division for the divided state party contests (with party donors choosing one candidate and Our Revolution picking another), in that 50 percent of the nominee's backers donated in the general election but only 19 percent of other candidates' backers did so.

Another way of examining party factionalism is to see which of these donors to Democratic primary candidates went on to donate to the Republican nominee after the primary election. Donating to the other party's nominee is a much more overt display of disloyalty than simple non-participation – we would expect very few people committed to a Democratic primary candidate to go ahead and back the Republican in the fall. However, we do see some evidence of this occurring in Figure 5.4. Among the whole sample, less than 2 percent of primary donors whose candidate won ended up supporting a Republican in the fall, while more than twice that figure did so among those whose candidate lost the primary. There was

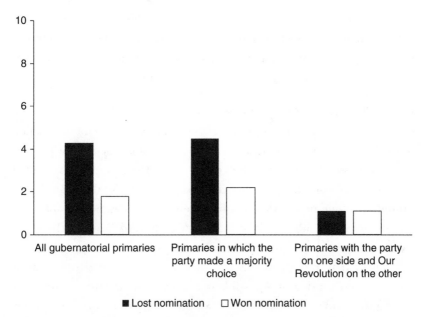

Figure 5.4 Percentage of Democratic primary donors contributing to Republican nominee in the general election in 2017–2018, by success of primary candidate

a similar split when we just look at those cases where a majority of party-and-candidate donors selected a candidate. In the most divisive primaries (those where the party was divided between establishment and progressives), however, we see no differences in GOP support based on whether the candidate won the primary.

The above analysis is somewhat incomplete, of course, in that a large percentage of the Democratic primary winners were essentially the party establishment figures. It would be helpful to isolate just those cases in which the Our Revolution-backed candidate defeated the establishment candidate in the primary, but there were no such cases in 2018 gubernatorial races. However, when we look at those races in which party donors and Our Revolution picked the same candidate (Florida, Georgia, Idaho, Illinois, Maryland, New York, Vermont), we still see substantial divisions. Within this subsample, 45 percent of backers of the winning primary candidate, and 15 percent of backers of a losing primary candidate, donated to a general election campaign. Similarly, 3.5 percent of backers of the loser went on to contribute to the Republican nominee, while less than 1 percent of the winner's backers did so in this subsample. Overall, the evidence here suggests that one's preferred candidate prevailing in the nomination contest makes a substantial difference in how involved, and for whom, a donor is in the general election.

Factionalism Prior to 2016

One question left unanswered by the above analysis is the extent to which the Clinton/Sanders divide was the *cause* of subsequent divisions, or whether those divisions precluded the 2016 Democratic presidential nomination. Generally speaking, are those who support the "ideologue" candidate in one nomination contest likely to be the same ones backing the ideologue in subsequent contests? Are Howard Dean backers, for example, the same people as Bernie Sanders backers?

I am unable to address this question in the very long term. But in a shorter time window, it is possible to compare the donation patterns in some gubernatorial primaries in 2018 with those from four years earlier, prior to the Clinton/Sanders rivalry. For example, the states of New York, Rhode Island, and Massachusetts, which saw competitive Democratic gubernatorial primaries in 2018, also saw such competition in their 2014 races. To what extent do donations in one race predict the other?

Tables 5.2 through 5.4 offer a bit of insight on this. The first shows the breakdown of the donors common to both the 2014 and 2018 gubernatorial Democratic primaries in New York. There were notable similarities

TABLE 5.2 *New York gubernatorial Democratic primaries*

2018 candidate	Cuomo '14	Teachout '14
Cuomo '18	99%	1%
Nixon '18	1%	99%

TABLE 5.3 *Massachusetts gubernatorial Democratic primaries*

2018 candidate	Berwick '14	Coakley '14	Grossman '14
Gonzales '18	65%	87%	79%
Massie '18	35%	13%	21%

THE PERSISTENCE OF FACTION

TABLE 5.4 *Rhode Island gubernatorial Democratic primaries*

2018 candidate	Giroux '14	Pell '14	Raimondo '14	Taveras '14
Brown '18	0%	5%	1%	5%
Raimondo '18	0%	95%	99%	95%

between these two contests, with Andrew Cuomo playing the role of the party regular, and a progressive reformer (Zephyr Teachout in 2014, Cynthia Nixon in 2018) challenging him from the left, in both. And indeed the donation patterns were strikingly similar. Cuomo retained nearly 100 percent of his donors from four years earlier, while over 99 percent of Teachout's donors from 2014 went to Nixon in 2018.

The patterns aren't quite so stark in the Massachusetts elections. There, party favorite Martha Coakley dominated donations and the primary in 2014, and 87 percent of her support went to party favorite and nominee Jay Gonzales in 2018. Indeed, Gonzales took the majority of donors from all three candidates from four years earlier, although not as strongly as he did from Coakley's supporters. Only 65 percent of progressive reformer Donald Berwick's supporters from 2014, for example, went Gonzales' way four years later.

Persistent donor patterns are even less in evidence in the Rhode Island contests. The 2014 Democratic gubernatorial primary there was split four ways, but donors between the two years overwhelmingly backed incumbent Gina Raimondo for nomination in 2018. The Our Revolution-backed Matthew Brown claimed no more than 5 percent of the donors from any of the candidates from four years earlier.

A LOOK AT 2020

The section above demonstrated that there are persistent factions within the Democratic coalition – we can call them progressive and establishment, for lack of better terms – that don't only show up in presidential races and weren't just a function of 2016. They structure other party contests, as well, and have something of a history. In this section, I ask whether this factionalism structured the 2020 presidential nomination contest also. As in the analysis above, assessing the ongoing divisions within the Democratic Party requires determination of just who the "party-preferred" candidate is in the presidential race. That in itself is a very interesting question. Yes, we know how the nomination ultimately unfolded, but could we see a party preference prior to the Iowa Caucuses? Who was the party's favorite in 2019? Or was it truly a chaotic, leaderless contest until the last minute?

To examine this, I looked at all the donations of over $200 made to all the Democratic presidential candidates during all four quarters of 2019 and the first month of 2020, just before the Iowa Caucuses. I also collected all the donations made to state or national Democratic Party committees during the same time period. Then I looked to see who the party-aligned donors seem to be leaning toward.

Doing the analysis this way required making some choices, and I want to be clear about why I made those. I only examined donations in excess of $200 because candidates are legally required to report those to the Federal Elections Commission. There were a great many donations made during this cycle lower than that figure – some just one or two dollars – to help candidates qualify for debate thresholds, which simply required a number of donations at any size. However, reporting those smaller figures was voluntary for the campaigns and thus less reliable. I have also limited this analysis to the time period beginning with January 2019 and ending at the end of January 2020, just before the Iowa Caucuses. The purpose here is to examine an aspect of party behavior prior to voters and caucusgoers weighing in.

Also, I should be clear that quite a few donors in this Democratic presidential cycle contributed to multiple candidates. In the third quarter of 2019, for example, more than 8 percent of people who'd given at least $200 to one presidential candidate had given at least $200 to another. For this analysis, I'm interested in calculating the share of unique donors supported by each presidential candidate. Because some of those donors give to multiple candidates, the totals across all candidates will often exceed 100 percent.

In Figure 5.5 below, I trace the total share of donors who gave to each of the top six fundraisers in the candidate pool. For example, in the first quarter of 2019, 22 percent of those who gave over $200 to presidential candidates contributed to Kamala Harris' campaign,

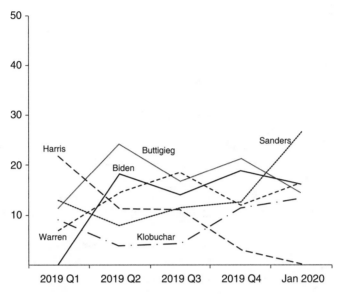

Figure 5.5 Lead candidates' share of total donors

although her share of those donors fell steadily over the course of 2019. Joe Biden, meanwhile, was not an active candidate in the first quarter, but posted solid figures by the second quarter, receiving donations from over 18 percent of donors, and he stayed in that range throughout the year. Bernie Sanders started modestly at 12 percent but closed the strongest, pulling donations from 26 percent of donors just before the Iowa Caucuses.

But that is the share of *all* donors. In Figure 5.6, I have limited the analysis to the candidates' shares of party-aligned donors, again defined as those who donate both to campaigns *and* to party committees. This figure tells a very different story. Sanders trails badly by this measure, never pulling donations from more than 8 percent of party-aligned donors. Elizabeth Warren is competitive here, and was the top fundraiser among party-aligned donors in the third quarter of 2019, but her success faded somewhat with time. Biden ultimately dominated in this measure. Not only was he the most successful fundraiser among party-aligned donors in the last two time periods, but he was actually drawing support from nearly a majority of them in January 2020, even in a very crowded

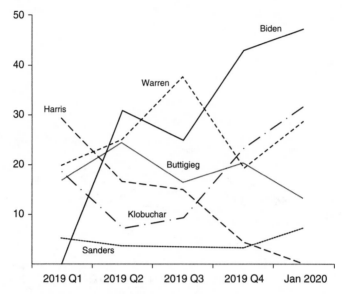

Figure 5.6 Lead candidates' share of party-aligned donors

field. By this measure, Biden appears to have become the party's pre-ferred candidate by the end of the Invisible Primary.

Some overall lessons stand out here. For one, Bernie Sanders was the only candidate with persistently lower shares of party-affiliated donors than of donors overall. As in 2016, Sanders was an accomplished fun-draiser in the 2020 cycle, and had considerably more money on hand than Biden did at the time of the first party contests. However, Sanders' money came almost entirely from those with no history of giving to the Democratic Party. Party-aligned donors overwhelmingly preferred Biden, even if he had less overall money to show for it.

This in itself is interesting and consistent with public impressions of the candidates. And it suggests that all money isn't equal – Sanders may have had *more* money, but Biden had the *right kind* of money, the kind that usually signals a nominee.

I next examined those donors who contributed to either Clinton or Sanders in 2016 *and* donated to a presidential candidate in 2020 to see how they leaned. The results of this analysis can be seen in Figure 5.7. The vertical axis shows the Clinton share of Clinton + Sanders donors;

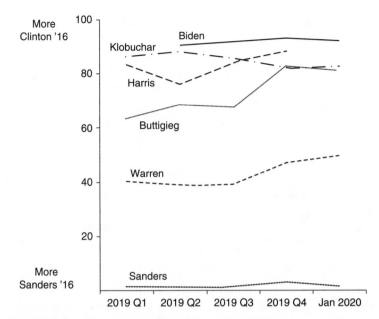

Figure 5.7 Candidates' share of Clinton donors from 2016

Notes: Vertical axis is the Clinton share of Clinton + Sanders donors from 2016 and how they donated to the 2020 presidential candidates. The lower the number, the more the candidate drew from Sanders '16 donors; the higher the number, the more the candidate drew from Clinton '16 donors.

candidates closer to 100 percent have the support of mainly Clinton donors from 2016, while those near zero have the support of mainly Sanders donors from 2016.

The interpretation here is similar to that above. Those who supported Hillary Clinton in 2016 were split in their loyalties among several leading 2020 candidates. Buttigieg drew from roughly two-thirds of Clinton donors and one-third of Sanders donors initially, and became more ensconced within the Clinton camp over time. Biden, Klobuchar, and Harris drew almost exclusively from former Clinton donors. Sanders, meanwhile, retained support solely from his own supporters from four years earlier. Sanders, that is, appeared to be holding his own coalition together, but failing to grow it. An interesting case is Elizabeth Warren, pulling a near-even mix of Clinton and Sanders donors from 2016. These data suggest that 2016 factions still cast a long shadow over 2020, with Sanders still the favorite of his faction, others competing for the support of the Clinton faction, and

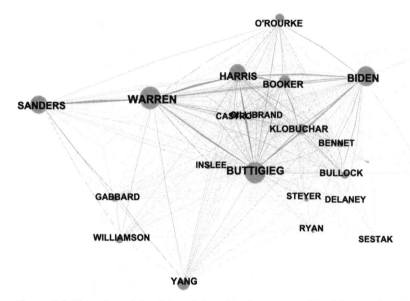

Figure 5.8 Network analysis of shared donations between presidential campaigns, 3rd quarter of 2019

Warren largely managing to bridge the divide throughout the Invisible Primary.

Here's yet one more way to examine the campaign finance data. I did a social network evaluation of just the donations in the third quarter of 2019. In that quarter, there were roughly 60,000 donations to the various Democratic presidential candidates of $200 or greater. The vast majority of those who donated to a candidate only did so for one candidate. However, a few donated to multiple candidates. In Figure 5.8, I draw out a network showing the links between candidates based on their shared donors. I used a computer program called Gephi that displays all the "nodes" (candidates) so that those with greater ties to each other (that is, more donors in common) appear closer to each other. The fuzzy balls indicating the candidates are actually dense clouds of donors giving just to one candidate, but the ties between those balls shows the shared donor patterns.

What we can see is that there was an inner core of candidates receiving the bulk of the donations and having most of the shared donors between them. This consists of the likes of Warren, Harris, Booker, Biden,

Klobuchar, and Buttigieg. Sanders is off to the far left. (Don't interpret any ideological statement from that – it just came out that way.) He had some shared donors with Warren, but pretty much none with the other major candidates. This is a way of saying that Sanders' support really was different from that of the other candidates. He certainly had a strong donor base, but those donors were not well tied to the rest of the party. And Warren was, again, at the nexus of the two factions, with ties both to the progressive community and the "establishment."

FACTIONS AND STAFFING

I'd like to examine one other aspect of factionalism in the 2020 campaign cycle. This involves campaign staff. The staffing of presidential campaigns doesn't often get a lot of media attention. However, campaign staff with a deep understanding of national politics and the skill set to run a presidential campaign are both essential and a scarce resource. Running a presidential campaign is complex. It requires making complicated decisions about fundraising and expenditure allocation, creating a communications program that's attuned to local customs and concerns, knowing how to manage an ambitious candidate and his or her family, understanding at least fifty sets of rules for primary and caucus participation along with ballot filing deadlines and qualifications, and more. Not very many people know how to do it, and even fewer are good at it.

In some ways, we can think of consultants, campaign managers, and others as gatekeepers to high office; with rare exceptions, candidates that don't get to hire these people don't get very far. As gatekeepers, elite campaign staffers play an important role in a political party. They help with the party's winnowing of candidates and determining who gets to be the nominee.

So where did the experienced campaign staff from 2016 go in 2020? To examine this, I drew on political scientist Eric Appleman's Democracy in Action data collection.[19] Appleman has put together lists of top staff

---

[19] www.democracyinaction.us/about.html. This is not obviously a complete record of all staff employed by these campaigns, but it is the most comprehensive such collection available.

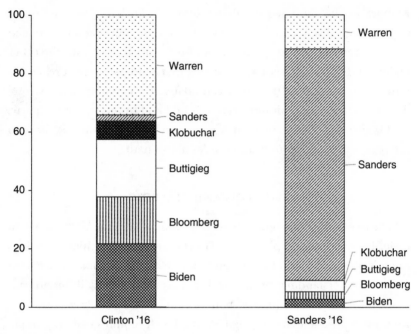

Figure 5.9 Percentage of Clinton '16 and Sanders '16 staffers working for various presidential campaigns in 2020

for all the presidential candidates and provided brief résumés for each. With the help of research assistant Colin Phipps, I examined the histories of 260 staffers who worked for Democratic presidential campaigns in 2016 and 2020. Among these staffers, 181 worked for Hillary Clinton in 2016, and 76 worked for Bernie Sanders that year, while 3 worked across both campaigns. Figure 5.9 shows the percentages of Clinton and Sanders staffers working for various 2020 Democratic presidential campaigns as of early 2020.

As the chart shows, Sanders largely retained his team – 79 percent of those who worked for Sanders in 2016 were working for his campaign four years later. Twelve percent of Sanders '16 staffers went to work for Elizabeth Warren, again demonstrating her ties to both factions, while just a smattering worked for other candidates. Clinton's 2016 staff, meanwhile, was spread across many leading Democratic campaigns in 2020. Thirty-four percent of them went to work for Warren, 22 percent for

Biden, 20 percent for Buttigieg, and 16 percent for Michael Bloomberg, while a handful went to work for either Sanders or Amy Klobuchar.

While this analysis suggests that the "establishment" wing of party staffers was hardly unified in its candidate preferences as of early 2020, there are clear signs of persistent factionalism. Sanders '16 staffers working across both campaigns largely stuck with Sanders. Clinton '16 staffers largely picked anyone *except* Sanders.

LASTING FACTIONALISM

In February 2020, Bernie Sanders tweeted, "I've got news for the Democratic establishment. They can't stop us." A week later, upon his South Carolina victory, Joe Biden said, "If Democrats want a nominee who's a Democrat, a lifelong Democrat, a proud Democrat, an Obama-Biden Democrat, join us." It wasn't like these candidates had suddenly discovered that the Democratic Party had factions. As the evidence I've shown in this chapter suggests, strong intraparty factional patterns persist from one election to the next, even from national to state-level elections. These patterns become more apparent when party factions communicate clear signals of difference, such as consistent party donors leaning toward one candidate and the "ideologue" faction publicly endorsing another. This divisiveness has important consequences, as well, with backers of a losing primary candidate far less likely than the winner's backers to help out the nominee in the general election, and also more likely to defect to the other party's candidate.

This study, of course, relies on a limited set of candidates and only covers one time period. It doesn't give us a basis to say whether the Clinton/Sanders divide is more or less potent than, say, the Clinton/Obama divide from 2008, or the Kerry/Dean divide from 2004. But the examination of 2014 and 2018 Democratic gubernatorial primaries suggests that there is some durability to these factions that precedes the Clinton/Sanders contest, and arguably structured it. The implication is that Democrats at the national and state level tend to be arrayed along the lines of durable factional groups, although the data here cannot determine the age of those factions.

It is also far from certain just how long we should expect these divisions to last. As the section on the 2020 Democratic presidential race suggests, much of the factionalism from 2016 persists. At the end of the 2020 Invisible Primary, Sanders' 2016 donors were still strongly for Sanders, and Clinton's 2016 supporters were moving toward Biden. The party "regulars," that is, were coming to an agreement on whom their candidate was, although from the beginning they had been quite clear on whom it was not.

At the very least, though, this chapter suggests that candidates and campaigns, whether at the national or state level, do not go into a nomination contest with a clean slate and get to decide how to position themselves. Important factions precede them and will determine to no small extent how that contest is shaped. And those factions remained potent in 2020, with the potential to divide the party's nomination process at least as much as in 2016.

It is finally worth asking how much such factionalism actually harms a party in a general election. There was at least anecdotal evidence mentioned above that the factional splits in the 1924 Democratic nomination contest undermined the party in that year's presidential election. Political scientists are not of one mind on this question today. Some recent studies find that by exposing flaws in the leading candidates and offending the supporters of the losers, divisive primaries can hurt the party's nominee in November.[20] Other studies find that more crowded and competitive primaries do not actually harm a party much in the general election,[21] particularly the closer the primary is to November,[22] and may even help the party with turnout.[23] But as evidence I showed

[20] Alexander Fouirnaies and Andrew B. Hall, 2020. "How Divisive Primaries Hurt Parties: Evidence from Near-Runoffs in US Legislatures." *The Journal of Politics* 82 (1): 43–56.

[21] Lonna Rae Atkeson, 1998. "Divisive Primaries and General Election Outcomes: Another Look at Presidential Campaigns." *American Journal of Political Science* 42 (1): 256–71.

[22] Gregg B. Johnson, Meredith-Joy Petersheim, and Jesse T. Wasson, 2010. "Divisive Primaries and Incumbent General Election Performance: Prospects and Costs in U.S. House Races." *American Politics Research* 38 (5): 931–55.

[23] Caitlin E. Jewitt and Sarah A. Treul, 2014. "Competitive Primaries and Party Divisions in Congressional Elections." *Electoral Studies* 35: 140–9.

above suggests, some of the losing factions' donors not only aren't enthusiastic about the nominee, but may actually end up supporting the opposing ticket on occasion. We have additional evidence that roughly one in ten of Bernie Sanders' supporters from 2016 ended up voting for Donald Trump.[24] While this is not a high figure historically, it does suggest that these factions pack some power and should not be taken lightly.

[24] John Sides, 2017. "Did Enough Bernie Sanders Supporters Vote for Trump to Cost Clinton the Election?" *The Monkey Cage / Washington Post*, August 24. www.washingtonpost.com/news/monkey-cage/wp/2017/08/24/did-enough-bernie-sanders-supporters-vote-for-trump-to-cost-clinton-the-election.

CHAPTER 6

How Narratives Change Voters

What I want is not impossible! I want someone who is not tainted by polarizing choices in the past, but who also has experience, who is knowledgeable but doesn't sound like she is lecturing, someone vibrant but not green, someone dignified but not dowdy, passionate but not a yeller, precise but not mechanical, someone lacking in off-putting ambition but capable of asking for what she wants, not accompanied but not alone, in a day but not in a month or a year, when the moon is neither waxing nor waning, carrying a sieve full of water and a hen's tooth. Easy!

That's why I'm so worried about our current slate of choices. A woman, sure, but – Kamala Harris? Elizabeth Warren? Kirsten Gillibrand? There are specific problems with each of them, entirely personal to each of them, all insurmountable. We need someone fresh. Someone without baggage. Joe Biden, maybe. But female! If you see. I can't wait to vote for a woman in 2020. A nameless, shapeless, faceless woman I know nothing about who will surely be perfect.

Alexandra Petri[1]

During a visit to Iowa in 2017, I spoke to an experienced political activist in Des Moines who had had a pretty negative interpretation of the 2016 election. "I really don't think nominating a woman is going to get us what

---

[1]   Alexandra Petri, 2018. "I'm Fine With Women in Power, Just Not This One Specific Woman Currently in Power." *The Washington Post*, November 16.

we need," she said. "The reality is we are an old state and it's that lack of willingness to accept women in those leadership roles." The results of 2016 suggested to her that it was risky to nominate a woman for president if the election was likely to be close.

A woman I spoke to in Manchester, New Hampshire, that same year had a similar take. She's a lifelong feminist and was an enthusiastic backer of Hillary Clinton's in both the 2008 and 2016 cycles. But, she said,

> based on what happened with Hillary, I think we now need to nominate a man. . . . Barack Obama's an incredibly strong man. He can't do what he did and not be a strong man. But he didn't project raging masculinity and I think you kind of have to do that. I hate to say that but . . . I'm gonna get kicked out of the women's club.

As these interviews suggest, post-election narratives can be very powerful, pulling people away from preferences and issue stances they've cared about for a long time. Up until now, I've mostly focused on how party activists argue over these narratives, how they inform party insiders about what direction to take their party, and so forth. In this chapter, I'm going to get into the very direct effect of a narrative on voters. Reading a narrative about the last election, it turns out, can directly affect how partisan voters are thinking about the next one. It can change what sorts of issues they think are important and what kind of candidates they think should be nominated.

In this chapter, I focus on one particular post-election narrative, the so-called "identity politics" narrative. This wasn't the most common explanation offered by the media or by the activists I've interviewed, although it was accepted by roughly a third of the activists and promoted in a similar proportion of news coverage. But importantly, it's a powerful narrative that has a built-in and highly consequential prescription for what the party should do next to avoid such losses. And it cuts to a lot of Democrats' concerns and insecurities about their own party.

This narrative argues that Clinton lost to Trump because of her over-emphasis on advocating for the needs of marginalized groups – women, African Americans, Latinos, LGBT members, and so on – without offering a broader vision accessible to all Americans. This, the argument goes, led white working-class voters, who might normally have voted

Democratic, to switch to the Republican side, where Trump was promising that such "forgotten" Americans would be remembered.

Again, for the purposes of this chapter, I'm not really interested in whether this interpretation of the 2016 election is correct. I'm trying to understand what kind of effect making this argument has on Democratic voters.

To investigate the effect of this narrative, I ran two separate survey experiments. The first of these was conducted in early 2018. I drew a sample of Americans and offered half of them a brief vignette saying that Clinton lost due to identity politics. Then I showed all the participants some brief information on six possible candidates for the Democratic presidential nomination in 2020. Those who saw the identity politics narrative seemed to hold women and candidates of color in lower regard than those who didn't. Those who saw the narrative also disproportionately wanted to see the Democratic Party reposition itself to the right.

I conducted the second survey experiment in two waves, one in late 2018 and one in early 2020, with political scientist Pavielle Haines. We surveyed a sample of Democrats and, as in the first study, gave half a vignette about identity politics in the 2016 and 2018 election cycles. Then we ran what's known as a *conjoint study*, asking people to evaluate different types of hypothetical presidential candidates: a man or a woman, a white or a person of color, someone advocating a universal economic message or someone advocating fixing workplace discrimination, and so forth. The effect here is telling – African Americans and white women, after seeing this narrative, abandoned some of their policy preferences and moved toward more conservative, male candidates.

The key lesson here is that the identity politics narrative had a substantial effect on Democratic voters, and that this effect interacted with both race and gender in an important way. It worked to systematically undermine women presidential candidates and candidates with more liberal policy agendas under consideration for 2020. To be sure, these are survey experiments – I can't say for certain how much they capture what went on in society at large. But the results suggest that the women, people of color, and more progressive candidates seeking the

Democratic presidential nomination in 2020 did so with one arm tied behind their backs. The shadow of 2016 limited their appeal.

IDENTITY POLITICS AND THE FRAMING OF AN ELECTION

Constructing a post-election narrative is quite common, especially for the losing party. Regardless of whether the explanation of why the party lost is true, that narrative can nonetheless provide direction for a party as it gears up for the next election, and it can be used as fuel in intraparty contests between factions.

But how do such post-election narratives actually affect voters? Here, it's helpful to think about the political psychology concept of *framing*.[2] Framing is a way to describe an issue in a way that encourages people "to emphasize certain considerations above others when evaluating that issue."[3] The language we use to describe an issue can sometimes produce major changes in public opinion. For example, a group of researchers did a study about how willing people were to limit free speech rights for hate groups. In one version of the question, they asked if hate groups should be allowed to hold a political rally "given the importance of free speech"; 85 percent said yes to that. But when they asked if hate groups should be allowed to hold a political rally "given the risk of violence," only 45 percent said yes.[4] The language matters.

Political activists, journalists, elected officials, and others sought some way to explain the surprising results of the 2016 election. However, one of the influential narratives to emerge in the days after the election was that of *identity politics*. (I described this fraught concept at some length in Chapter 2.) While identity politics can mean many things, here I'm using it in a specific way – it's the argument that blames the

---

[2] James N. Druckman, 2011. "What's It All About? Framing in Political Science." In Keren, Gideon, ed., *Perspectives on Framing*. Hove: Psychology Press, pp. 279–302.

[3] Dennis Chong and James N. Druckman, 2007a. "Framing Public Opinion in Competitive Democracies." *American Political Science Review* 101: 637–55.

[4] Paul M. Sniderman and Sean M. Theriault, 2004. "The Structure of Political Argument and the Logic of Issue Framing." In Willem E. Saris and Paul M. Sniderman, eds., *Studies in Public Opinion: Attitudes, Nonattitudes, Measurement Error, and Change*, Princeton: Princeton University Press: 133–65.

identity claims of Democrats, especially women and people of color, for an election loss. One of the clearest distillations of this argument comes from humanities professor Mark Lilla's *New York Times* op/ed "The End of Identity Liberalism,"[5] published just a week after the 2016 election. At the core of Lilla's argument was a critique of the Clinton campaign and Democrats at large for appealing to narrow demographic subgroups of the electorate at the expense of the whole:

> Hillary Clinton was at her best and most uplifting when she spoke about American interests in world affairs and how they relate to our understanding of democracy. But when it came to life at home, she tended on the campaign trail to lose that large vision and slip into the rhetoric of diversity, calling out explicitly to African-American, Latino, LGBT and women voters at every stop. This was a strategic mistake. If you are going to mention groups in America, you had better mention all of them. If you don't, those left out will notice and feel excluded. Which, as the data show, was exactly what happened with the white working class and those with strong religious convictions. Fully two-thirds of white voters without college degrees voted for Donald Trump, as did over 80 percent of white evangelicals.

Complaints about the Democrats' "political correctness," accusations that Hillary Clinton sounded too much like a "schoolmarm," and arguments that white voters' "economic anxiety" (regardless of their actual economic circumstances) made them more receptive to white identity claims are all folded into this narrative.

In this chapter, I'm investigating the effect of this election narrative on voters, especially Democrats. To be sure, Republicans rely on loss narratives and identity politics no less than Democrats do, but I'm primarily interested in understanding how the 2016 election loss caused Democrats to evaluate potential candidates for 2020.

I make the assumption that there are important differences across race and sex in the way these loss narratives are interpreted. White men are often treated as the default reference group in the United States and many other countries. There's a Ladies' Pro Golf Association, historically

---

[5] Mark Lilla, 2016. "The End of Identity Liberalism." *The New York Times*, November 18.

black colleges and universities, political consultants who specialize in women's issues or minority issues, and so forth. But for white men, there's just golf, college, and issues.

Relatedly, race and gender are heavily tied up in party identities and coalitions. Women have been voting more Democratic than men for decades and have become an increasingly prominent segment of the Democratic Party. They comprised nearly 60 percent of the Democratic primary vote in 2016[6] and a substantial proportion of the party's leadership. African Americans made up roughly a quarter of the Democratic primary vote in 2016[7] and also a good portion of the party's leadership. (The DNC was chaired by Rep. Debbie Wasserman Schultz until her forced resignation in 2016, followed by Donna Brazile, an African American woman.) The fact that the party's most recent presidential nominees were Barack Obama, a liberal black man from Chicago, and Hillary Clinton, a lifelong feminist and a multi-decade target of conservatives for refusing to conform to traditional gender roles as First Lady, was not lost on Democratic African Americans and women. Nor was the fact that Clinton's general election opponent had decades of documented sexist and racist tirades, was the target of multiple sexual predation accusations, had been investigated by the Nixon administration for discriminatory housing practices, and had been caught on tape bragging about committing sexual assault. It would be difficult to concoct a more gender- and race-salient election than the 2016 presidential contest.

Yet many influential Democratic Party figures are convinced, and often publicly proclaim, that there are political risks to nominating a woman or person of color for high office because such candidates are less electable. (This is far more a perception than a data-driven conclusion, but the perception is difficult to dislodge.) Thus the election loss narrative that focused on identity politics – a claim that Clinton and her party lost for focusing too much on the needs of marginalized

---

[6] Ronald Brownstein, 2019. "2020 Democrats Face the Most Diverse Electorate in History." CNN, February 12. www.cnn.com/interactive/2019/02/politics/dem-primaries-exit-polls/.

[7] Jennifer Pinto, 2016. "Who's Voting in the Democratic Primaries?" CBS News, May 17. www.cbsnews.com/news/democratic-primary-electorate-key-findings-from-the-exit-polls/.

communities – may have had a particularly pernicious effect on Democratic women and people of color. It essentially placed the blame for the loss on them. The subtext of the argument was, if they had asked for less – a more moderate candidate, a male candidate, a candidate who didn't focus so much on addressing systemic inequalities in American life – their party would have won. For white men, however, the identity politics narrative was less jarring, essentially confirming many of their longstanding beliefs that politics is properly focused on their concerns (which they see as general, not special, concerns) and that straying from those invites problems. This identity politics narrative will likely have very different effects depending on who is hearing it.

In this way, the identity politics narrative is fundamentally different, and more consequential, than most of the other election loss narratives. If you believe that for Democrats to win, they needed better polling data, a more thoughtful message, higher-impact advertisements, a better staffed and trained field operation, a more inspiring nominee, less Russian interference, and so on – it could have any or all those things in the next election without forcing key constituent members to reassess their place in the party. But if the claim is that the party lost because it embraced and highlighted its diversity, because it elevated the needs of underrepresented groups, that can force some deeply uncomfortable assessments, both of voters and candidates, and cause the party to change its stance toward the people it has been championing for decades. The price for accepting this narrative is a steep one.

APPROACH AND ANALYSIS

To test this idea, I have conducted two separate survey experiments. The first of these was a short survey, designed and conducted online using Qualtrics, and I recruited subjects using Amazon Mechanical Turk.[8] The

---

[8] Amazon Mechanical Turk (or mTurk) is a crowd-sourced electronic marketplace in which people can be hired to, among other things, fill out short surveys. There are some biases associated with mTurk samples, but some recent studies suggest that they are a reliable method of examining political and psychological behavior. See, for example, Christoph, Bartneck, Andreas Duenser, Elena Moltchanova, and Karolina Zawieska, 2015. "Comparing the Similarity of Responses Received from

survey was conducted between January 24 and 27, 2018. Eight hundred and three subjects completed the survey, 443 of whom described themselves as Democrats or independents who lean Democratic.

Near the beginning of the survey, I randomly presented half of the subjects with the following explanation of the outcome of the 2016 presidential election:

> According to some political experts, Hillary Clinton lost the 2016 election because she focused too much on identity politics. She appealed directly to African Americans, Latinos, gays and lesbians, and women voters whenever she spoke, but she never painted a broader picture of American life or addressed basic issues like jobs and health care that are of concern to all Americans.

This is the "identity politics" condition. The other subjects, in the control condition, were shown a brief message about the use of painkillers in the treatment of children after surgery.

I was first interested in knowing whether seeing this identity politics narrative affected the way people evaluated possible Democratic presidential candidates. I asked the people in the study to provide a feeling thermometer evaluation of six prospective candidates for the Democratic presidential nomination in 2020, each of whom had at least been considering a run as of early 2018. (They did this by moving a slider scale from any position between zero and 100, with 100 being the warmest possible feelings toward a candidate.) These were:

- Former Missouri Secretary of State Jason Kander
- Former Maryland Governor Martin O'Malley
- US Senator Elizabeth Warren (Massachusetts)
- US Senator Kirsten Gillibrand (New York)
- US Senator Cory Booker (New Jersey)
- Former Massachusetts Governor Deval Patrick

Studies in Amazon's Mechanical Turk to Studies Conducted Online and with Direct Recruitment." *PloS one* 10: e0121595; Scott Clifford, Ryan M. Jewell, and Philip D. Waggoner, 2015. "Are Samples Drawn from Mechanical Turk Valid for Research on Political Ideology?" *Research & Politics* 2: doi:2053168015622072; David J. Hauser, and Norbert Schwarz, 2016. "Attentive Turkers: mTurk Participants Perform Better on Online Attention Checks Than Do Subject Pool Participants." *Behavior Research Methods* 48: 400–7.

Survey participants saw brief descriptions of the candidates and their photos. Notably, the candidates included two white men, two white women, and two African American men, although they were not described as such in the text. I selected candidates that have appeared in numerous newspaper listings of likely Democratic competitors for 2020, even if few had national political profiles at the time this survey was done. (My guesses were reasonably good – four of the six ended up formally running for president.)

I also wanted to see if the narrative caused them to change their evaluation of the Democratic Party. I did this through two questions. First, I asked them to ideologically place the current Democratic Party, using a slider scale from 0 (the most liberal position) to 10 (the most conservative position). Then I asked them to place where the Democratic Party, in their opinion, should be, again ranging from 0 to 10. If a participant said that the Democratic Party should be to the right of where the participant said the party currently is, I categorized them as desiring moderation for the Democrats.

RESULTS OF FIRST EXPERIMENT

Figure 6.1 shows the average thermometer score for each of the candidates across both groups of participants, those in the experimental (identity politics) condition and those in the control (use of painkillers) condition. This figure is limited to the 443 participants identifying themselves as Democrats or Democratic-leaners. Interestingly, the average thermometer score for all six candidates was lower among participants in the experimental condition. This may suggest that viewing the identity politics condition lowered evaluations for Democratic candidates across the board, even among self-identified Democrats. Yet it is clear that this effect was not uniform across candidates. Notably, there is a substantial difference between the control and experimental conditions for evaluations of Elizabeth Warren, both for Democrats and for the whole sample.

In Figure 6.2, I have calculated the effect of the identity politics message by subtracting the control condition from the experimental condition. I have broken down the results by demographic subgroups. For example, white men in the control group were 8.4 points more

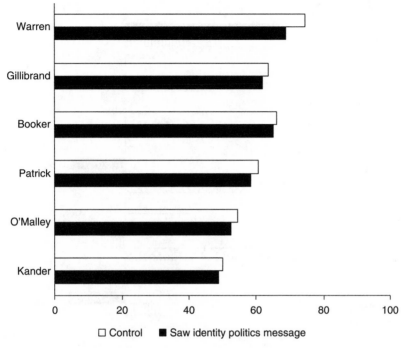

Figure 6.1 Feeling thermometers for candidates among Democrats

positive in their thermometer evaluations of Warren than white men in the identity politics group were. Seeing the identity politics message cost her 8.4 points among this subgroup. I don't want to make too much of the results among different subgroups as the numbers get somewhat small here – there were only eighteen African American men among the Democrats in this sample. But the overall trends can be revealing.

As the results suggest, the most consistent effect was for Warren, who lost support among all subgroups from the identity politics message. Kirsten Gillibrand and Deval Patrick lost significant support among white men and African American women who saw the message. Cory Booker actually saw a very modest increase among African American men, but a 15-point decrease among African American women. Overall, the two African American candidates saw significant drops in support among African American women, the women candidates saw

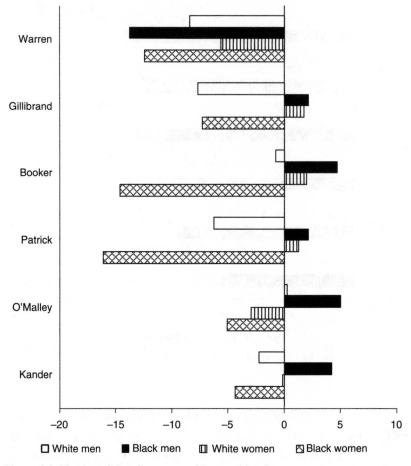

Figure 6.2 Identity politics effect among demographic subgroups

drops among many groups, although more consistently for Warren, and
the effects were smaller and mixed for the white candidates.

These figures suggest that the narrative had a mostly negative effect,
particularly for women and candidates of color.[9] But given that it seemed

---

[9] I ran a regression analysis to control for a lot of competing variables, and these results
held. Those who saw the identity politics narrative, on average, held each of the
candidates in lower esteem than did those who did not see the narrative. However,
the effect for Warren was at least twice the size of the others', and it is the only one that
achieved statistical significance.

to affect a broad range of candidates, I was curious what kind of effect it had on evaluations of the Democratic Party.

To examine this, I asked the Democratic subjects two questions about the ideological placement of the Democratic Party: where they think the party is now (as of January 2018), and where they think it should be. On a 10-point scale, with 0 the most liberal position and 10 the most conservative, the Democratic subjects on average rated the current Democratic Party as relatively liberal, with a mean of 3.3. They thought the ideal position for the Democratic Party was slightly left of that, at 2.8. Democrats, on average, wanted the party to become somewhat more liberal.

So did viewing the identity politics narrative change this calculation? To test this, I compared the percentage of Democrats who believe the Democratic Party should move right to those who believe it should move left. Only 25 percent of Democratic participants in the control group wanted to see their party become more conservative. However, 31 percent of those who saw the identity politics narrative wanted a more conservative party. This effect appears to be most powerful among white participants, who became more than 10 percentage points more supportive of seeing a more conservative Democratic Party after seeing the identity politics argument. A separate and more sophisticated statistical analysis found these results to be statistically significant.[10]

FIRST EXPERIMENT SUMMARY

The evidence I presented above suggests that hearing the argument that Hillary Clinton lost in 2016 because of an emphasis on identity politics causes Democrats to think less of some Democratic presidential candidates, especially women and candidates of color. Evaluations of Senator Elizabeth Warren, in particular, dropped among all subgroups after exposure to the election narrative. There were substantial drops for Deval Patrick and Cory Booker, as well, particularly among African

---

[10] Seth Masket, 2018. "Learning from Loss? How Interpretations of the Last Election Affect the Next One." Paper presented at the annual meeting of the American Political Science Association in Boston, Massachusetts, September 1.

American women who heard the argument. Meanwhile, exposure to the identity politics argument apparently made some Democrats, especially white Democrats, want to see their party become more conservative.

These findings are suggestive about the trajectory of the Democratic Party between 2016 and 2020. Again, the identity politics narrative wasn't the only narrative out there, and it wasn't necessarily the most popular or persuasive. But it clearly packed some power, convincing some Democrats that they needed a more moderate party, and they should maybe consider a white male for a nominee.

RESULTS OF SECOND EXPERIMENT

The first survey experiment suggested a potentially important role for the identity politics narrative in affecting Democrats' evaluations of women and candidates of color. To examine this possibility in greater detail, I conducted a second experiment with political scientist Pavielle Haines. We conducted this in two waves, one in November of 2018 and one in early 2020.

Our approach was to use what is known as a choice-based *conjoint analysis*. A conjoint analysis is useful when trying to figure out people's preferences when there are a lot of variables in play. For example, if voters seem to prefer a white male moderate over an African American female progressive, how do we know whether race, gender, or ideology is more important to that choice? Conjoint analysis breaks their options down into a series of A-or-B choices. We can present them with a choice between two candidates which vary by gender, race, ideological stance, and campaign platforms. This helps us see which candidate traits are most important to voters, and also which can be affected by some kind of political message.

In this survey experiment, we started the survey by telling participants that the Democratic Party was strategizing for the 2020 election and that we were interested in their opinions on several potential Democratic candidates. Participants were then asked to read a fictitious news clipping from the *New York Times* to "refresh their memory" about the Democrats' performance in the 2016 and 2018 elections before giving their opinions. In the control condition, the news clipping simply mentioned

Democratic losses: "Hillary Clinton lost the 2016 presidential campaign. Although the Democrats managed to take back the House in the 2018 midterm, they were unable to win the Senate. The stakes of the 2020 election are incredibly high for the Democratic Party." In the experimental treatment, the news clipping attributed Democratic losses to identity politics:

> According to some political experts, Hillary Clinton lost the 2016 election because she focused too much on identity politics. Others note that although the Democrats managed to take back the House in the 2018 midterm, their continued focus on identity politics likely prevented them from winning the Senate. Hillary Clinton and other Democratic candidates appealed directly to African Americans, Latinos, women, and LGBT voters, but failed to pain a broader picture of American life or address basic issues like jobs and health care that are of concern to all Americans. The stakes of the 2020 election are incredibly high for the Democratic Party.

After that, we straightforwardly asked participants whether they thought Clinton lost in 2016 because she focused too much on issues pertaining to women and minorities. That is, we were basically asking them whether they believed the identity politics narrative. This was a way of finding out just how effective that political message was. If it didn't really change anyone's minds, then the people in the control condition should have similar answers to those who saw the message.

As Figure 6.3 below shows, there were substantial differences in reactions to this question among demographic subgroups. White men were the most likely to initially accept the idea that Clinton lost because of her identity politics appeals – nearly 30 percent believed this, and this figure didn't change once they'd been shown the identity politics election narrative. African American men, however, started off much less likely to accept the argument – only about 16 percent believed it – but moved about 10 points more toward accepting it after seeing the message. There was an even greater effect for white women, as only about 10 percent initially accepted it, but that rose to 26 percent after seeing the message. The message had somewhat less effect among African American women, who remained the least supportive group of the argument, but

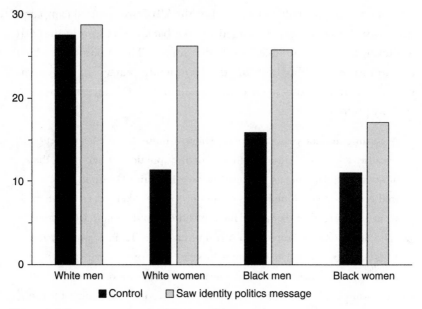

Figure 6.3 Percentage accepting identity politics narrative

they still reacted to the message. Perhaps one of the most interesting takeaways here is that African American men and white women were much less accepting of the identity politics narrative initially than white men were, but upon seeing the political message, their preferences came to closely mirror that of white men.

Now we move to the more complicated conjoint study results. We showed participants a screen with two candidate profiles, as in the example below (Table 6.1). The instructions asked participants, "Which of these candidates would you be more likely to vote for in the 2020 Democratic presidential primary?" Each respondent evaluated ten pairs of candidates. Candidate characteristics were randomly varied on four characteristics related to identity politics: *gender, race, ideology,* and *key policy issue.* Each attribute could take on multiple values. For instance, key policy issues could take one of four values: "Support women and racial minorities in accessing high paying jobs with good benefits"; "Support economic reform to incentivize high paying jobs with good benefits"; "Reform the criminal justice system to discourage disproportionately harsh sentences for racial

TABLE 6.1 *Example of trial heat between two candidates in conjoint study*

	Candidate 1	Candidate 2
Policy issue	Support women and racial minorities in accessing high paying jobs with good benefits	Reform the criminal justice system to discourage disproportionately harsh sentences for racial minorities
Gender	Man	Man
Ideology	Very liberal	Slightly liberal
Race/ethnicity	Black	Hispanic

TABLE 6.2 *Attributes of candidates used in conjoint experiment*

Attribute	Values
Gender	1) Man 2) Woman
Race	1) White 2) Asian American 3) Hispanic 4) African American
Ideology	1) Slightly liberal 2) Moderately liberal 3) Very liberal
Policy platform	1) Support economic growth to create high paying jobs with good benefits ("good jobs") 2) Reform the criminal justice system so that non-violent offenders receive fairer sentences ("justice reform") 3) Support policies to combat workplace discrimination against women and people of color ("fair employment") 4) Reform the criminal justice system so that people of color are treated fairly ("fair sentencing")

minorities"; or "Reform the criminal justice system to discourage harsh sentences for minor crimes committed by non-violent offenders." For each of the issues we offer (economy, crime), we offer an anti-discrimination (identity politics) version and an ostensibly neutral and universalistic version. The full range of candidate traits and values can be seen in Table 6.2.

To get a sense of the results of this study, Figures 6.4 and 6.5 boil down the results of a statistical analysis, the details of which are described in a separate paper.[11] These figures are a bit complicated so I want to

---

[11] Pavielle Haines and Seth Masket, 2019. "'You Had Better Mention All of Them:' Gendered Effects in Election Loss Narratives." Paper prepared for the annual meeting of the American Political Science Association in Washington, DC, August 29.

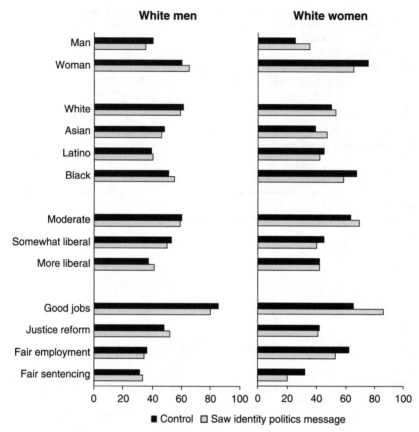

Figure 6.4 Effect of identity politics narrative on support for candidates of various traits, white Democrats only

explain what they show. They translate the results of the conjoint analysis into the predicted probabilities that a candidate with a given trait would "win" against a candidate without that trait among the people we surveyed. I have divided up the responses among white men and women, and black men and women.

Now, what should we interpret from these figures? Let's start with white Democrats, seen in Figure 6.4. Just to draw an example, if we look at the top left of the figure, we see that white men in the control condition (that is, they didn't see the identity politics message) had about a 40 percent chance of preferring a male candidate. That dropped to a 35 percent chance among those in the treatment condition (that is, they saw the identity politics message). This isn't a large or statistically significant difference.

And in general, the identity politics narrative didn't seem to change the preferences of white men very much at all. However, the identity politics message seemed to change the preferences of white women significantly. In particular, white women became less likely to support a woman candidate and more likely to support a man. It also made them more likely to support a candidate pushing an economic message, and less likely to support one favoring progressive policies like criminal justice reform, sentencing reform, and redressing workplace discrimination. White women became moderately less supportive of nonwhite candidates and liberal candidates, as well. Overall, the identity politics argument had a powerful effect on Democratic white women, inducing them to abandon a number of progressive policy goals and inclusiveness and become more likely to favor the nomination of a moderate white man.

The lesson is a bit different when we examine African American respondents (Figure 6.5). African American women, in many ways, reacted similarly to white women in their responses to the identity politics message. Even though their results do not meet tests of statistical significance, black women who saw the message generally became less supportive of Asian American and Latino candidates, as well as those who support addressing discrimination in the workplace. They became more supportive of candidates favoring a general economic message. Black men had a similar reaction with regards to their support for candidates favoring progressive reform policies, although they interestingly became somewhat more supportive of Latino candidates and Asian American candidates. The results for African Americans are perhaps not quite as stark as those for white respondents, but still tell basically the same story – the identity politics message didn't change the attitudes of white Democratic men, but it made others move away from more progressive candidates, and in many cases made them less likely to support a woman of a candidate of color.

SECOND EXPERIMENT SUMMARY

The results of this second experiment show that the identity politics narrative had a powerful effect on Democrats, an effect that varied

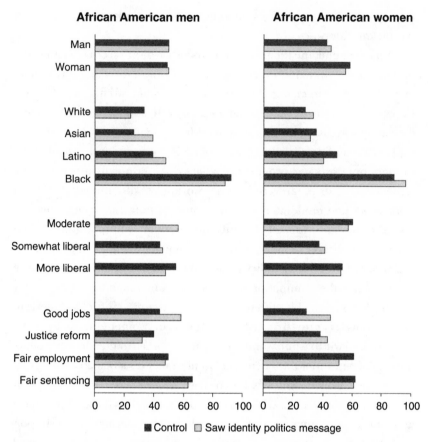

Figure 6.5 Effect of identity politics narrative on support for candidates of various traits, African American Democrats only

importantly by race and gender. The argument did little to affect the types of candidates white Democratic men were willing to support. One explanation for this is that the narrative simply confirms the beliefs many white Democratic men already held. They were already concerned about elevating issues related to inequality above those related to the economy, and they already had some worries about nominating non-white candidates and women. Other Democrats, however, sharply changed their preferences in responses to the identity politics narrative, often becoming substantially more likely to favor a moderate white male nominee. White women abandoned some of their support for a woman candidate. African American women abandoned their support for some candidates of color. And white Democratic women, along with African American Democrats, saw the message and became substantially less supportive of candidates favoring redress of workplace and criminal justice discrimination.

The results here are consistent with a number of findings about race and gender politics. A recent political science study found that nonwhite Democrats are less likely to support an African American primary candidate if they think the general election will be very competitive.[12] And I mentioned a number of studies back in Chapter 2 that suggested that many people believe African American candidates and women to be more liberal (and thus less competitive in a general election) than they actually are.

We also see some interesting evidence in here of white men's unwillingness to compromise on their candidate preferences; although they comprise a shrinking minority of the Democratic party, they continue to have disproportionate influence due to their status as society's "default group." By contrast, white women and African Americans within the Democratic coalition are regularly told that they need to sacrifice some of their preferences for the sake of their party's competitiveness.

THE NARRATIVE SHAPES THE NOMINATION

There are a number of important takeaways from the studies in this chapter. For one, they demonstrate that election narratives affect more than pundits and party elites. Even a fairly modest treatment – a few sentences at the beginning of the survey – showed rather dramatic effects on voters' evaluations of the political scene. It didn't take very much to get Democratic voters to turn against women and candidates of color or abandon anti-discrimination policy goals.

And importantly, party insiders *know* this about Democratic voters. They heard arguments being made, and may have even made or

---

[12] John A. Henderson, Logan Dancey, Stephen Goggin, Geoffrey Sheagley, and Alexander G. Theodoridis, 2019. "Primary Divisions: How Voters Evaluate Policy and Non-Policy Differences Between Co-Party Politicians." Unpublished manuscript.

amplified those arguments themselves, that made Democratic voters more likely to support a moderate white male candidate. If you see voters believing these arguments and are tempted to believe them yourself, it's difficult to ignore them. Many Democratic Party insiders certainly advocate for greater inclusivity and equality; as I've argued, it's the party's central ideology. But it is also a goal many – including members of the underrepresented groups themselves – are willing to scale back on if they come to believe that it's costing them elections. This was not necessarily the most common narrative emerging from 2016 but it was a powerful one, and it made the nomination of a moderate white man for 2020 more likely.

I should close by noting that these narrative interpretations aren't written in stone, and evidence suggesting one interpretation can yield to conflicting evidence from a subsequent election. For example, at the beginning of this chapter, I mentioned a Democratic activist and feminist in Manchester, New Hampshire, whose take on the 2016 election was that Democrats needed to nominate a white man for 2020. I followed up with her on this question in early 2019, and she said she'd changed her mind, thanks to the results of the 2018 elections. The increased turnout and the successes of many women candidates and candidates of color suggested to her that a broader range of presidential candidates could succeed:

> I'm of the opinion that people want someone competent and not crazy ... who will move the country forward, and it doesn't matter if they're a woman or a man or white or a person of color. I don't think that's really going to matter. .... Given who is in the field I think it would be disconcerting if there wasn't a woman on the ticket or someone of color, or both.

This activist ended up backing Kirsten Gillibrand, just a few weeks before the New York senator withdrew from the race. She would end up supporting Elizabeth Warren shortly before the primary.

In some ways, it's possible that the damage had already been done – the field of candidates had been shaped earlier by those with a similar interpretation of 2016 thanks to the identity politics narrative. But it may also be different narratives emerging from 2018 that compelled Joe Biden to commit to naming a woman as a running mate.

CHAPTER 7

The Invisible Primary Becomes Visible

We can't choose a candidate we don't believe in just because we're too scared to do anything else.

Elizabeth Warren

I would rather win with Lucifer than lose to the Republicans again.

Don Fowler

The previous chapters set the stage for this one. In those chapters, we saw party activists divided over the perceived lessons of 2016. We saw party officers arguing over matters of election interpretation and race. We saw party donors split into factions. We saw media narratives undermining how many Democrats, especially women and African Americans, saw themselves as fitting into the party and what sorts of candidates they should support.

In this chapter, I examine how all these divisions and interpretations played out in the year leading up to the first voting in Iowa and New Hampshire. I look at several aspects of how the contest unfolded. I'll talk about what happened in the early primaries and caucuses of 2020 and how the factions quickly consolidated around their favorite candidates. As has been the focus of this book, I am studying not so much the candidates and their campaigns as the party actors trying to make decisions about them. However, I'll spend some time toward the end of the chapter examining the fates of three of the finalists in the contest – Joe Biden, Bernie Sanders, and Elizabeth Warren – and what those tell us about the power of election narratives.

MAKING A CHOICE

At this point I want to lay out how party activists went about evaluating the candidates and deciding on a favorite. I provide some context by examining a variety of publicly available data – polls, endorsements, and fundraising – examining the behavior of voters and party insiders. From there, I'll dig into the choices made by the activists I interviewed between 2017 and 2020.

WHO LED? The idea that a presidential nomination is a *contest*, with people who are leading and people who are trailing, is misleading. Candidates are not on a racetrack and the winner is not necessarily the one who does the most campaign tasks the best. Rather than a contest, a nomination is a *decision*. Party insiders are evaluating various candidates based on their perceived likelihood of winning elections and delivering on party goals once in office. We should be focusing on the people making the decision and trying understand how they're making it, rather than just asking which candidate was ahead.

That being said, I'm going to break my own rule here a bit and examine the 2020 nomination as a horserace, just for the sake of providing a high-altitude overview of the nomination leading up to the election year.

There are, of course, a lot of ways to do this. A few election cycles ago, there weren't many ways to determine who was "winning" the Invisible Primary. There were a few polls, of course, but they were sparse, and polling a presidential nomination is a tricky thing. We can observe national polls, but they don't always tell us what's going to happen in early primary and caucus states, and those early contests can have an outsized impact both on the national race and on each other. But beyond limited polling evidence, people interested in knowing who was likely to be the next presidential nominee would need to judge for themselves from punditry, spin, and experience.

But as I've suggested at various points throughout this book, we have a number of useful metrics today that give us an idea how the party is leaning in its decision-making. None of these methods are flawless, and even when they're working well, they sometimes give different answers.

But it's worth reviewing what evidence we had as the Invisible Primary drew to a close.

POLLING. Polling, as I suggested, is of limited value in informing us who is most likely to become the party's nominee. Early polls are often heavily distorted by name recognition, and are part of the reason that forecasted nomination winners include the likes of Howard Dean in 2004, Hillary Clinton and Rudy Giuliani in 2008, and Newt Gingrich in 2012. Also, national polls, even if conducted well, can be unrealistic; states conduct their contests sequentially, and the candidates spend far more time in the early-contest states and get far more media attention there. Early-state polls can be useful, but they, too, have limits. Typically, several candidates will drop out after poor performances in the Iowa Caucuses, which will affect how downstream contests turn out. Polls of a Super Tuesday state measuring support for a dozen candidates seem wanting when only a handful of those candidates will still be in the race when the contest occurs.

That said, early polls still have some predictive value, and for what it's worth, the polls during the Invisible Primary were relatively stable compared to contests for other years. Unlike, say, the Republican presidential contest in 2012, in which many different candidates took the number one spot in the polls for a few days at a time, Biden led the Democratic 2020 contest pretty much from the moment he entered. It was never an overwhelming lead, but it was a stable one; he commanded between 25 and 30 percent of Democratic support for the whole second half of 2019. (Remarkably, his average polling level was the same in December 2019 as it was in December 2018.[1]) His support dipped somewhat after a particularly memorable attack from Kamala Harris during the first debate in June 2019, but his dip and her bounce evaporated after a few weeks. Senator Warren had numbers close to his in the early fall of 2019, but then her support eroded. If Biden's support was just sustained by his name-recognition advantage over other candidates, we would expect to see his lead erode with time as people learned more about the other candidates; but that didn't happen. Bernie Sanders, meanwhile,

[1] https://twitter.com/gdebenedetti/status/1210192402792747008.

maintained relatively stable numbers in the 15–20 percent range throughout 2019, and then began to rise into the 20s as January came to an end.

Early-state polls showed a much closer and more volatile contest. By the end of 2019, polls showed Iowa Democrats split between Sanders, Biden, and Buttigieg, with Warren only a few points behind them. The poll leader there had jumped around several times during the fall. New Hampshire polls basically showed a four-way tie. Biden maintained a modest lead in Nevada as the year ended, and his support in South Carolina was substantial – more than 20 points ahead of his nearest competitor throughout 2019.

These polling positions would prove especially volatile once voting began. After strong performances in Iowa by Pete Buttigieg and Bernie Sanders and a weak showing by Biden, the former vice president's numbers plummeted, only to recover later in February. But for the duration of the Invisible Primary, Biden was in a strong position.

CAMPAIGN FINANCE. There are a number of different ways to examine campaign donation leadership. During 2019, Bernie Sanders was by far the donation leader, pulling in $74 million. Warren and Buttigieg were in second a third with $60 million and $51 million, respectively. Biden, the poll leader, was in fifth place with $37 million.

But campaign finance totals are rarely predictive of nomination success. Instead, the donation patterns of party-loyal donors tend to be a good predictor of who will receive the nomination, at least in congressional races.[2] And as we saw in Chapter 5 a plurality of people who gave to both a presidential candidate *and* a Democratic Party committee strongly preferred Joe Biden in by the last quarter of 2019 and the first month of 2020. He had won the support of nearly a majority of these donors.

In many ways, campaign finance is an insufficient measure of candidate support, especially in a contest that featured two billionaires, each of whom was pursuing very different strategies. Tom Steyer, for one, pursued an aggressive fundraising campaign to ensure he qualified for

---

[2] Hans J.G. Hassell, 2017. *The Party's Primary: Control of Congressional Nominations.* Cambridge: Cambridge University Press.

debates, while Michael Bloomberg essentially ignored the debates but devoted hundreds of millions of dollars to an advertising campaign in late 2019 and early 2020. Their ability to self-fund makes it harder to deduce just how much party leaders wanted these candidates in the race. But for those who were raising money, Biden's and Sanders' positions were telling. Sanders was raising a lot of money, but not by people with strong ties to the party; Biden was raising less money, but was raising it from the right places.

ENDORSEMENTS. One of the most reliable predictors of modern presidential nominations is endorsement patterns, as described at length in *The Party Decides*.[3] Of course, this measurement is only as good as party elites allow it to be. It's predictive when party insiders collectively choose a candidate and rally behind that person, as happened for Hillary Clinton in 2016, Al Gore and George W. Bush in 2000, and so on. But that, of course, didn't happen on the Republican side in 2016. Those few party elites that made an endorsement marginally preferred Marco Rubio, but most just didn't make a pick at all, leaving the decision to party voters. In such a case, early polling is a far better indicator of what's going to happen.

FiveThirtyEight maintains an endorsement tracker consisting of just governors, members of Congress, former presidents and vice presidents, DNC members, and state legislative leaders.[4] Following that measure, in the case of the Democrats in 2020, the endorsement leader was the same as the national poll leader. Joe Biden maintained a healthy lead over the other candidates throughout 2019, having secured the endorsements of a broad range of party elected officials, as well as former DNC chairs Ed Rendell and Chris Dodd, and 2004 presidential nominee John Kerry.

It would be a mistake to suggest that endorsements just tracked polling, however. The candidate with the second-most endorsement "points" in the *FiveThirtyEight* tracker throughout much of 2019 was Kamala Harris, prior to her December withdrawal. Elizabeth Warren and Cory

---

[3] Marty Cohen, David Karol, Hans Noel, and John Zaller, 2009. *The Party Decides: Presidential Nominations Before and After Reform.* Chicago: University of Chicago Press.

[4] https://projects.fivethirtyeight.com/2020-endorsements/democratic-primary.

Booker trailed her. The mismatch between the public and party insiders was interesting here. Both Booker and Harris had impressed local and national party leaders across the country, yet this support hadn't really translated into general popularity. Meanwhile, during Warren's fall polling surge, she hadn't managed to secure many endorsements.

Bernie Sanders was in fifth place in endorsement points by the end of 2019, having secured the support of several DNC members and three of the four members of "The Squad" – Representatives Alexandria Ocasio-Cortez(NY), Ilhan Omar (MN), and Rashida Tlaib (MI). By *FiveThirtyEight*'s measures, Sanders had acquired just shy of 60 endorsement points by the end of January 2020, more than four times as many points as he'd garnered during the entire 2016 nomination cycle.[5] While considerable evidence suggested that Sanders had not particularly expanded his base of support between 2016 and 2020, the supporters he retained across cycles had increased in stature, with many of them becoming elected officials during the 2016 and 2018 cycles.

Joe Biden's end-of-Invisible-Primary total of 230 endorsement points put him well behind past consensus party nominees like George W. Bush (523), Hillary Clinton (453), Bob Dole (388), and Al Gore (355), but ahead of other eventual nominees like George H.W. Bush (136), Walter Mondale (119), Mitt Romney (109), Barack Obama (64), and Bill Clinton (51) at the same point in their election cycles.

Political scientist Boris Shor ran a separate project[6] to determine how Democratic state legislators across the country were endorsing in the presidential nomination race. As of late January 2020, according to Shor's data, Biden was leading in these endorsements substantially. Biden held 225 state legislative endorsements, while Elizabeth Warren was in second place with roughly half that figure. Then there was a precipitous drop-off to Bernie Sanders (60), Amy Klobuchar (49), and Pete Buttigieg (25). Biden held a particularly strong advantage among state legislators in South Carolina and Nevada, although Klobuchar dominated legislative endorsements in Iowa, and Warren

---

[5] https://projects.fivethirtyeight.com/2016-endorsement-primary/.

[6] https://research.bshor.com/2019/10/16/october-2019-update-on-state-legislative-endorsements-of-2020-democratic-presidential-candidates/.

did the same in New Hampshire. A separate analysis of endorsements by the authors of *The Party Decides*, which included interest group leaders, labor unions and others besides Democratic officeholders, had Biden in the lead right before Iowa, with Bernie Sanders a distant second.[7]

Judging by these three common metrics for evaluating presidential nomination contests – national polling, party-aligned donations, and endorsements – Joe Biden was the clear, if not overwhelming, leader in all of them at the end of the Invisible Primary. That doesn't mean events were fated to turn out as they did, but to the extent a party can make a decision, it had largely done so before anyone started voting in the 2020 cycle.

ACTIVISTS DECIDING. At this point I want to return to the activists I interviewed and discussed in Chapter 3. I followed up with these activists with an online survey conducted every two months between December 2018 and February 2020. I asked them a number of questions about changes in the political environment and the Democratic field, but also made sure to ask them some questions about their candidate leanings.

In Figure 7.1, I chart out their candidate preferences over time. I start with fifty-eight activists with whom I spoke about candidate preferences and the figure charts the total number of candidates supporting each candidate.[8] The figure suggests several interesting trends. For one, activists were deciding, slowly but steadily throughout 2019. The number of undecided activists dropped from fifty-two in the first survey to twenty-three at the beginning of 2020. However, they didn't seem to converge on any particular candidate. By February 2020, twelve were backing Biden, nine backed Sanders, and Warren had eight. No other candidate had more than three supporters.

---

[7] Marty Cohen, David Karol, Hans Noel, and John Zaller, 2020. "The Party No Longer Decides." *Politico*, February 3.

[8] The results here are based on a survey conducted every two months. Typically, only around thirty activists responded to each survey round. I filled in additional candidate endorsements based on media reporting. If an activist didn't respond to a survey, they were presumed to hold the same preference that they did in the previous survey unless their candidate withdrew or they publicly stated otherwise.

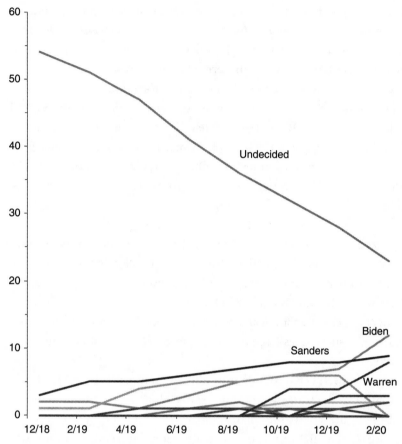

Figure 7.1 Candidate preferences among activists, December 2018–February 2020

What does this suggest? I should again note here that I'm not claiming this group of activists to be broadly representative of the Democratic Party. I also have not monitored this particular group of people in previous election cycles, so it's difficult to draw direct comparisons. However, these are, for the most part, influential and very active local political figures. Their behavior here appears to be a willingness to pick a favorite – more than half of them had done so by the time of the Iowa Caucuses. They had not really agreed on a consensus candidate by this point, although they had essentially narrowed down the race to three alternatives.

I obtained some additional information about their behavior by asking them which candidates they were *considering* supporting. This is

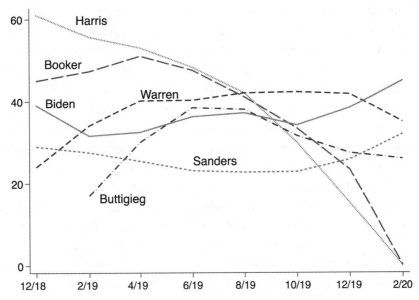

Figure 7.2 Percentage of activists supporting or considering leading candidates

a much softer level of commitment, of course, and I allowed them to pick multiple candidates for this. This doesn't represent overall enthusiasm for a candidate so much as the candidate's acceptability to party activists.

Figure 7.2 shows how this measure of candidate consideration varied between December 2018 and February 2020 among a selection of candidates. For this, I have summed the percentage of activists saying they were supporting each candidate and the percentage saying they were considering that candidate.[9] By this measure, the nomination contest was much more dynamic than it appears in other measures. Kamala Harris was named by more than 60 percent of activists as someone they were considering in late 2018, far more than any other candidate. (Interestingly, no activist in my sample ever claimed they were committed to her.) But her support dwindled over the course of 2019.[10] Cory Booker faced

---

[9] If an activist was supporting a candidate, I treated that candidate as their only consideration. Only for those activists uncommitted to a candidate did I tally their considerations.

[10] Harris withdrew from the contest while the December 2019 version of this survey was in the field. Thus some people still named her, but those who answered after her withdrawal simply ignored her name.

a similar trajectory, first rising in prominence and then fading somewhat with time. It is notable that the two most prominent African American candidates in the field were broadly being considered by activists even if they had few committed supporters or voters.

Warren had a modestly upward trajectory during her time as a candidate, managing to win over a number of skeptical activists over the course of 2019, but ultimately waning in the final wave of the survey. Biden came in initially strong, suffered a bit throughout 2019 as he endured some negative coverage related to some campaign performances, but then rebounded at the beginning of 2020 to reach the most support of any candidate. Sanders' numbers largely held steady with time, and he enjoyed a slight uptick prior to the Iowa Caucuses. Buttigieg's pattern appears to be one of rapid rise and slow fall.

But this picture is incomplete. Consideration of a candidate is not the same as support, and the extent of acceptance of a candidate is not a perfect measurement of that candidate's appeal among a range of factions.

We see another approach to this in Figure 7.3 below. For this, I asked activists in the same survey whom they did *not* want to see become the nominee. This is obviously related to the question about whom they're considering, but it's not quite the same. It's possible for a candidate to measure low in both likes and dislikes if activists just aren't thinking very much about them at all. It's also possible for a candidate to have to have a reasonably large number of both supporters and detractors if they are a very factional candidate.

Of the candidates depicted here,[11] Sanders by far has the most detractors – roughly 50 percent of the activists said they definitely didn't want him to become the nominee in early 2019, and that figure grew to over 60 percent over time. Sanders, that is, had a set of enthusiastic backers, many of whom had been with him since 2018 or earlier, but his ability to grow that coalition looked minimal. Meanwhile, Biden's popularity increased as Iowa approached, while

---

[11] Seventy percent or more of activists regularly said they would not consider several other candidates, especially spiritual author Marianne Williamson and Rep. Tulsi Gabbard, for the nomination.

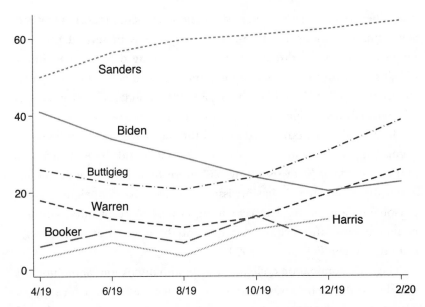

Figure 7.3 Percentage of activists who do not want to see candidate become nominee

his detractors became fewer. By February 2020, Biden was the most popular and the least unpopular of the major candidates – a good position for a prospective nominee. Buttigieg's detractors increased toward the end of the year as critical accounts of him grew. Meanwhile, Warren's, Booker's, and Harris' lines remained under 25 percent, suggesting that they were broadly acceptable to multiple factions within the party, although Warren's detractors were growing.

What does the above evidence suggest to us about the nature of the 2020 Democratic presidential nomination? As with the overall national evidence shown earlier, these activists reveal a party that had largely winnowed down a very large field of candidates to just a few viable possibilities, and the overall lean was toward Joe Biden.

This narrowing – the signals sent by endorsers, activists, donors, and others that they were leaning toward Biden and only considering a few other alternatives – had an effect on the shape of the race. In the middle of 2019, there were, by most measures, twenty-four presidential candidates vying for the Democratic nomination. By the end of January 2020, there were eleven. No one had voted those other thirteen candidates out of the race. They were, in many cases, pushed out by a lack of support. A few had some support – Kamala Harris, for example, was in second place in endorsements and had qualified for an upcoming debate – but simply didn't see a path to the nomination given the arrangement of the party. The activities of the Invisible Primary, and the candidates' interpretations of those activities, helped to winnow down the field considerably.

But they didn't winnow it down all the way. Given these candidates' regular appearances in the District of Columbia and the early primary and caucus states, activists surely had more than enough information about the candidates' behavior, issues preferences, campaigning style, personality, and more. The remaining critical piece of information – could they win an election? – could only be guessed at until people started voting in February of 2020.

The 2020 nomination cycle was replete with discussions about not just why the candidate field was so large, but why it stayed so large for so long. The eleven candidates competing in Iowa still constituted a record-sized field for that point in a cycle. It is certainly plausible that candidates, even those without substantial backing, were staying in because the signal from activists and partisan voters was vague; they had not converged on a candidate, and many suggested that they could switch their support.

In an interview[12] after his withdrawal from the presidential contest, Colorado Senator Michael Bennet said that he stayed in the race as long as he did because of encouragement he was receiving from voters and activists: "There were people in New Hampshire saying to me, 'Please don't drop out of this race. ... We're looking at the field and we think you're the only one who can beat Donald Trump.'"

I spoke with Bennet's wife, Susan Daggett, separately, to get a sense of these requests, as she played a leadership role in the campaign. Local party leaders, she said, repeatedly told her,

"We don't know how this is going to shake out. And your voice is really important and you have a set of qualifications that nobody else in the race has. And it's not your fault that the attention hasn't yet turned to you, but it's too early to know definitively that that won't happen." I think New

[12] https://youtu.be/It1v2P39rVU?t=6592.

Hampshire deeply remembers Gary Hart coming out of the blue and winning. ... And I've spent hours of my life calling party chairs in Iowa and talking to them and they almost to a person say, "It's too early. People haven't decided. People are still talking."

Daggett noted a sharp disconnect between this encouragement from local party leaders and a coolness from the national party, whose debate qualification rules functionally prohibited the participation of Bennet and similarly placed candidates. Those rules largely favored well-endowed candidates with national reputations, and Bennet hoped to simply stay in the race until the early contests just to see what happened at the local level.

I certainly don't claim these reflections speak for all the candidates in the field, but they are telling. They suggest that "the party" was not necessarily speaking with a unified voice, and that national and local party figures might have very different agendas. They also suggest an important lesson about the nature of winnowing. Candidates are rarely explicitly told to leave the race. Indeed, sometimes local party officials go out of their way to encourage competition and embrace even long-shot candidates. But eventually candidates see some of their competitors doing better, getting more attention and support, and determine to either go broke shooting for the next debate threshold or simply cut their losses and withdraw.

AT THE END OF THE INVISIBLE PRIMARY

As the Invisible Primary drew to a close, we saw a general signal by party insiders, examined at a variety of levels, in favor of Biden's nomination. But this was not a consensus position. Judging from my interview evidence and from other observational data, Bernie Sanders had not really grown his coalition much from 2016, but he hadn't lost very much of it, either. He had a substantial wellspring of very enthusiastic support. Elizabeth Warren had done well by a number of measures, as well – she'd been one of the top recipients of party-aligned donations, she was in second place in endorsements, and so on. So while Biden's nomination seemed likely by the end of the Invisible Primary, Sanders and Warren looked to be credible alternatives.

At this point, I need to get into the events of late February and early March 2020, which quickly narrowed the race down to a Biden–Sanders contest. This was a fascinating moment of party coordination that also reveals party insiders attempting to learn from past losses.

The Democratic Party of mid-February 2020 was in an unusual state. It had signaled a preference for Joe Biden, but he had significantly underperformed in Iowa and New Hampshire, coming in fourth and fifth, respectively. Bernie Sanders, meanwhile, received the support of the most caucusgoers in Iowa (while Pete Buttigieg won in state delegate equivalents), and won handily in New Hampshire. Elizabeth Warren was underperforming against expectations but still came in ahead of Biden in those states. Biden's polling support plummeted in the wake of those contests, dropping from an average of 26 points on the day of the Iowa Caucuses to an average of 15 points just three weeks later. A particularly important feature of these early contests was that, unlike in earlier cycles, very few candidates were treating their losses as a sign to quit.

The factionalism within the party was highly relevant here. The progressive faction appeared to be strongly united behind Sanders. Warren had attempted to make some inroads into that camp but had largely found it unresponsive to her appeals. She and the rest of the candidates were essentially competing for the remaining two-thirds of partisan voters, who had repeatedly demonstrated a great deal of indecision and impermanence in their candidate choices. As long as Sanders had one faction unified, and there were multiple viable candidates competing for the remainder of the party, it was plausible that Sanders could win upcoming primaries and caucuses with 30 to 40 percent of the vote but secure a plurality, or even a majority, of convention delegates.

FiveThirtyEight's convention forecast model, which used polling and past performances to determine probabilities for delegate shares, went from a nearly one in two chance of a Biden nomination in early February, to roughly the same chance of Sanders getting it a week later, and then to a better than 60 percent chance that *no one* would secure a majority of delegates, which would then lead to a contested convention for the first time since 1952. The candidates even seemed to be preparing for this event. At a February 19 debate, moderator Chuck Todd asked the candidates whether they would pledge to support whomever had a plurality of delegates prior to the convention as the party's nominee; Sanders said yes, the others said no.[13]

To no small degree, the Democrats seemed to be following in the path of the Republicans four years earlier. One of the questions I asked at the beginning of this book was whether the Democratic Party of 2020 was as weak as the Republican Party of 2016 – whether it still had the ability to control its nomination system and prevent the nomination of a candidate much of its leadership found unacceptable. Many Republican leaders in 2016 were clearly and deeply uncomfortable with Donald Trump's candidacy. They worried he wasn't loyal to the party's agenda, and they feared he would cost them a winnable election. They had many opportunities to thwart his rise and repeatedly failed to do so. A number of prominent party and conservative movement leaders issued warnings, of course, but they never picked an alternative or convinced fellow partisans to rally around that candidate.

Sanders was not precisely the same threat to the Democrats that Trump appeared to be to the Republicans four years earlier. For one thing, Sanders was hardly as hostile to the Democrats' agenda as Trump had seemed to his party's. The main threat that many Democrats perceived in him was that he would lose to Trump in November and take many down-ballot candidates with him, jeopardizing the party's prospects for controlling Congress. *New York* magazine's Jonathan Chait, sounding warnings not unlike the *National Review*'s about Trump in January 2016,[14] summed up the critiques of Sanders at the end of January 2020:

> The totality of the evidence suggests Sanders is an extremely, perhaps uniquely, risky nominee. His vulnerabilities are enormous and untested. No party nomination, with the possible exception of Barry Goldwater in 1964, has put forth a presidential nominee with the level of downside risk exposure as a Sanders-led ticket would bring. To nominate Sanders would be insane.[15]

---

[13] Adam Gabbatt, 2020. "Debate Shows Bernie Sanders Could Win Most Votes but be Denied Nomination." *The Guardian*, February 20.

[14] *National Review* Editors, 2016. "Against Trump." *The National Review*, January 22.

[15] Jonathan Chait, 2020. "Running Bernie Sanders Against Trump Would Be an Act of Insanity." *New York Magazine*, January 28.

For a time, Democrats perceived their party much as the Republicans had four years earlier; unable to winnow the field and prevent a divided vote, likely to nominate a candidate many thought unelectable, and powerless to do anything about it. Then came the Nevada Caucuses of February 22nd. To be sure, Sanders won this contest handily, taking 47 percent of county delegates. Biden, however, came in second, with 20 percent of county delegates. This was hardly a spectacular showing by a recent vice president and the party's purported choice, but in his speech that night, Biden claimed a victory of sorts – "The press is ready to declare people dead quickly but we're alive and we're coming back and we're going to win!" The media largely went along with his "comeback" framework, and Biden promised a strong showing at the upcoming South Carolina primary, where he had led with large margins for months and where the electorate's substantial African American population had long signaled a strong preference for him.

Now, it's interesting to note how party insiders themselves were reacting to these early contests. Pete Buttigieg had done unexpectedly well in Iowa, but the party didn't move toward him. In the three days that followed the caucuses, he got just two new endorsements – those of Indianapolis Mayor Joe Hogsett and US Rep. Andy Kim of New Jersey – according to *FiveThirtyEight's* endorsement tracker. Sanders dominated in New Hampshire and Nevada, but in the three days following those contests, he picked up only the endorsements of former presidential candidates Bill de Blasio and Marianne Williamson.

Party insiders were very different in their treatment of Biden. A few days before the South Carolina primary, US Rep. Jim Clyburn, considered the godfather of Palmetto State Democratic politics, endorsed Joe Biden. "We know Joe Biden," said Clyburn. "But more importantly, he knows us."[16] Biden won the contest definitively. A stunning 47 percent of primary voters there said that Clyburn's endorsement was an important factor in their vote.[17] Biden had vowed all month that he could deliver

---

[16] Eric Bradner and Paul LeBlanc, 2020. "South Carolina Rep. Jim Clyburn Endorses Joe Biden Ahead of Primary." CNN, February 26.

[17] Deborah Barfield Berry and Ledyard King, 2020. "How Rep. James Clyburn, a South Carolina Icon, Helped Biden Score his Big Comeback." *USA Today*, February 29.

the votes of African Americans, and events bore out the prediction. He won 48 percent of the primary vote – including 61 percent of the African American vote – besting Sanders by nearly 30 points overall. Unlike with Sanders and Buttigieg, in the three days following South Carolina, Biden picked up *thirty* endorsements, including those of former senator Harry Reid (NV) and former DNC chair Terry McAuliffe. Many who were holding back their support rushed to publicly back Biden. The strong South Carolina victory was the demonstration they needed.

Former DNC Chair McAuliffe, during an election-night appearance on CNN, urged a number of candidates to rethink their bids, specifically mentioning Michael Bloomberg, Pete Buttigieg, Amy Klobuchar, and Tom Steyer. "I would ask these candidates – not after Super Tuesday but tomorrow – do you have a pathway? And if you don't have a pathway, who is it that you think is the most electable and can help the Democratic Party from the top to the bottom in all the local races and statewide races?"[18] Shortly following the election's conclusion, Klobuchar and Buttigieg saw the way the race was unfolding and abandoned their bids and endorsed Biden. Beto O'Rourke, who had withdrawn from the race in November of 2019, endorsed Biden at this point, as well.

With this strong signal of support – a very loud message from the party that Biden was the person who could deliver the party's platform and defeat Trump – and a smaller field, suddenly Biden had real strengths on Super Tuesday. The candidacy that looked to be on life support a few days earlier won most of the state contests on Tuesday. It was telling that those Super Tuesday states where Biden did the worst and Sanders did the best – especially California, Colorado, and Utah – were the states with substantial early voting. Roughly half the ballots had been cast prior to the late winnowing, and many of those votes went to candidates who were no longer in the race. Shortly after Super Tuesday, *FiveThirtyEight* updated its forecast and gave Biden an 88 percent chance at the nomination, Sanders only a 2 percent chance, and just a 10 percent chance for a contested convention.

If the speed of this party coordination was remarkable, so was the timing. The framework for this book has been the assumption that much

18 https://youtu.be/ytS6nO3-QL0.

of the party's coordination, if any actually occurred, would take place prior to the Iowa Caucuses. To be sure, some of it happened then. But there's been a trend since roughly 2004 of party insiders winnowing the field down somewhat prior to Iowa and then using the candidates' performances in the early contests as helpful information in picking a favorite. In 2020, it was as if insiders treated the first four states as straw polls that were informative about the vote-getting ability of candidates, but not determinative of very many delegates. But Super Tuesday, with roughly a third of the total delegates at stake, had to be taken seriously, and so party insiders coordinated very shortly before it. And Democratic insiders were no doubt motivated to avoid what they saw as Republican insiders' failure four years ago.

In this sense, the Democratic Party's "establishment" faction learned from its Republican counterparts' loss four years earlier. They demonstrated that a modern party could still narrow down alternatives and pick a favorite, suggesting that the Republican Party *could* have done that four years earlier for Marco Rubio, Jeb Bush, Scott Walker, or someone else. Obviously this would be a pretty different country if they had.

BIDEN AS THE CHOSEN ONE

In many ways, Biden was a fairly obvious choice for a party having a difficult time making a decision. He had universal name recognition, was attached to a popular recent two-term presidency, and had a long reputation as someone basically right at the ideological middle of the party, neither unusually conservative nor liberal.

Perhaps even more importantly, he was the logical answer to many of the narratives that emerged from 2016. If Democrats had lost points because of "identity politics," their nomination of Biden would blunt some of those objections. If Democrats had pushed too far in terms of egalitarianism and representation, seeking to succeed the nation's first African American president with its first woman president, Biden was a tactical retreat from that. Moderate whites in swing states wouldn't find him inherently objectionable.

But nor was he a complete abrogation of egalitarianism. As a year of polling and a day of voting in South Carolina demonstrated, many

African Americans within the Democratic Party were not only accepting of but enthusiastic about his candidacy. His decades of outreach and his close ties with Barack Obama helped convey a shared cause with the broader African American community. There were, after all, a number of prominent African American candidates in the presidential race, but they failed to secure significant support from potential black voters, who largely leaned toward Biden.

This point deserves a bit of elaboration. Political scientist Julian Wamble demonstrates that African American voters often prefer candidates who have shown, through social connections or political or physical risk, some sort of "commitment to prioritizing the racial group's interest over their own self-interest."[19] Wamble's research focuses mainly on the appeals of black politicians, such as when US Rep John Lewis cites his physical beatings at the 1965 Selma march or when Sen. Cory Booker describes choosing to live and run for office in Newark, NJ. But this extends to white politicians, as well. Bernie Sanders sought black support by describing his own participation in the March on Washington in 1963. Elizabeth Warren did so by communicating knowledge of the ways racial disparity affects virtually every public policy debate in the United States, supporting plans for desegregating housing patterns, providing reparations for the descendants of slaves, and so forth.

Joe Biden had a much more immediate and emotional connection to the African American community; Barack Obama had twice named him his running mate. What's more, the two seemed to have had a genuine affection for each other and a strong working partnership, a relationship that perhaps culminated when Obama presented a teared-up Biden with the Presidential Medal of Freedom, referring to the Vice President as "my brother," shortly before leaving office. Biden hardly had a spotless record of support for causes valued by the black community throughout his career, but Obama's figurative and literal embrace of him spoke loudly. In a popular brief essay shared on social media in early March, educator

---

[19] Julian Wamble. n.d. "The Chosen One: How Community Commitment makes certain Representatives More Preferable." Working paper.

Laurie Goff explained the symbolic attachment many African Americans have for Biden:

> This old rich white man played second fiddle to a black man. Not just any black man but a younger black man, a smart black man. Not just for a day. Not 1, not 2, but eight years. . . . He was willing and proud to be his wing man. Not once did he try to undermine him, this black man. Instead Joe walked in lockstep with him. . . . You tell me what 40+ year "establishment" white politician has ever done that. Joe Biden is cut from a different cloth. And black folks understand that and for good reason. He has shown it. This is what showing up and being an ally looks like. When black people say they know Joe this is how we know.[20]

What's more, African American voters were at least as concerned with perceptions of candidate electability as white voters were. As we saw in the polling evidence back in Chapter 3, black voters (especially men) punished Kamala Harris and Cory Booker the most, saying they would wave a magic wand and make those candidates president, but didn't think they could win a general election. They were supporting Biden in part because they thought he could win. In an early February 2020 poll, 40 percent of African Americans said that Biden was the most likely to defeat Trump in the general election; 14 percent said Sanders and only 2 percent said Warren could.[21]

More generally, Biden was a natural choice for a party that prized electability above all else. As many voters and activists revealed, both within this book and elsewhere, they were unusually interested in finding someone who could defeat the Republican nominee in 2019–2020, prioritizing that over the candidate's stances on a great many issues. Democrats during this cycle, even though they'd just been out of power a few years, were acting like a party that had lost the last three or four presidential elections in a row. They were hungry for a win and willing to give up quite a bit for it.

An obsession with electability leads to the prioritization of candidates with certain traits. Moderate candidates are perceived to be more

---

[20] https://twitter.com/lloki08/status/1236493650189680641.

[21] Chryl N. Laird and Ismail K. White, 2020. "Biden Lost his 'Electable' Claim. That's Why Black Votes are up for Grabs Again." *The Washington Post*, February 24.

electable than relatively extreme ones, with considerable evidence to support that claim. Male candidates and white candidates are also perceived to be more electable, and while the evidence is far less clear on this, it is difficult to shake people of those beliefs, particularly when they see the stakes of a general election as so high.

Now none of this pointed automatically to Joe Biden. There were plenty of other options earlier in the race, but none as tested and familiar to so many different groups within the party as Biden was. If Democrats were generally seeking a more moderate white man for the job, as long as Biden was there and campaigning reasonably well, he'd be a convenient choice.

At the beginning of this book I mentioned the example of New Coke, which Coca-Cola executives were confident would be better tasting and better received by soft drink customers. When it unexpectedly and catastrophically failed, after much internal debate and blame casting, the company ultimately decided to re-release its original formula, nominally rebranded as "Classic Coke." In many ways, this was what Democrats came up with in 2020; they fell back on a tried-and-true brand in the hope of winning back market share.

SANDERS AND FACTIONALISM

Bernie Sanders' playbook did not evolve significantly between 2016 and 2020. He campaigned in similar ways, sounded similar themes, and, importantly, appealed to similar blocs within the party.

The shadows of 2016 and of the party's internal reform efforts in the years that followed it hung heavily over the 2020 contest. There were something like three main groups within the Democratic National Committee who struggled with nomination reform during the 2017–2018 period. These were Sanders' progressive supporters (who sought changes to open up nominations, dethrone longstanding insiders, and otherwise increase the likelihood of the nomination of Sanders or someone like him), Clinton's African American supporters (who resisted efforts to disempower party insiders like themselves in favor of those with less experience within the party), and Clinton's white supporters (who were eager to move past the controversy and demonstrate unity).

The final showdown on the Democratic side between Sanders and Biden, although it was not terribly long-lived, looked similar to the Sanders–Clinton primary of 2016 and was a logical consequence of internal party debates in 2018. The candidate that the vast majority of Clinton supporters from four years earlier, along with most African Americans in the party, were comfortable with had a clear path to the nomination, and Sanders and his supporters were, at least for a time, trying to brand that path as wrong, illegitimate, and insufficiently progressive.

ELIZABETH WARREN AND ELECTABILITY

Elizabeth Warren dropped out of the race a few days after a disappointing Super Tuesday performance. Despite having a substantial number of activists, party-aligned donors, and other insiders supportive of her candidacy, she came in at fourth or fifth place in nearly all the contests from New Hampshire through Super Tuesday, and even lost her home state of Massachusetts to both Biden and Sanders.

Why did her campaign fail? I want to be clear here, and this applies broadly: In a field of twenty-four candidates, twenty-three are going to lose, and one does not need to construct a separate theory for each of those failures. The days following her departure from the contest saw a broad range of punditry, many blaming sexism for her loss, some blaming her own campaigning decisions, some faulting her stances on Medicare For All, and so forth.

I'll just weigh in a bit here. *Of course* sexism played a role, the same role it played when Hillary Clinton ran and when so many other women candidates run. Warren and other women presidential candidates, even when they were relatively popular, were found to be disproportionately "unlikeable," were criticized for their ambition and tone and the sounds of their voices, and were blamed for things men just don't get blamed for. Voters with more sexist attitudes, even within the Democratic Party, were less likely to support her.[22]

---

[22] Ella Nilsen and Li Zhou, 2020. "Why Women are Feeling so Defeated after Elizabeth Warren's Loss." *Vox*, March 6. www.vox.com/2020/3/6/21166338/elizabeth-warren-loss-2020-primary-sexism.

But this, in many ways, is an insufficient answer. Just because sexism hurt Warren's campaign, and the campaigns of several other candidates, that does not mean that she lost because of it. That would be the equivalent of saying that if you could somehow remove prejudice from party nominations then only the wisest, most eloquent, and most decent candidate would become the nominee. That is a *very* charitable view of history.

But other answers are equally problematic. Yes, it probably hurt Warren to embrace Medicare For All, long a goal of the Sanders campaign, and then to develop a finance plan for it, because then Sanders was getting the credit for the proposal and she was getting the blame for its specifics. But had she not done this, would we really expect her to have become the Democratic nominee? All the Tuesday-morning-quarterbacking explanations of her failures generally place too much weight on the decisions and actions of individual candidates. As I've tried to demonstrate throughout this book, decisions of party insiders were far more important here, and they structured the contest in a way that made it very hard for her to succeed.

Seen in this light, Warren failed for the same reason Biden succeeded – the narratives emerging from 2016. Many in the party saw in her the same things they had seen in Hillary Clinton – feminism, mastery of policy details, a confident intellect, and so on – and it worried them. Many were gripped with the idea that these qualities had cost the party votes in 2016. An analysis by political scientists Brian Schaffner and Jon Green demonstrated that *secondary sexism* hurt her candidacy substantially. That is, many Democrats themselves wanted to nominate a woman, but they were concerned that *other* voters wouldn't support such a candidate, so they didn't support her.[23] Similarly, as I noted earlier, many Democratic activists, while committed to egalitarianism and representation, were willing to backtrack somewhat on that for what they perceived (without much evidence) as a better chance at victory.

---

[23] Brian Schaffner and Jon Green, 2020. "Sexism Is Probably One Reason Why Elizabeth Warren Didn't Do Better." *Data For Progress*, March 5. www.dataforprogress.org/blog/3/5/sexism-one-reason-why-warren-didnt-do-better.

THE NARRATIVE NEXT TIME

At the beginning of this book, I noted that I'd initially been motivated to write about the Republican Party, which seemed due for a significant self-analysis after its inevitable loss in the 2016 presidential election. Of course, that conversation has been postponed. But should that party lose control of the White House in 2020, suffering the defeat of an incumbent president for only the fifth time in the past century, there will be a quick contest within the GOP to define just why it lost. Does the party need to change the way it nominates candidates? Could it adopt some of the processes and traditions that Democrats have shown in culling their candidate field? Should it attempt something like super-delegates? Was Trump cruising for a reelection until an unforeseen pandemic came along? Was it just a matter of waiting a few years for a more favorable environment?

Similarly, a Democratic loss in 2020 would produce a profound wave of narrative creation and internal arguments. Those who came out of 2016 worried that the party lost that contest because it nominated a liberal women essentially "won" the post-election narrative battle; they got a moderate white man into the top ballot position. Should that formula prove inadequate, other factions within the party may find themselves ascendant in the next cycle. A lot of the party's controversial practices and decisions from the 2020 cycle – caucuses, the early position-ing of Iowa and New Hampshire, top-down party management of debate access thresholds, a prioritization of small donors, early voting, and so on – could well find themselves on the chopping block for 2024. The prioritization of electability above policy concerns will undoubtedly come under fire if the chosen candidate from that environment doesn't get elected.

While the cycles of blame and narrative attribution don't really end, I'd just like to close by noting that many of these narratives are, if not flat out wrong, not particularly right either. The race or sex of a candidate, where she campaigns, how she speaks, whom she chooses as a running mate, and so on, while hardly irrelevant, are probably less consequential for the outcome of an election than other factors, such as how electoral college votes are distributed across the states, who has an easy time voting and who doesn't, how well the economy is performing nationally and is experienced in people's daily lives, which issues the media choose to discuss and which they ignore, and so forth. Yet those latter issues receive far less scrutiny by a political party in the wake of a loss. What will also likely get little discussion is the role of random chance; in an era of close and competitive presidential elections, more than a few can simply end on the equivalent of a coin toss. But for a few random twists of fate in late 2016 Hillary Clinton would have been in the White House between 2017 and 2021 and I'd have been interviewing Republicans trying to figure out how they blew such an obviously winnable election.

Of course, parties can only control so much. One of the interesting lessons of the 2020 cycle is that the Democratic Party, at least, demonstrated some significant organizational power. On both formal and informal levels, it made some decisions, sorting between narratives and settling on a candidate. It was not clear to me when I started this project that the Democratic Party was actually a stronger party than the GOP. It is considerably clearer now.

In January 2018, Oprah Winfrey gave a passionate televised speech at the Golden Globe awards ceremony, addressing a number of ongoing political concerns but specifically noting the Me Too movement. "I want all the girls watching here, now," Winfrey said,

> to know that a new day is on the horizon. And when that new day finally dawns, it will be because of a lot of magnificent women, many of whom are right here in this room tonight, and some pretty phenomenal men, fighting hard to make sure that they become the leaders who take us to the time when nobody ever has to say "Me too" again.

The speech drew widespread coverage and praise. After the show, Meryl Streep told a reporter that Winfrey "launched a rocket tonight. I want her to run for president. I don't think she had any intention [of declaring]. But now she doesn't have a choice."[24]

That candidacy, of course, never happened. Winfrey told reporters that after considerable reflection and prayer, she decided, "I don't have

---

[24] David Smith, 2018. "Oprah Winfrey for President: A Wild Idea that Just Got Dramatically More Real." *The Guardian*, January 9.

the DNA for it. That's not for me."[25] Nor did other celebrity candidacies manifest for the Democratic ticket. Now, obviously a Winfrey bid for a presidential nomination is not the same as a Donald Trump bid. But there was at least some interest in the job from a wealthy, well known, and powerful potential candidate, and she apparently found the party uninterested. This was not what Trump found four years earlier.

So the Democrats have some power as a party. But if power truly comes with responsibility, we will learn a lot about just how responsible the party is in the election cycles to come.

---

[25] Carly Ledbetter, 2018. "Oprah Says She Would Run for President Under One Condition." *Huffington Post*, February 28.

Index

Note: Page numbers in **bold** refer to tables; those in *italics* refer to figures